GREAT BRITAIN?
THE SECRET DESTINY
OF THE BRITISH
AND THEIR ISLES

GREAT BRITAIN?
The Secret Destiny of The British and Their Isles

By Richard Abbot

natural living
BOOKS

Natural Living Books & Passerine Publishing
Northamptonshire, UK

International Standard Book Number: 978–0–9554758–8–7

First edition: 2016

Typeset, printed and bound by CPI Group (UK) Ltd, Croydon, CR0 4YY

This is a Natural Living Books Illumination Device ID33

History repeats itself.
Though never exactly.

Look to the British Empire as a necessary lesson
in the formation of the Human Empire.
For Great Britain, as was, is no more.
Only upon her re–incarnation shall the essence,
which originally entered her, come again.

CONTENTS

Forces…*Music as Rebellion, or Conformity?...The Numerology of the SNP…Four More Forgotten Lands…The Role of the Group Consciousness.*

Britain & Europe: *What is Europe, anyway?...Resistance to the EU…The Numerology of UKIP…Religious Freedom…Does Europe Help Britain Resolve its Karma or Fulfil its Destiny?*

Powerless Britain? *Powerless? The Numerology of Transnational Corporations… Powerless? USA! USA!...Powerful? The Numerology of the Green Party…Balanced? The United Nations…Britain's Gift to the World… Prescription for a Renewed Nation…You Are the Land and the Land is You…Voting Matters.*

Notes on The Method. *The Rumsfeld Paradox & Beyond…But No Method is 100%.*

The Secret Conclusion. *Not printed here. To be revealed at the Time of Reckoning*

APPENDIX A: The Places of Britain

APPENDIX B: Foreign Relations

APPENDIX C: British General Elections

APPENDIX D: The Full Names & Numbers of the Nations

APPENDIX E: The Tarot of the Union Jack

Bibliography

Great Britain? Who Cares?

Throughout all history the lay of the land has caused different peoples to live differently. The people at the top of a hill move along a different path of development than those who live in the forest, each gifted and deprived of resources in differing ways. The tribe inhabiting a warm climate is blessed with more fruits and berries than the tribe in the cold region, yet that shivering tribe has access to cold, clear water where others do not. Thus the people of the Earth are divided, by land, water and air, such that they might come together through exchange, co–operation and exploration.

Over time differing tribes formalised themselves into nations and defined themselves by the particular things they could do that others could not. They found, over time, that certain lands suited certain endeavours. For example, hut and wheel makers found that they worked better near the forest where they had plentiful raw material, and that their works could not be achieved as efficiently elsewhere. Thus the idea of different nations became embedded, though its initial drivers subsequently forgotten.

To support the particular things that could be done in particular lands the people formulated different languages. Over time different tribes and nations started to call like things by differing names. The tree became the arbre (French), the albero (Italian), the baum (German) and the boom (Dutch). Or perhaps those words became the tree? Or perhaps they sprang from another root altogether? Regardless of how it occurred, differences in identification and disagreements about method came more to the fore.

Many now look back and say that these tribes, with their differences in language and location, are the cause of war and conflict. I would suggest that these differences are the triggers, but not the causes. Many speak now of a Global Village, Earth Consciousness and One World. Yet we are as divided as ever we were by language and geography as well as genetics. For example, most of the world is lactose intolerant and cannot drink milk, yet due to a freak genetic mutation that occurred around five hundred years ago Northern Europeans, especially the British, mostly can. Different things continue to occur in different parts of the world and the essential possibilities of the nation state, as I will demonstrate, are not yet exhausted. There are things that can be done in each individual country – for our purposes, Great Britain – that cannot be done elsewhere, due to land, climate, people and history.

Great Britain is, was, and always will be different to, say, France. Not least because the traveller has to cross water in order to get here, and is then changed by that act of crossing. This remains true whether the journey is under or over the sea, by car, train, boat or plane. Once arrived the visitor will then be compelled, in one way or another, to speak a different language, to join in a common communication with his fellows. As we will shortly see, it is a fallacy to believe that one can live fully and functionally in England without speaking English. The language is the nation. This is true across the world.

In all cases the differences between Great Britain and any other nation are more pronounced than, say, between France and Germany, or between the states of America. This is due to the geography, the nature of Britain as an island, and the identity of its people as an island race. In this sense only, race matters. Not in the sense of superiority, but of difference. There are seven billion different individuals on the planet and, as there are individual differences, there are also group, tribal and national differences. It is easier to walk into a country where there is no border than to cross a sea. People born and raised on an island are not the same as those born and raised on the continent, but each needs the other, for knowledge, skills and trade. Superiority cannot be claimed by the islanders or by the mainlanders.

Many, at this point, will be tempted to draw breath and frame these ideas as racist, discriminatory, divisive and ultimately war–like. Yet this would be incorrect for destruction is not a product of national difference, as much as it is of the Dark Side; that deliberately hateful tendency of all human beings which seeks to manifest regardless of what they call themselves or where they come from. A planet dictated to by a supposedly beneficent One World Government will be the most repressive system in all history if the Human Dark Side – the innate tendency to hate and destroy – is not checked. The true reality is that to be British is not to be Chinese, and only haters will find these factual words discriminatory. The Law of the Planet is limitation, of age, height, size, time, abundance and intelligence. Location and geography are but another form of this. Settlements limited by natural phenomenon, as the British Isles is by the sea, must therefore develop differently than others. This book is the story of that development and where it must inevitably take us.

On top of the natural geographic differences, thousands of years of history have been created to support the notion of the difference of Great Britain. From the apocryphal 12th century tales of Geoffrey of Monmouth who told of the founding of London as Troia Nova – New Troy – by Brutus sometime around 1100BC, through tales of the land of Albion (under which the Greek God Zeus lies sleeping, awaiting his time of return), to archaeological realities such as Stonehenge, to the legends of King Arthur and Camelot, the daring–do of the British Empire and last redoubt of freedom in the Battle of Britain, the thread of nation is old. The generations before us made this history, but now it re–makes us, everyday. The sense of something special endures in these islands, beneath and beyond Manchester United football shirts, 24 hour drinking, Indian street food and Porsche driving bankers. The legends of King Arthur – one of the most powerful components of British exceptionalism – will not be easily forgotten. He waits, it is said, and will return in the country's darkest hours.

Today's mundane reality, though, is that Great Britain – as it was in history and myth – no longer exists, destroyed already by those impatient for change. Its material and physical life is already diminished and its identity undermined. But what might Great Britain represent? What aspects of it might live on, in the dimensions we cannot see? Can the life of the nation be restored, or is such a notion backward and obsolete? Is a break up of the most successful national alliance in recorded history a cause for concern? Is the legacy of Empire a positive or negative one? We will address all these questions through esoteric lenses. We will incorporate history, politics, economics and monarchy into the equation, although this is not really a book about any of those things. It is a book for those who visit Great Britain, whether for a lifetime or for a holiday, and for those ready to move beyond the standard explanations for Britain's status and condition in the world; its lucky positioning as a beneficiary of the Gulf Stream, its central time zone position, and its murderous Imperial past. But we will discover many more and better, occult, reasons for Great Britain to exist and to continue to exert its influence on every single person on the planet.

Some might wonder at this point, in a connected world of globalised trade, travel and technology, where one can just as easily hop off to Venice, Copenhagen or Tallinn for the weekend as Edinburgh or Cornwall, why we should limit our scope to one slightly odd, old–fashioned collection of rocks in the North Atlantic? For me the answer is simple and profound – because I, along with tens of millions of others, live here. Because of this, and although the book is a connection with high minded, esoteric and historic principles, it is also an explanation of why you cannot find a parking space in the town centre, why your internet connection is so bad, why you cannot get your children into the local school, and why so many Brits have so much yet are so miserable. The secrets behind this have now been opened where every small issue conceals a big one. This is, therefore, the hidden story of a nation that continues to exert influence upon all of us.

What Is It About The British?

Travelling around Great Britain today it is hard to see how we ever managed to accumulate the largest Empire in human history, though it is far easier to see that we have always done things differently. How, for example, has it come to pass that almost every other nationality learns English to communicate with us, yet we rarely bother to do the same in return? How is it that British post boxes are red yet in almost every other country of the world they are blue or yellow ? Why do Brits drive on the left hand side of the road, while mostly everyone else drives on the right? And why do Brits complain about almost everything yet often fail to do anything about their complaints? The desirability of these aspects of British–ness is secondary to the fact that they are very real and persist to this day.

No discussion of Britain can go far without tackling the existence of Empire, yet almost immediately we are flung into contention and recrimination over the nature of Imperial Britain. The path I will seek to take throughout this book is the middle one. I do not accept that extremities of viewpoint are ever valuable, let alone true. Human beings the world over are grey, combinations of black and white, good and bad, enlightened and ignorant. These human traits are not exclusive to Britain and they are imprinted on the ground everywhere that humans walk. The British Empire was neither the murderous adventure painted by some nor the unalloyed joy that it was celebrated as at the time. Or perhaps it would be more accurate to say that it was both these things, delivering a great – as well as murderous – legacy, founding systems of government around the world that successfully endure to this day, as well as creating partitioned states which are the fault lines of modern conflict. The flag has been waved in enlightened victory as much as it has been in massacre and there is not one nation on the planet that can claim purity or innocence in this regard. The actors of the Empire were great intellectuals, artists and innovators, as well as pompous and repressed morons. The landed gentry were both noble and ignorant, while the working class was ignorant and noble. And there has always been in Britain an intelligent but self–loathing tendency, those who articulately argue that the nation is responsible for every crime under the sun. There is nothing new to see in this regard, short of placing their opinions in context with others.

We must, therefore, be careful to distinguish the Eras of Britain from one another. The Great Britain after the New Millennium differs both from the Empire and from the Britain of thousands of years of history. The illusion of modernity is ever present, for every generation feels itself somehow more advanced than its predecessor. Superficially the Britain I now inhabit is very different to that which I grew up in. This is most apparent in London, where the condition of the city compared to twenty years ago is as night to day. A great deal has changed in Britain during my 43 years here, but I suggest that the essential characteristics of the nation are unchanged in one hundred years.

Indeed it cannot be otherwise for all that we see and experience around us is created by language.

Our language defines us. It sets the parameters of our reality. Songwriters and novelists know it. Polemicists, pollsters, politicians and TV producers know it. They all know that restriction of language means restriction of thought, and thus eventually of behaviour. I wrote about the negative effects of this, what I called "Speech Creates", in *Emergence Book Zero: Darkness*. Now we are able to understand the hidden influences of our language, by recognising that wherever there is a letter there is also a number.

Numerology 101

"There is a Divine Source which is ultimate Truth…this Truth can be expressed by means of numbers…and that, if followed correctly, these principles can be expressed with infinite variety to produce Beauty." – Prince Charles.

Numerology states that numbers *form patterns* and *generate meaning*. Numbers are everywhere, and therefore pattern and meaning are also everywhere. I present a detailed explanation of the intricacies of numerological methods in *The Secret Language of Numbers* and *Emergence Book One: Law*, but for now we can proceed with a mode of transferring letters into numbers, attributed to the Ancient Greek Pythagoras, famous for his well known mathematical theorem about triangles and angles. This is the Pythagorean Key, and we will use it to transpose letters for numbers throughout this book:

1	2	3	4	5	6	7	8	9
A	B	C	D	E	F	G	H	I
J	K	L	M	N	O	P	Q	R
S	T	U	V	W	X	Y	Z	

Accordingly, whenever a particular letter is written or uttered (even if it is a silent sound) then the corresponding numerical vibration is activated. Words, being collections of letters, form greater vibrations, which can be analysed numerically to reveal the energy hidden behind the word. This then tells us what is actually said, as distinct from what is meant, intended or heard.

We pair each letter of the English language with a single digit numerical equivalent. Each letter of a word is numerated in this way and then added together to give a two–digit number. We note if these two–digits sum to between 1 and 22 inclusive, or 33. Two digit numbers are known as *compound numbers*. We then take the individual digits of the compound number and add those together until we reach a single digit number. This step is called *reduction* and it produces what we call the *root number*. Those two numbers then offer us two levels of numerological interpretation of any word, or name. The compound number offers us higher lessons and bigger picture stuff, while the root number gives us finer and more fundamental details. Students of numerology should note that there are an impossibly large number of alternative and derivative methods. Many have merit and all show us something. I detail many of these in *Emergence Book One: Law*, but the methods found here have proved to be the most accurate, tested to destruction over the last twenty–five years. But wait;

"Not everything that counts can be counted. And not everything that can be counted counts"–Albert Einstein.

In other words, we must, partially at least, heed the warning of the mathematician who shuns numerology with a cry of 'Reductio ad absurdum!' We must not fall down a rabbit hole. We can ascribe letters to numbers using consistent methods and look for any patterns that might emerge, checking our prejudices and desires as well as our calculations. We can interpret those patterns through a prism where numbers are energy and energy is alive, wishing to show itself through those words. We can suggest that to a great extent, things are whatever we name them. But we must not see patterns where they do not exist, nor conjure them up wherever we wish.

Nonetheless, I guarantee that you will find – as I did – the repeated numerological patterns in this book shocking and amazing. Or perhaps it would be more accurate to say that your Ego – like mine – is the thing that will be amazed. For the inner soul, the essential self knows that amazing things happen every single day, but the Ego wishes to keep your awareness as far away from true wonder as possible.

The truth awaiting us is that numbers *allow* much more than they *tell*. It is through a process of absorption in numbers where connections of which we were previously unaware become apparent. We are neither using numbers for tenuous self–justification, nor trying to reveal a hidden codex pre–programmed by some section of the Illuminati. We are simply accessing portions of a bigger picture that we would not normally see, through a series of defined methods. We are not looking to statistically prove anything, nor are we looking to get lost in a bubble of the infinite in a search of God. We are simply choosing to think differently, to approach old questions in a new way. This is what numerology allows us to do. Numerology is valuable for the truth that it reveals, not that which it contains.

We will calculate five data points for each word or name under analysis. Each data point has been given an identifying name, for ease, to help us see repetition and pattern. It is through these that we will be able to read the Numbers of Britain, using consistent methodology.

Some Rules
Common numbers from different data points suggest some meaning or resonance between words.
Repeated instances of common numbers across words suggest a pattern.

All resonances and connections are noted, including any that are absent when we might expect otherwise.

Whenever we deal with a root number we are also directly dealing with its multiples and indirectly dealing with its compounds. For example, to have 3 is to connect to 6 and to 9. To have 6 is to become aware of the possibility of 15.

Five Data Points

Expression
The addition, and reduction, of the numbers from all the letters in the whole of a word or name.

ENGLAND
$5 + 5 + 7 + 3 + 1 + 5 + 4 = 30$
$3 + 0 = 3$
Thus, England's Expression = 3

SCOTLAND
$1 + 3 + 6 + 2 + 3 + 1 + 5 + 4 = 25$
$2 + 5 = 7$
So, Scotland's Expression = 7

This is the most important data point, whose numbers represent the message that the word is trying to deliver. As the word, or name, is written or spoken so the Expression number is brought to life. We can immediately see that in the case of ENGLAND (3) and SCOTLAND (7) the numbers are very different. 3 does not fit with 7 cleanly, and 7 (being much larger) certainly cannot be absorbed into 3. As it is mathematically so it is numerologically. England does not fit with Scotland very cleanly, and Scotland certainly will not be swallowed by England, even though geographically and by population it is much smaller.

An easy doorway into numerology is to imagine that each number produces a two–dimensional shape. For example 4 would produce a square, 5 a pentagram, and so on. In the example above England produces a triangle, yet Scotland produces a heptagon. At this simple level of interpretation we can see that these are two shapes that cannot interlace or fit perfectly and cleanly side by side.

Soul Urge
The addition, and reduction, of the numbers from only the vowels (a, e, i, o u) in the whole word or name.

ENGLAND = E, A
$5 + 1 = 6$
So, England's Soul Urge = 6
SCOTLAND = O, A
$6 + 1 = 7$
So, Scotland's Soul Urge = 7

These numbers show us the inner motivations of the word, what it wants and where it is seeks to go. Mathematically, England's Expression of 3 is divisible into its Soul Urge of 6, showing us numerologically that the nation's soul can be easily expressed. In Scotland's case we have a repeated number (7 again) where Scotland straightforwardly expresses its soul, and in turn finds that through all its expressions that its soul is revealed. This is akin to wearing its heart on its sleeve.

Secret Desire
The addition, and reduction, of the numbers from only the consonants in the whole word or name.

ENGLAND = N, G, L, N, D
5 + 7 + 3 + 5 + 4 = 24
2 + 4 = 6
So, England's Secret Desire = 6

SCOTLAND = S, C, T, L, N, D
1 + 3 + 2 + 3 + 5 + 4 = 18
1 + 8 = 9
So, Scotland's Secret Desire = 9 (influenced by its compound, 18)

This reveals the hidden, possibly unexpressed, but implicit drive of the word. Sometimes this is unrecognised, denied, is shown through challenge and difficulty, or goes unfulfilled. It is somewhat more difficult to harness than the Soul Urge. Here England's Secret Desire (6) harmonises nicely with its other numbers (3 and 6), while Scotland's Secret Desire of 9 reveals a new factor in the identity of that nation, a nonagon to fit with the previous two heptagons. 9 is always recognised as a powerful force in numerology, being the highest possible root number. There is, therefore, ambition for more deep in Scotland's psyche.

First Letter
The number of the first letter of the word or name. This is the letter –and thus the number –which makes the initial impact when spoken or written.

ENGLAND = E
E = 5
So, the First Letter/Number of England = 5

SCOTLAND = S
S = 1
So, the First Letter/Number of Scotland = 1

These numbers lead and are the first things produced by utterance or transcription of the name. 5 is the middle number in the sequence of 1 to 9, occupying the middle station of a nine square grid. This is a powerful and pivotal number capable of multi–directional movement, expansion and travel. While the 1 of Scotland is the first and the solitary, able to only move in one direction for, unlike mathematics, numerology has not yet developed to incorporate minus numbers. Thus we have an England that initially seems much more (5) than it is (3, 6, 6), while Scotland seems much less (1) than it really is (7, 7, 9).

Repeating Letters
Any repeating letters in the word or name that correspond to the same number. For example, A and J though different letters correspond to the same number (1). The earlier in the word the letter/number repeats the more weight it is given during interpretation.

ENGLAND = E, N, N = 5

SCOTLAND = S, A = 1

In these examples we have revealed the same numbers that we had in the First Letter Data Point. This emphasises the interpretation we just made. This will not, however, always be so.

So, we have five numbers for each name. But what else do they mean?

Common Meanings & Behaviours of the Root Numbers

The meanings and behaviours of numbers are suggestive, which is to say they are not fixed or always identical. Each number produces a spectrum of possibilities – from full expression of the number's force, to complete denial of it. Yet even when the essential behaviour of a number is suppressed it is still apparent and can be traced back to its root. The numbers therefore have multi–valence (many meanings), but not omni–valence (any meanings). The Prime Law of Numerology states that 1 is 1, but 1 is not 2. Thus, within bounds there are many meanings to each number, but all those meanings are related. For example, ONE can be many types of singular, but it is never plural.

A good analogy is the prism, which captures pure light and refracts it, distributing it out again in more readily recognisable forms. Over the page are the 9 root manifestations, which show themselves, as indicated, wherever and whenever they appear – in words, names, dates and places, large or small, human or impersonal.

1	Independence. Drive. Innovation. Invention. Leadership. Entrepreneurship. Pioneering. Self–determining. Or the lack of/need for these things. Does not take direction well. Can be impatient.
2	Partnership. Co–operation. Diplomacy. Negotiation. Harmony. Balance. Emotions. Sensitivity. Or the lack of/need for these things. Often needs others to give it a lead, but must resist domination by others. Can be indecisive. Must resist the urge to prove strength by force.
3	Creativity. Self–expression – music, arts, literature. Fame, celebrity, notoriety. Shows and celebrations. Openness. Or the lack of/need for these things. Often poor financial management and inability to recognise mistakes. May come in for a great deal of criticism.
4	Order. Rules. Traditions. Systems. Building and construction. Hard work, organisation and efficiency. Or the lack of/need for these things. Equally determined to succeed and stubborn in the face of change. All endeavours must be built on solid material foundations.
5	Travel. Adventure. Freedom. Discovery. Movement. Change. Versatility. Adaptability. Education and teaching. Or the lack of/need for these things. Operates best within a loose framework of guidelines, is rebellious against strict rules.
6	Togetherness. Society. Family. Community. Social cohesion. Looking after one another. The house and home. Or the lack of/need for these things. Prone to interfering in others' affairs.
7	Privacy. Aloofness. Detachment. Nature, animals, the elements. Knowledge, science, technology. Spirituality. Eccentricity. Thoughts, more than feelings. Or the lack of/need for these things. Dreamy, muddling through. Strong connections with water. Affinity with the past. Can become solitary and isolated. Can develop an overly critical nature.
8	Money. Wealth. Power. Finance. Control. Strength. Force. Or the lack of/need for these things. Can be dictatorial and aggressive. Can be self–critical and too quick to find fault.
9	Humanity. Charity. Compassion. Kindness, openness. The bigger picture. Big spirit and big heart. Or the lack of/need for these things. Could be downtrodden and oppressed.

This table is a summary, for in truth we could produce a large volume of meanings and associations for every number, such is the detail associated with each. But a basic interpretation for oneself can always be achieved by following the invisible thread that runs Number –2D Shape –Pattern –Tarot card. We will develop this further later on.

Numbers are to all intents and purposes alive and sentient, their precise existence shaped by, though not reliant upon, context. Their energy is neither created nor enlivened by our awareness of them. Numbers are everywhere, we cannot stand outside of them. They operate around us and through us, even dictating how aware we might be of their very existence! The behaviour of a number thus becomes the behaviour of any entity that owns that number – be it through word, name or date. Any life that also belongs to that entity, or uses its name, is then also influenced by it. As soon as we create names and words (even though our intentions will themselves be defined by previously existing numbers) they continue their operation in the world regardless of our belief and recognition of them.

The Root Numbers of the Nation

Officially the current name of the country is the **United Kingdom of Great Britain and Northern Ireland**, although variants are often used. Internationally, within the United Nations and the European Union it is officially known as the United Kingdom, often just shortened to UK. Yet informally this is interchanged with Great Britain, and sometimes simply Britain, the name as to which the country has long been referred, although technically Great Britain does not include Northern Ireland. From the Acts of Union in 1801 until the establishment of the Irish Free State in 1922 the whole nation was officially known as the United Kingdom of Great Britain and Ireland (without a distinction for Northern). The six counties of the north of Ireland only became known as Northern Ireland after the British government's partition of the island in 1921, exercising their negotiated opt–back–in to Great Britain the following year. Indeed, to some the name of those six counties is Ulster. There was even serious discussion, in 1949, of changing the name of the whole nation to the United Kingdom of Great Britain and Ulster, though nothing came of this in the end. And not long before all of that the usage of the term British Empire was commonplace, whilst even further back there is good evidence that the nation was once named Albion. Confused we are indeed. What do we write in that box marked 'Nationality'? For it matters very much what we are called. It affects how others see us, and therefore how they treat us, and therefore potentially how we ourselves respond.

The uninitiated should now prepare for a mass of numbers to wash over and into them. Be happy in the knowledge that you do not know what they mean, yet secure with the possibility that you already know what they mean, even though you do not know that you know. Get comfortable in the confusion and contradictory wash (or freeze!) of information in your mind. This is akin to learning a new language, or perhaps re–learning it, for if you are an inhabitant or visitor to these isles then you have already connected with the meaning of the nation in some way or another. None of the answers we seek may present themselves consciously or logically. Any unexpected flashes of insight are as jewels amongst wreckage, and that is what we seek. This is the key to understanding numerology.

As GREAT BRITAIN (7) we recognise the stiff upper lip of aloofness and detachment, our long involvement with science and technology, going back even before the Industrial Revolution, and our self image as a nation of animal lovers. In this 7 we have all things impractical, our Heath Robinson make–do–and–mend approach and an attachment to the past. We see the same in SCOTLAND

Country	Expression	Soul Urge	Secret Desire	First Letter	Repeating Letters/Numbers
United Kingdom of Great Britain and Northern Ireland	8	9	8	U (3)	N, E (5)
Great Britain	7	7	9	G (7)	R, I (9)
United Kingdom	(11) 2	5	6	U (3)	N, E (5) D, M (4)
England	3	6	6	E (5)	E, N (5)
Scotland	7	7	9	S (1)	S, A (1) & C, L (3)
Wales	6	6	9	W (5)	W, E (5) & A, S (1)
Northern Ireland	(22) 4	8	5	N (5)	N, E (5) & I, R (9)
Ulster	5	8	6	U (3)	U, L (3)
Ireland	9	6	3	I (9)	I, R (9)
British Empire	7	1	6	B (2)	R, I (9)
British Isles	5	5	5	B (2)	R, I (9)
Britain	1	1	9	B (2)	R, I (9)
Albion	8	7	1	A (1)	none

(7), one of the driving forces in the creation of Empire. 7 is also the number of dreams and fantasies, which often do not survive contact with reality. Both Great Britain and Scotland are the lands of dreamers. As the BRITISH EMPIRE (7) we saw thinkers and preachers on unrealistic missions to civilise the globe. Interestingly, now that we are under the influence of the UNITED KINGDOM OF GREAT BRITAIN AND NORTHERN IRELAND (8) we relate everything through the prism of money and power, and assume that was the driver of old Empire, whereas the truth may have been more noble and delusional (7). The High Victorian Tory Prime Minister, the dour Lord Salisbury, may have been even nearer to the heart of this matter when in 1861 he is supposed to have remarked, when discussing the purpose of continuing vast Imperial defence spending, *"it is to indulge in the sentiment that the sun never sets on our Empire."* His words capture the very essence of 7 and the numbers suggest that the British Empire was formed from the mixture of a noble motive of togetherness (Secret Desire 6) by pioneering and selfish methods (Soul Urge 1) in the quest to spread reason and knowledge (Expression 7), but that the whole thing was a bit of a fantasy (7).

Today's nation is a different story, dominated by its expression 8. Since its birth in 1922 this has shown itself through all things of power; the military, territory, law, sovereignty and money have been the many factors in our modern story. We are certainly playing out a deep relationship with these things, the most visible of which is money. Much more on that later.

Elsewhere, the prominence of 7 reveals separation, distance and aloneness. Here we can clearly see the desire of the nation and empire to be distinct from the wider world, the reinforcement of the separate island–race mentality, our failure to integrate fully into the EU and now the approaching culmination of centuries old Scottish dreams of separation. Being nations of 7 the further suggestion is that this *is* just a dream. Traditional British reserve on the other hand is a product of the desire for privacy (7), repressed self–expression (negative 3) and emotional disconnection (negative 11/2).

7 is a number with long tentacles, of which Great Britain and the Empire forms an integral part. The author Rod Chapman wrote extensively about the appearance of the number in his fascinating book *Seven*. Seven Wonders of the World, Seven Seas, Seven Traditional Planets, Seven Days of the Week, seven stars in the Pleiades and the Plough. There are many, many others, including appearances closer to home such as the terrorist bombings of 7/7, in the year 2005 (2+0+0+5 = 7).

Merry Old ENGLAND (3) fulfils its nickname well, expressing the number of optimism, confidence and good times together with overspending and lack of restraint. England (3) with its Three Lions, sits well alongside WALES (6 = 2 x 3) and IRELAND (9 = 3 x 3) though not with SCOTLAND (7), the numbers 3 and 7 relating to each other in precisely no way at all. By including the Soul Urge and Secret Desire we see a great symbiosis between the three nations England (3, 6, 6), Wales (6, 6, 9) and Ireland (9, 6, 3). Yet still, by this measure,

Scotland stands semi–detached (7, 7, 9), as does to a much greater extent NORTHERN IRELAND (22/4, 8, 5). The message is clear, by the continued usage of the component country names the whole nation is fractured and divided. Surely it is just a matter of time until the holes can no longer be patched? At this point we should note that 9 - at the forefront of Ireland and in the background of Scotland - is the number of extremes. It is the biggest, most charitable and open number, as well as the most oppressed and victim-like. This reflects a history of subjugation, whether it be Catholics by Protestants, Ireland by Rome or the EU, and both Scotland and Ireland by the English.

It is perhaps to the UNITED KINGDOM that we must look for something uplifting. Here we lead with the Letter U (3), the number of the arts, fashion, music, literature and self–expression. The need for attention and recognition, but a dislike of others getting the same. A cynical and sarcastic streak, good at talking, but not always listening. Demeaning and censorious. And always –accidentally on purpose –the one of whom others disapprove. The Expression of 2 brings into play the need for harmony, tolerance and accommodation. 2 seeks balance in all things, which to some just seems like muddling through, or being junior partner to another, but nonetheless comes into its own when placed in a diplomatic balancing role. 2 is the number of now – the 2000's AD – and as such the United Kingdom keys into the current and future world in ways we cannot yet see. Yet like all numbers there is a negative side to take into account. 2 can bring weakness and fear and in the extreme negative, although the number is emotional, it also produces emotional repression and a busy–bodying attitude. It is often hard for the negative 2 to find a fulfilling place within a group – swinging from dominance over other members, to over–reliance on other members. With a Soul Urge 5, travel, adventure, rebellion and education are all well indicated, and the appearance again of 6 in the Secret Desire reveals the appeal of family and togetherness.

Depending on the precise method of calculation the UNITED KINGDOM reveals a compound number of 11 (1+1 then equalling the 2). This is a Master Number, a higher vibration requiring a more complex interpretation. Master Numbers act as bigger versions of their root, thus everything we have said about the United Kingdom and 2 becomes larger, truer, more powerful and more difficult. At its core it is the number of genius and invention through science and mathematics, but also of magic, spirituality and religion, together with intolerance and extremism. All shades of life appear through the doorway of the 11 – knowledge and ignorance, wealth and poverty, success and ruin. There are very few countries in the world that possess an 11. The two other most significant examples are FRANCE (11) and GERMANY (11), though not DEUTSCHLAND (3). When interacting, like Master Numbers are either the best of friends or mortal enemies, such is the strength of their respective energies. It might also be noted here that NORTHERN IRELAND sums to 22. This is an even more powerful and extreme number, with the potential for great things yet with self–destructive tendencies. The current and past expression of this has undoubtedly occurred on the level of 4 – repression, heaviness, tradition and downward looking. But 22 brings a hidden dimension into the life of NORTHERN IRELAND. Many will recognise this, yet will attribute it to The Troubles. We might say that The Troubles are attributed to the numbers. All these factors – and more – are at play in the names of the nation. They indicate the issues that the nations must work with and solve. Inevitably we will find ourselves (as individual components of the nations) working our way along the spectrum generated by each number. To work effectively with the diplomacy of 2 for example, we might first find ourselves powerful without any need for diplomacy, only to lose our power and in the process, by necessity, come to learn all about diplomacy. Numbers do not only indicate character, personality and behaviour. They show us the paths of evolution. So, just to make the point in a lighter way, let us look at three unofficial, yet evocative, names.

Country	Expression	Soul Urge	Secret Desire	First Letter	Repeating Letters/Numbers
Britannia	7	2	5	B (2)	R, I (9)
Cool Britannia	7	5	2	C (3)	R, I (9)
Little Britain	7	6	1	L (3)	T, B (2) I, R (9)

As we can see from the continued repetition of 7 it does not really matter what we, as a family of four nations, call ourselves, for we cannot escape from the 7. Cool Britannia though itself a reaction against Empire and Conservatism is as British as Queen Victoria while Lou and Andy from Little Britain connect as much to the soul of the nation as Charles Dickens did more than one hundred years before.

A Note about Language

The re–introduction of Welsh, and to a lesser extent Gaelic, into common usage, along with the popular migrant languages of Polish, Punjabi, Urdu, Bengali and Gujarati across the nations makes it hard to apply the lessons of the letters and the numbers universally. These languages are spoken in small though significant amounts and do not fit into the 9–stage Pythagorean Key. Some work is being done with regards to creating a Polish Numerology but as a Slavic language with many additional letters this is not an easy task. All such attempts are made harder by the fact that equivalent or replacement letters from English often do not exist and that translations between languages are always imperfect.

The deeper lesson here is that to speak a different language is to literally call a spade a shovel. To speak a different language is to approach the world differently, and to name things differently is to interact with them differently. Thousands of Poles, for example, live in Scotland (7), but if their English language skills are not good, and/or they have not been here very long then as far as they are concerned they may live in Szkocja (1). Their quality of interaction with the surroundings is then changed. They are literally walking around in a different world than the rest of us. Absolutely no racial superiority or discrimination should be inferred from this, but it cannot help community cohesion if one group are walking around, interacting with and seeing 1, while everyone else is dealing with and working in 7. It is neither better nor worse to be in 1 or 7, but it is different. The ramifications of all this are significant so, with a few exceptions, the examples in this book are therefore necessarily limited to the English language.

A Note About Prejudice

I approach this work neither from the perspective of Britain Good, nor Britain Bad. When people claim to hate Britain or to love Britain what they really mean is that they love and hate *parts* of Britain, parts that are inevitably subject to change and will, over time, flower or fade. We will see that there is an essential soul to the nation, or maybe a collection of souls, which endures and weaves through fashion, politics, celebration and scandal. In today's interconnected global world we may be so assailed by outside, international influences that we cannot any longer discern the national character. Yet it lives on, regardless of our connection to it.

Stereotypes always contain a grain of truth, which is why they offend people so easily. Yet they never tell the whole story. England is still as much the home of stuffy old Colonel Blimps as it is eccentric, cunning men and women who live down the end of the lane selling herbs and reading Tarot cards. But it is also the place of Polish shopkeepers and Indian restaurants. Diversity of thought exists on pristine cricket pitches in Surrey just as much as diversity of music, ethnicity and dress exist on Geordie council estates. They are just different types of diversity. The Lancashire Working Men's Club plays host to bigotry and racism just as much as the Bullingdon Club. It just expresses itself differently. And the indentured labour that worked the fields of the aristocracy hundreds of years ago does not seem so far removed from the mortgage tied wage slaves who now undergo daily multi–hour commutes just to sit at a desk and perform a job that in one hundred years will be done in a fraction of the time by a robot. Yes, we must be very careful in asserting enlightenment to ourselves, or prejudice to others.

Therefore the numbers provide a commentary of awareness, and can never indicate a rightness of outcome or behaviour. Be very sure to understand this point for regardless of individual preferences, appearance, race, skin colour, clothing, religion, language, gender, sexuality, wealth, or education, everyone involved with the life of Great Britain is playing their part in working the spectrum of the numbers revealed by the names of the nation. Every British life, native born or otherwise, is an expression of British identity, British success and British failure. Every lesson learned by an individual is an advancement of the nation, whilst every refusal to learn is a retardation of the nation. Advancement and decay occur in every family, street, and town across the nation. Yet all these contradictory actions, so visible now in a transparent society, are themselves merely acts on the stage of the grand old play known as Great Britain.

The Matter of Britain

Great Britain is a land of stories, tales and legends (3 – England). Through these we immerse ourselves in the past (7 – Scotland, Great Britain) and connect deeply with notions of love and romance (6 – Wales) though we may be undemonstrative about this (4 – Northern Ireland). These traits are as apparent in William Shakespeare and Edward Elgar as they are in Harry Potter and Amy Winehouse. Our favourite tales of King Arthur and the Knights of the Round Table are fundamentally stories of romance, as are The Adventures of Robin Hood, Richard the Lionheart, Henry VIII and his Six Wives, Queen Victoria's forty–year mourning of her beloved Albert, as well as the tragic life and death of Princess Diana. Whether we demonstrate it or not, the United Kingdom is a land of deep emotion (11/2).

The Arthurian canon, together with the legendary naming of the island by Brutus of Troy and the subsequent tales of Old King Cole and King Lear (later further romanticised by the English Storyteller–in–Chief William Shakespeare, as well as many others) all form part of what is known as The Matter of Britain. The work is rich, complex and deeply interwoven into the national psyche. It involves a study of great literature and appreciation (if not a belief) in ancient, pre–Christian Gods and practices. Essentially the Matter of Britain speaks to five key things:

1. The Nature of Britain

The Matter implies, if it does not state outright, British exceptionalism. Here the names of the nation are often different, and much of the Matter could arguably be attributed more to Wales or Ireland than any other part of the Isles. Nonetheless, threaded throughout are stories of which there is no compare elsewhere in the world; richer, older and deeper even than the Matter of Rome. Though the Romans bequeathed us a great deal of archaeology, the Britons passed on an oral tradition in which the beauty of the land is often spoken of, as are the wondrous things that occurred in the reign of Arthur. According to some, though now lost to history, the realm of King Arthur extended as far afield as Northern Norway, Iceland, Greenland, Eastern Canada, and Western France. The suggestion is always that a nation divided is a people lost, but a nation united and expanding is a people proud and free.

2. Ideals of Behaviour and Values to Aspire to (or overcome)

Every archetypal character is contained in the Arthurian Tradition. There is the strong, yet flawed leader King Arthur, who gets stuck between love for his beautiful wife Guinevere and loyalty to the office of King. Tales of chivalry extend to individual Knights, some successful and brave, others less so. A utopian community is centred on the egalitarian Round Table, within the city of enlightened values, Camelot. All this is constructed by King Arthur's bravery and virtue, yet none of it would be possible without the wise counsel of the wizard–sage Merlin and the forces he invokes. All of these characters and situations are readily apparent – in modern form – in today's world. From the industrial estate to the sports field, via the school gates and all places in between, Lancelot, Guinevere, Arthur and Merlin together with all of their dramas, in whole or in part, repeated yet never fully resolved, are everywhere to be seen.

3. The Promise of Salvation

A key appeal of the myth of King Arthur is that he never died, and is merely sleeping, waiting to take up his rightful place as *Restitutor Britanniae*, The Restorer of Britain. The idea that significant British figures do not die and instead go into some kind of holding space is a powerful and enduring one. It was a strong current after the death of such icons as The Duke of Wellington in 1852, Lord Kitchener in 1916, and again with the passing of Winston Churchill in 1965. In both Kitchener and Churchill's case there were many contemporary accounts of how otherwise rational people simply refused to accept that their hero was no more. We have long been infatuated with the idea that one man (or woman) can save us from ourselves. With the furore surrounding Jeremy Corbyn's successful bid to lead the Labour Party in 2015 we can see that nothing has really changed in this regard.

At the heart of the Matter lies the promise of the return of King Arthur when the land and people need him. Whether any of this is true or not is secondary to the invisible power of the story in shaping beliefs and culture, even in a society that overtly disregards such things. Redemption and restoration, of the land and people, live on through these tales. They are witnessed today in every TV property makeover show where an old relic is converted to modern use. Central to the value of these myths is the assertion that Britain is Great and made to a Grand Design when it is forged by noble men and women who are themselves guided beyond reason by invisible forces they do not understand.

4. Sorcery: What Might Merlin Say?

Merlin is every sorcerer, wise man, sage and counsellor that has ever existed in Britain. He shows himself through the Whitehall Mandarin, the Oxford academic, the Druid, the Wiccan priest, the New Age Life Coach and the Strategic Business Consultant. He is the Adviser, the Hermit and the Wise Old Man. Whether his voice can be heard or not is, of course, another matter. But he embodies these traits in a peculiarly British way. Merlin's guardianship of Britain is recognised in the alternative name of the nation *Clas Myrddin* (Merlin's Enclosure). Connection with him is intensely necessary for any understanding of the nation, so tightly are the two interwoven. Such a connection might go like this:

"What is your nature, Merlin?"
"Wild and free, independent. Of the rain and the wind."
"How can this nature return to the land?"

"It cannot. But it can be re–born in new guises."
"How so, Merlin?"
"Cultivate invention, non–conformity, awkwardness and eccentricity. Be these things organically, birthing and returning to the soil, enriching the next generation."
"What about belief? Socialism, liberalism, these things are British, right?"
"No, these things are alien to Britain, though fairness is British. Simply be the tree. Trees crowd out other trees only when badly planted."
"Where might we find the essential nature of Britain?"
"Search The Forgotten Lands. It is not one country but four."

5. Sovereignty: Who Rules the Land?

Merlin performs an essential role in that he is the only one strong enough to speak truth to power – in this case first Uther Pendragon and then King Arthur. King Arthur is every monarch and Prime Minister that has ever existed. And every leader needs a wife (or husband) to provide their balance and their sanity. This is Guinevere.

Central to the Matter of Britain is the three–pronged relationship of the People to their Leader and the Land. The Land, in Arthurian tradition, is not some inanimate thing that is taken for granted. It is alive, and identified as female in recognition of its fertility. This can also be seen in the Goddess Minerva, often taken as the symbol of Britannia. Those who seek rulership of the People must take the Land into account, the true nature and name of which is only revealed to the one she chooses. No one can govern the People against the wishes of the Land. No one can rule the Land who cannot rule themselves. No one can hold the Land who cannot hold their wife or husband. This level of governance is way beyond what is derived from the ballot box and can be recognised in the successes and failures of our various leaders over time. Many are the leaders who have attempted to govern without the consent of the Land. Their efforts were always disastrous.

"You are the Land and the Land is You. As you grow, the Land will prosper. As you falter so the Land shall perish." Merlin to King Arthur. Excalibur (1981)

The Forgotten Lands

Many have searched the geography of the nation for clues and signs as to the hidden nature and power of Britain. Yet the secret does not lie in Westminster Abbey, on Lindisfarne, atop Glastonbury Tor, or beneath Rosslyn Chapel. It lies hidden in plain sight in the four Forgotten Lands.

Taken literally this suggests parity of importance between England, Scotland, Northern Ireland and Wales. Often, culturally, when people say British they actually mean English, and this is then sometimes taken as a slight and used as a wedge, highlighting how the three smaller nations are bullied and overlooked by the English. It is a complex political and constitutional problem which can only be truly resolved by recognising that the four component nations are very different, as shown by their numbers, in character, behaviour, values and energy.

Some attempts to address these issues have been made, with many decision–making powers devolved to the component nations, with many other policies decided in Westminster but implemented differently across the four nations. In this way we can see that the nation is already fractured and diminished.

But the nation cannot really be understood so superficially. To deeply connect with The Forgotten Lands is to do nothing less than re–awaken the Ancient Gods of the Elements: Earth, Water, Air and Fire, under the direction of the supreme fifth element – Akasha. This is a powerful occult operation, performed under the alchemical formula VITRIOL – *Visita Interiora Terrae, Recificando Invenies Occultum Lapidem.* Visit the interior parts of the earth, by rectification thou shalt find the hidden stone. The interior parts of the earth are the Forgotten Lands.

These Lords of Change are the real component nations of Great Britain. They exist in varying measure throughout the world, but are rarely recognised or called upon. A notable exception to this was in the run up to Pearl Harbour when the Japanese Emperor Hirohito marked them in a challenge to his generals, saying, apparently repeatedly, that *"the seas of the four directions are all born of one womb..."* History however shows us that Great Britain was once most effective in gaining the co–operation of these Gods. The Empire was the proof of this, its missteps and mistakes a product of man's frailty and disconnection from those Gods. Man's belief in his own might, forgetting just as King Arthur did that it was the Gods working through him that created the magic, caused the downfall and broken connection. Somewhere, in the midst of Empire we lost sight of the secret – that recognition of the Forgotten Lands must always breed a greater and more active involvement with them. Thus, through this practice, the Land and the People prosper, and without it both fail.

EARTH

We see the impact of the Gods of the Earth in all things that move slowly and endure. Traditions, customs, laws and history are all the domain of the Earth. The countryside, farming, agriculture, quarrying and mining dwell here too. Practical people engaged in ordering, construction and manufacturing, working with materials – coal, iron, paper, glass – and fabrications of all kinds – brick, steel and wood – come under the auspices of the Earth. Earth is not interested in simply assembly, but in turning raw, natural material, by skill and craft, into useful form. Along with the by products of this (dirt and waste) nobility and purpose is found in work. When the Gods of Earth are dominant then the atmosphere can be heavy and unimaginative, yet reliable and consistent. In the same way that some component nations of Great Britain are mistakenly ascribed less importance than others, so Earth is, mistakenly, treated the same. Regardless of technological advancement the need for the Gods of the Earth to be actively harnessed in pursuit of a better life is a great as it ever was. Where matters of the Earth are disregarded, or we believe we have somehow ascended beyond them then we will always be reliant upon others for our material welfare.

A successful modern nation, with the co–operation of the Gods of the Earth, would value and encourage maker communities of artisan crafters right alongside large-scale high tech manufacturing plants, each working new types of materials and finding new processes for old materials. Materials technology, recycling, repair and restoration would all grow under the blessing of Earth. Mining, maybe through the extension of clean burn coal technologies, would begin a resurgence. Both the love affair and the hostility to mining in Britain, particularly of coal, are doctrinal and outdated. Trades Unions may honestly seek only protection of their workers, but the militant miners in the 1970s and 1980s crafted the death sentence for their own industry. A post–Scargill, post–Thatcher revival is now required. Safety concerns and environmental worries are artificial barriers to the British actively engaging with the Gods of the Earth. With just one proviso.

Permission and Thanks

Anything that man appears to achieve for himself is actually only ever done with the co–operation of the Elements or, as we call them here, the Gods. (The efforts of women and the co–operation of Goddesses in equal measure is implicit throughout). The sea will always overwhelm the sailor if it wants to, and there is nothing the sailor can do about it. The earth will swallow the miner, if it wants to, and there is nothing that the miner, his friends, or his safety technology, can do about it. A successful Britain would be respectful of the role of these Gods, and seek permission from them at all times. A good example of this is in the currently controversial topic of fracking.

We urgently need to train an army of sensitives to be able to ask the Earth whether it agrees to be fracked. These people must be able to hear the answer of the Earth, as distinct from the answer of their own prejudices, or their community's propaganda. I say this because it is not at all clear that the Earth would be resistant to giving up her fruits if we asked correctly, undertook the work respectfully and gave appropriate thanks afterwards. Coal miners of old would wax lyrical about the almost spiritual nature of their connection to the Earth, and this was no romantic illusion, for they recognised the awesome power of the Earth and possibly came to glimpse that through sympathy, communication and co–operation the Gods will grant whatever is in their remit to give. But if the Gods do not want to play ball then they will see to it that their domain is not interfered with. Some modern Druids believe they have already had this conversation and received the answers. I would want to be much more certain about this before placing myself in the anti–fracking community.

All things material and natural are ruled by the Gods of the Earth. Crops grow bountifully under their guardianship, the soil fertile and vibrant. Metals forge and mix well, the ore plentiful, with co–operation. The Gods are generous through co–operation and respect, but can rarely be coerced. Gold and silver remain hidden or are discovered, as the Gods allow, not as man desires. Great

Britain could be at the forefront of this kind of enlightened approach, for this is not about a regression into superstition. This is very much about the future and the hidden principles that lie beyond science and apply to all things of and from the Earth.

So many things of and from the Earth have an economic value, which is often where the problems start. But economic problems are fundamentally elemental problems, and that is the level on which we should approach them. We may live in a globalised, financial, knowledge economy, but fundamental, real, and lasting wealth is only ever generated by the creation of *value added*, the transformation of low value raw material, through innovation, skill, enterprise and effort, into higher value saleable product. Economic success is as much a matter of alchemy as the mystical quest for the Philosophers Stone. All the great wealth creators of history knew this and honed their own personal formulae, but when man turns away from the Gods of the Earth then his factories output less and less, his plant breaks down more and more and the quality of his product gets worse and worse. This was the fate of many British industries in the second half of the twentieth century.

Property, whether commercial or residential, is a matter of the Earth. Land ownership, fences and boundaries, planning permissions and rights of way all fall under the Earth's rulership, as does the shopping centre, the council estate, the affordable new–builds and the conservatory extension. The statue in the town centre and all the materials involved in its construction are Earth based. Kevin McCloud from TV's Grand Designs clearly seeks to channel the Gods of the Earth every day.

Currency is a further aspect of the Earth. Inflation, devaluation, the restriction or expansion of the money supply, the debasement of the coinage, debt, and taxation – all these things affect and distort our relationship with the Gods of the Earth. This is not a book about economic history but such a thing would be enormously revealing from an occult, numerological, elemental point of view. To borrow money without paying it back; to expend enormous sums on interest payments to international bankers; to devalue the coinage such that money in the hand buys less each day, and to heavily tax the poor whist allowing the rich loopholes – these things are *elemental suicide* and a slander to the Gods. To call out the evils of the current debt–based economic system is not to advance a socialist revolution, but a reconnection of the People to the Gods of the Earth in an appeal for their co–operation.

The Strange Case of Decimalisation

The fundamentals of a nation are formed from its numbers. Dates of birth of key figures, the names of its leaders, the establishment dates of organisations, coronations, inaugurations and funerals are all numerical, capturing and dictating the energies all around us. The UNITED KINGDOM OF GREAT BRITAIN AND NORTHERN IRELAND is conducting a long and intense relationship with money through its expression number 8. This is the number of finance, insurance, cash, credit and banking – all expressions themselves of power and control. In order to feed or even to resolve this, Harold Wilson's Labour government of the late 1960's agreed to abandon the currency system, first originated in Roman times, of Pounds, Shillings and Pence. This represented a numerical movement away from 12 (1 shilling = 12 pence, 1 pound = 240 pence) to 10 (1 new pound = 100 new pence).

The final implementation of this took place on Decimal Day, 15th February 1971 (15+2+1971 = 1988. 1+9+8+8 = 8). For a financial issue (8) to be dealt with on a financial day (8) in a nation conducting a tempestuous relationship with money (8) is just one of the many co–incidences–too–far that litter the story of the nation, as told in this book, for decimalisation was no mere cosmetic change, but a clear attempt to alter the relationship between the people and the Gods of the Earth. Harold Wilson's Labour cabinet is supposed to have nodded the change through, in 1966, with very little discussion; Wilson himself supposedly remarking, "why not?"

It was only the general public; dealing with the real–life effects of the change, who were unnerved, for to interfere with the currency is to interfere with the lifeblood of the nation. There are few things more fundamental to national well–being than the condition, names, and numbers of the money in the peoples' pocket. A great upheaval will likewise take place should Britain ever join the Euro, for regardless of political reassurances you only have to look at the change in appearance of British notes and coins over recent years to see how they are slowly being harmonised with the Euro.

What Wilson did not understand – or possibly even care about – was that to pass Shillings in payment for goods in 1960 was to connect directly with someone who had done the same three hundred years earlier, such was the length of time that the currency had been in operation. To change the currency was to interfere with the energy, symbolism and connection to the long–lived Gods of the Earth. This was the profound issue at stake, not the red herrings of standardisation and modernisation which Wilson cast out. To touch the currency is to interfere with the connection that people have with the Gods of the Earth and no government can survive this. Wilson was voted out, unexpectedly, in 1970. His successor, Edward Heath, who implemented Wilson's decision, was removed four years later. Wilson then returned again but was by now a shadow of his former self and lasted only two years.

Returning to other spheres of influence of the Gods of the Earth we find traditions, laws and customs. In order for people to govern a large expanse of land it must be divided into administrative regions. This has been done through the system of Shires ever since the Anglo–Saxons. These have largely survived centuries of political wrangling, including the most recent attempts at change by John Prescott and his regional assemblies. Though the quality of elected representatives can be poor the real problem lies in the maladministration of the land through constituency gerrymandering. The effectiveness of any elected or appointed representative is rooted in his or her connection to the People and the Land they represent. Both. Not just one or the other. Any drawing and redrawing of electoral or administrative boundaries that takes into account collections of red or blue voters but disregards rivers, hills, roads, and ancient landmarks is a disrespect by man of the Gods of the Earth. And this can only bring ruin on all of us.

Another aspect of Earth is the law. Matters of law are always complex and tricky to follow, and like roots in the soil, their effects are far-reaching.

Imagine an impossibly large round table, within which exists the full range of human possibilities, actions, trade, art and science. Common Law systems (which originated in Great Britain, but have now spread across the Anglo-Saxon world) tend to allow this range of human experience to continue unmolested until something goes wrong and legislation is passed in a particular area to correct that wrong. Subsequently an area of illegality is created – for example speed limits on roads – but all other areas remain untouched. This process is often criticised as being too slow and too reactive, lawmakers always behind the curve in adapting legislation to events.

Elsewhere on another impossibly large round table full of human possibilities is the governing system of Civil Law. This system, which is widely operative in Europe, tends to take a view across the range of human experiences and seeks to specifically allow and encourage certain – so called desirable – aspects. The implication within this system is that everything else is not permissible.

The differences between these two systems are of course not that clear cut, but Common Law – as practiced in Great Britain, though only partly in Scotland – seems to facilitate greater freedom while civil law tends toward the ongoing creation of 'well-behaved' societies, rather than free ones. If the difference between the two styles seems tiny or irrelevant then maybe that is because we have already forgotten what it means to be free? Freedom (5) sits at the heart of the numbers of the United Kingdom, England, Wales and Northern Ireland, though it features hardly at all in Scotland, which interestingly possesses its own hybrid legal system, part Common, part Civil, distinct from the other component nations. We might also carefully note that Sharia Law attempts to regulate all areas of the Table of Life according to the tenets of Islam.

Traditions also play a major part in the sustenance of the nation, and we forget them at our peril. It is only lately however that I have come round to this point of view. For many years, and well into my thirties, I railed against tradition, custom and all things established. British traditions, I mistakenly thought, were boring, backward and restrictive, the preserve of the male, pale and stale. Yet I now realise that we deride these things at our peril.

Customs are cohesive, and heritage is a steadying influence. Like everything it can be too much and the weight of history – due to the age of the nation – is great. But we risk going way too far in socially cleansing ourselves of the past. British traditions – roast beef, fish and chips, Wimbledon and the Grand

National – can be enjoyed and revived (and maybe should be) by Polish, Pakistani and Latvian migrants as much as the older members of the bowls club. There is no reason why the organising committee for Bonfire Night should not include the Asian corner shop keeper, the boss of the local Polish car wash as well as the retired mayor and former garage owner. All these people are British, by adoption if not birth, and are part of the nation and its evolving customs. Migrants may even bring their own customs to enrich, enhance and complement our own – but not to replace them, or be a substitute for them, without very good reason. For to discard the old without thought, in preference of shiny novelty is another slight upon the Earth. To embrace May Day, warm beer, Morris Dancers, Pearly Kings and Queens, and folk music should be the goal of everyone. And if we cannot embrace it then we must at least tolerate it and encourage the Morris Dancers to live stream or tweet their performance into the 21st Century. We must move beyond the stereotype of these people as discriminatory and closed minded, for paradoxically a great deal of derision and bigotry seems to stem from their progressive critics, utterly intolerant of that with which they disagree.

Alongside this the commemorative days of the National Saints George, Andrew, Patrick, and David should be heartily celebrated throughout the nation and effort given over to revere these things and gain understanding from them, because once we abandon the cohesive nature of tradition and custom the only way that society can hang together is through coercion by the law.

I can understand that free thinkers, creatives and revolutionary spirits often cannot abide these things of the Earth, but these people – of which I have been one – must learn tolerance of those who are slower, heavier and more fixed than they, and acceptance of the fact that a society gets on together or fails separately.

All of the Forgotten Lands are rooted in the Classical Elements and as such have many relevant occult correspondences. The Forgotten Land of the Earth is traditionally positioned in the North. Many occultists go to great lengths to resist applying their correspondences literally, constantly asserting that the North does not actually mean compass North. I do not agree however, for it is self–evident that one of the Forgotten Lands of our nation is Scotland. We will explore what can be done about this mountainous, craggy, Earth–bound place later on, but for now, we might call upon the co–operation of the ruling Angel of the North, Uriel, and the cold Wind of the North, Borus. These things are alive, if we take a moment to connect with them.

Food is another important aspect of the Earth, yet here is where modern society has not only forgotten the Gods, but seeks to actively disrespect them. Ready meals and processed foods are not a product of, or in alignment to, the Earth. We have formed no relationship to processed foodstuffs or to items shipped half way around the world. To eat British is to be British and to strengthen the nation. To cook what you grow, or be part of an allotment share is to deepen your connection to the Gods of the Earth. We might even have a thriving agricultural industry if we prioritised respect for the land over the worship of profit. We might even find ourselves amply rewarded for it. British food is long past being boring. Cornish Pasties, for example, can be cooked healthily using interesting varieties of ingredients, including the most British of British foods – curry. That's right, the first curry house is supposed to have opened in London in 1810, decades before the first fish and chip shop. Curry is as British as afternoon tea with the cricket at Lords.

In all these areas of the Earth we can see how there is much work to do, how far we have deviated from our relationship with these Gods, and how in certain cases we have perverted or destroyed our connection to them entirely. Observe the collection by town halls of vast tax receipts sitting side by side with their enormous profligacy and waste. See the obesity crisis alongside malnutrition and undernourishment. See how we have lost the skills of manufacture and fabrication and how very few of us want to get our hands dirty in any way at all. See how we can neither seem to build new homes nor keep in good order older buildings. Notice land banking, neighbour disputes about fence boundaries, and over zealous parking control firms. These are not purely political, social or economic arguments, for those things themselves flow from the influence of the Elements and the beneficence – or otherwise – of the Gods of the Earth. It is we who have departed from the Gods, not them from us, and we must stop mistreating the Earth – in all its manifestations – before it is too late.

"The Land is not safe when the people are unhappy, and the people are not safe when the Land is unhappy."– Benjamin Disraeli.

WATER

"Sea faring nations are in the business of constant accommodation, where as land locked nations believe there can be a perfect answer and a fixed end."– Gisela Stuart, German born, British Labour MP for Birmingham Edgbaston from 1997.

The Gods of Water hold powerful sway over the British Isles, whose nations have always succeeded when those Gods have been respected. Britannia ruled the waves because the Gods of Water co–operated in the creation of the Empire, and if they had been unwilling then it would not have flourished in the way that it did. Time and time again the Gods of Water have rescued the nation, assisting in the defeat of the Spanish Armada, the naval battles of World Wars One and Two and the discovery and extraction of North Sea Oil.

Yet many of today's inhabitants, of what was once the world's leading maritime nation, don't even like the rain! Whatever linkage we once possessed to the Gods of Water has all but disappeared. We have given away many of its manifestations. We no longer control our own fishing waters nor – to any scale – build our own boats. The great shipyards of Harland & Wolff in Belfast and those on the River Clyde in Glasgow no longer operate to anywhere near their historical extent. How did a nation that ruled the oceans less than one hundred years ago so utterly destroy its own connection to the sea?

We now need new connections with the Gods of Water. Wave power, maritime innovation, undersea research, and marine conservation –all these are things at which the British can excel. But we must address our relationship to water, boating, swimming, and the rain first.

We might restore these in part through a re–appreciation of such symbolic rituals as the Oxford and Cambridge Boat Race, school swimming competitions, Cowes Week, a thorough restoration of our seaside towns, and a return to active management of our waterways and wetlands. Many of these things, whether high or low, have fallen into disrepair or disregard, yet the whole nation benefits from their restoration, and we all languish from their decay. We have seen docklands through the UK – London, Salford, Gloucester, Bristol – restored successfully but it requires farsighted policy and brave decision making to create the necessary conditions to do this in, for example, Grimsby. Yet the condition of the waterfront in Grimsby is just as important as the presence of shops and housing in Gloucester Docks.

All things flowing, cleansing, and purifying come under the rulership of Water. Water is a deeply emotional force, deluging and overwhelming that which needs it. Water is therefore the most recognisably human of all the Gods, and it urges compassion for our fellow man, nudging us toward charity and concern for the poor and vulnerable. This is visible in the annual rituals of Comic Relief and Children in Need. Yet whilst the Gods see the humanitarian instinct in us they may not be so pleased when every aspect of public discourse becomes overwhelmed with woe, victimhood, grief and tears.

Continuing the human theme of Water we can see a connection to one of the most British of British things – migration. The story of Britain is the story of human migration. From the known history of Roman, Saxon, Viking and Norman invasion and settlement, to the departure of Britons in the creation of the Empire and the world as we know it, to the recent influx from Eastern Europe, North Africa and the Middle East, migration is the number one topic which defines and divides the nation.

The Necessary Deceit of New Labour

The objective of New Labour's open door immigration policy, from 1997 to 2010 was never disclosed until the very end of their time in power. Senior Labour figures have now admitted that their objective was nothing less than to utterly change the nature of the social fabric. If this had been overtly stated as policy then it is unlikely they would ever have been elected. So they had to lie and dissemble in order to get their way.

Prior to 1997, both the scale and the originating countries of immigrants into Britain were very different. Before New Labour the annual gross and net inflows were low, maybe in the tens of thousands, the vast majority of whom were from the ex–colonies. As such their ways of life, customs, and to some extent language were not that different, and even when they were the overall quantity made assimilation and integration that much easier. Granted there was very real and significant colour prejudice, but many Caribbean, African, and Asian families would willingly and swiftly adopt and improve British norms and values.

Here is not the place for a discussion about the socio–political–economic benefits and drawbacks of immigration. I mean only to layout what has happened and view it through the lens of the elements, numbers and letters. For the big shift post 1997 was the large scale introduction into the language of very different sets of words originating from Poland, Latvia, Lithuania and Czech which use the Slavic alphabet, not the Roman one.

Numerologically – and thus energetically – this makes a big difference. For example, the letters K (11 and 2), V (22 and 4) and Z (8) are much more prominent in the words of the Polish language, than they are in English. Men, women and children from Poland have names containing these letters, much more than the British do. As time passes and British people marry Polish people, passing hybrid names onto their children so the language of society changes. This is compounded by the all British couple with friendly Polish neighbours who are inspired them to call their first, British, child, Suzanna, for example.

Please take a moment to think carefully and coolly about what is being said here. Through large–scale immigration the language is slowly changed. As night follows day, if the language changes then the very nature of the country must also change. It is unavoidable. And very, very necessary.

A nation can only operate within its language structure, which is proscribed by the names it gives to things. In an everyday sense a British woman called Monica ($4+6+5+9+3+1 = 28$, $2+8 = 10$, $1+0 = 1$) will view the world and operate within it very differently to a Polish woman called Monika ($4+6+5+9+2+1 = 27$, $2+7 = 9$). Their differences will be partly to do with their nationally, but much more to do with their names. Monica (1) will be independent, bordering on selfish, while Monika (9) will be open and loving, bordering on naïve. This is far truer than many are prepared to accept, for names define us. Names are formed by letters, which are always connected to numbers.

Of course New Labour probably did not think this through when they embarked on their deceit. Their conscious calculation was more likely a political one, figuring that migrants would be less conservative in their views and more likely to vote Labour. But their true, now admitted, motivation was to utterly and completely change the nature of the country. In this they were successful.

Whether we like our Latvian neighbours, appreciate the work ethic of Polish builders and feel comfortable hearing Czech spoken on the bus – or not – is secondary to the fact that in order to renew the life of the nation we must constantly attract and retain people of a different vibration, conjoin the best of them with the best of us and together make a much better future for all. As the gene pool tends to stagnation over time so the language pool does the same. And if the language pool is restricted – by underuse or overuse of certain letters and numbers – then evolution stalls. Migration revives the language, and thus the nation. Having said that, the latest waves of migration have tended to introduce a lot of 4, through names beginning with the letter M. The negatives of 4 are ultra-conservatism and unwillingness to change. 4, in bulk, can be a dark energy.

Returning to other Watery connections, the corresponding direction is to the West, which takes us to Wales and Northern Ireland. These are by repute the most emotional, and wettest, parts of the Kingdom, ruled by the Angel Gabriel and influenced by the damp Winds of Zephyrus. Humanity and togetherness thus become more important in these regions, though of course the negative expression – division – would also be greater. Through this lens the only possible resolution to the Irish Question is compassion, empathy, and tolerance.

Emotional repression – the negative appreciation of Water – is a hallmark of the British, yet rarely is this seen in our relationship with wildlife and pets, whom the British are often accused of loving more than their fellow human beings. Whilst we are less emotionally demonstrative than say the Italians or Spanish, our stiff upper lip sometimes collapses, as witnessed in the aftermath of the death of Princess Diana in 1997.

The Gift of Diana

There have been few greater jolts to the national psyche than the unforeseen and unexpected death of Princess Diana in Paris on 31st August 1997, the numerology of which marks her indelibly with the sign of the Gods of Water.

DIANA (4+9+1+5+1 = 20 = 2) is a name of Water, always emotional and deep feeling. In the Roman myths she was the goddess of the Moon and childbirth. But in Norfolk, on 1st July 1961, she was simply an uncertain girl named Diana Spencer. Her date of birth reduces to 7, marking her out – even at that young age – as connected to one of the main numbers of the nation, 7.

The root number of DIANA is 2, the same as that of the UNITED KINGDOM. Charles and Diana were married on 29th July 1981 (29th = 2+9 = 11). 11 appears as the higher vibration of 2, bringing extremes of emotional expression. The number connected Diana to the heart of the nation and both rejoiced, at least temporarily.

The numbers 2 and 11 are threaded together by Water. On 20th November 1995 (20th = 20 = 2) she disclosed the true state of her marriage on BBC's Panorama programme. (PANORAMA = 7, same as her date birth). Her divorce then came through on 28th August 1996 (28+8+1996 = 2032 = 7, and 1996 = 25 = 7) and after the tragic events in the tunnel in Paris she died on 31st August 1997 (31+8+1997 = 2036 = 11).

In the end she may have been no Goddess, but through her numbers she enabled centuries of repressed emotion to flood out in preparation for the coming

Millennium of Water (2000's = 2). No conspiracy theory is needed to explain the supposedly unexplainable events of her life. The numbers do it perfectly.

There is one final area under the command of Water, which we must get back under control. Too much Water is overwhelming, bringing melancholia and ultimately depression. These connect with a key British weakness – negativity. We have distorted our bridge to the Gods when our default position in the face of obstacles is 'cannot'. Across vast areas of Britain the prevailing meme is one of depression, sadness, defeatism and negativity. If you are unaffected by these things then rejoice. But recognise that others, close by, are. These are not matters of mental health. They are matters of our individual and collective relationship to the Gods. Water shifts, moving wherever it can, submerging and engulfing whatever it can. Water – without sunlight – is a deep, dark, cold and foreboding place, which requires a different form of navigation.

In 1577, Dr John Dee, mathematician and mystic to Queen Elizabeth I, wrote a pamphlet entitled *The Perfect Arte of Navigation* explaining how Britain should go about gathering the wherewithal to extend its exploration of the seas in order to create an Empire. To our eyes today the manuscript contains nothing more than propaganda and a series of statements of the obvious, such as (paraphrasing) 'ships are made best from wood, and Britain has lots of trees'. It is therefore easy to dismiss his ideas, but we ought to remember how alien the concept of British sea power was in 1577, the known world being dominated by the Holy Roman Empire, with the ascendant nations of Spain, Portugal, Holland, and France competing with and mostly surpassing Britain in strength and influence. The relevance of this is that we need – right now – a new Perfect Art of Navigation, detailing how an individual human being might navigate their own way on the Seas of An Emotional Life. Feelings – of like, dislike, hate, and love – absolutely dominate the lives of many people in Britain today. Very little of life (and much less than many would prefer) seems solid. The currents of life seem to shift tremendously from one minute to the next and life, for many, is akin to being lost at sea, in a boat that seems too small, among waves that threaten to engulf. In these circumstances it seems preferable for many to self–medicate, be it through drugs, drink, food, or sex. These things are, of course, no kind of resolution and only mask the inherent uncertainty of life on the ocean waves. Even if that life takes place in a semi–detached in Birmingham.

Technology and science have no connection whatsoever to the Gods of Water, and we are foolish in the extreme if we think that, due to our technological advancement, we can forget about Water; for the more we deny its influence the more it will gather its forces until one day it sweeps us all away. Human beings of today can no more hold back the tide than could King Canute. We might recall that his story was primarily designed to demonstrate to his foolish councillors the limits of human power.

The sooner we demonstrate faith in the sea by restoring our waters and our shipyards to national ownership (be it private or state), the better off we will all be. The sooner we reinstate our own fishing industry, where we fish in an environmentally sensitive ways – but under our own aegis – the more at ease the nation will be. The quicker we extend our national waterways, a key feature of the Industrial Revolution, the better our lives will flow. If we want economic growth then we must first achieve energetic harmony and restore our relationship to the Gods of Water, who have always looked after us when we have looked after them. The rivers that run through our great towns and cities demand this and when we are consistently insensitive to the needs of Water – through inappropriate building, lack of dredging, poor river management, or pollution – then we must pay the price. These are not economic, environmental or political arguments. They are much more important than that.

AIR

Each of the Gods regulate different areas of life. In some regions the Gods rule unequally – for example in a city of high–rise buildings Air would be more prominent than Water. But across the four nations of Great Britain, and even within each component nation, the four Gods exert, overall, an equal influence. Humans, of course, over time develop preferences for one and disregard another. This is only natural, even though it is ruinous.

The Gods of the Air are instantly apparent to the British. They are embodied in Shakespeare, Chaucer and Dickens as well as JK Rowling, Terry Pratchett and Jeffrey Archer. They are found wherever there is conversation in a pub or café as well as in the national discourse of newspapers, TV and radio. They appear in the realm of dreams, tales and myths as well as through science, mathematics and spiritualism – all of which run strong and clear in British history.

Yet recently Air too has been despoiled. Air functions through education and free speech yet we are one of the few nations on the planet to hold the intelligent in contempt, seeking to educate all a little, but none too much. Witness the disdain that great thinkers such as Alan Turing and Clive Sinclair were held in, during their time. Sinclair is great case in point, for whatever else he was he was undoubtedly a vessel of Air, yet has been cast aside in the national consciousness in favour of the man who financially rescued him, Alan Sugar, now extolled as a Lord, but unquestionably a man of very low Earth.

Air is always the ruler of openness, and while this has not always been the most dominant of social forces – at either end of the wealth spectrum – it was at least once tolerated in academia. But no longer, where university campuses are now subject to the imposition of 'safe spaces' where discussion is severely limited lest the students' fragile little minds become subject to challenging opinions.

The mode of Air is invisible and neutral, all pervading, yet colourless. This is also the true nature of ideas. Like electricity, ideas can be used to power the electric chair or the operating theatre, but a diminution of ideas, a restraint of Air, can never produce progress. The full airing of views is essential to any functional society, and this does not mean only the right kind of views. In this sense Jeremy Kyle and Loose Women are as British as Panorama and the News at Ten.

The expansiveness of Air is seen nowadays in the form of Twitter, which has democratised opinion, broadening it if not yet deepening or extending it. The Air is the place where it is truly safe to release controversy and divergence, for it is immediately – if it has no value – swept away. Witness the controversy around the BNP leader Nick Griffin's appearance on BBC Question Time in 2009. It quickly become obvious that neither his words, nor ideas, could fly – literally – and that was the high point of his popularity. Divergences such as Nigel Farage and George Galloway can make their words soar in arenas such as this, though the longevity and impact of both remains to be seen. It is only those who are disconnected from the Gods of the Air that cannot bear to hear words and ideas with which they disagree.

Music is another important product of Air, and Britain has long been marinated in sounds and tones. From the songs of Empire –Pomp and Circumstance, Britannia Rules the Waves –the chimes of Big Ben and the coronation anthem of Zadok the Priest, to TV and advertising jingles, Songs of Praise and the BBC's in–between programme idents, sound and music plays an integral role in the life of the nation. Patriotic music, whether sung by Adele, Katherine Jenkins, or Vera Lynn, makes people stand, literally giving their attention to the nation. Whether it is Robbie Williams at Knebworth or The Prodigy at T in the Park, music lifts the nation. Like pure ideas, music in diversity is always colour blind and non discriminatory. Appreciation of this is as strong at Glastonbury as it is at Glyndebourne and the Last Night of the Proms.

The National Anthem, though now hopelessly maligned and mischaracterised, is a cohesive force, and a re–assertion of the national spirit. The USA has not lost sight of this, yet the British have, which causes them to lose sight of who they are. Much that is bad has been done under the sound of the anthem and the wave of flag, yet only when these things are retired and evil *still* stalks the world might we realise what was lost.

That said, plurality of opinion is what really counts under the auspices of Air. Britain has a fine tradition of investigative journalism – from the Sunday Times through to the Guardian and Private Eye –and when we abandon the desire to hunt out wrong doing, in favour of not giving offence, then we do ourselves a great dis–service.

Propaganda is a perversion of the powers of Air. So much that is presented now as news is little more than opinion, and organisations like the BBC tend to be circular and limited in what they will address. Much more on the BBC later.

Air encourages dissent, and Britain has a long tradition of this. In Robin Hood, the Chartists, Tony Benn, Owen Jones and Russell Brand, Air is strong. Air can both contain and release many divergent points of view. The patriotic fervour of the Proms can easily cope with a balloon or firecracker, and a coronation ceremony can easily withstand a snarky editorial from Polly Toynbee, for all these things form part of Great Britain, which can easily withstand mockery in the form of Austin Powers or Kingsman. The Gods of the Air can tolerate dissent and even refusal of their existence, so long as it is honest and heart felt. What the Gods of the Air seem to dislike is those who speak with forked tongue, who present war as peace and slavery as freedom. It is those people that the Gods desert. Any opinion – however strong – can be tolerated, and if necessary contained, in Great Britain if its owner speaks with clarity and honesty.

With Air we have expansion, but without Earth to anchor it we have dreaminess and impracticality. Britain is the home of many an impractical dream and Heath Robinson bodge–up. It is even said that the modus operandi of the British Establishment is simply to muddle through. Yet many great inventions and innovations have occurred in Britain, by the British. Great Britain is the place of open skies and expansive views, the most famous recent manifestation of which was Tim Berners–Lee's gift to the world – the World Wide Web.

Air resides mainly in the East, ruled by the Angel Raphael sweeping the strong forces of Eurus though our lives. Listen for this and it will be apparent to you, but you will require an optimistic and noble vision coupled with a desire for learning and expansion in order to draw its powers near.

To harness the powers of Air we must again make the nation a free one, where all shades of opinion can be expressed. Feelings are but one aspect of life, and if a nation is to flourish it must be able to unchain its mind and learn to value again the principles of expansion and discovery. All things technological, scientific and mathematical can be developed easily when minds are unchained. New ideas can take hold and prove their worth – without being imposed upon the nation – when minds are open and administrative processes are clear, straightforward and transparent, yet when officialdom and procedures are opaque, complex and time consuming then the national mind is caged and cannot fly. It can only obey.

We once walked side by side with the Gods of the Air, who facilitated the spread of British ideals, language, literature, music and invention around the entire globe. With occasional, notable exceptions in recent times, this has happened less and less.

FIRE

If Air is the Land of Hope, then Fire is the Land of Glory, desire and enthusiasm. Goals and quests, uplifting endeavours and all grand things are possible with the co–operation of the Gods of Fire. But much caution is required for with bad material the flames will flicker only dimly, yet with the wrong intention they will rip out of control. Much can be accomplished through Fire – be that creation or destruction.

This again is the story of Britain, a tale of one scorched Earth after another. From the battlefields of Hastings, to the Civil War, the Great Fire of London, the Blitz, Margaret Thatcher's purging of old industry and socialism in the 1980's, to New Labour's abandonment of town centres to the 24–hour drinking of alcohol (Fire–water) the history of the nation is often of the destructive application of Fire.

Many of the great leaders of the nation attained their credentials through war and destruction. Winston Churchill's bloodthirstiness was well known before World War Two, and he never toned it down. Churchill – though arguably the saviour of the nation – was burning with Fire all his adult life, as exemplified through his reckless love of adventure coupled with bravery, fuelled by cigars and alcohol.

Another aspect of Fire is the revolutionary current that runs deep in Britain, burning with injustice and sometimes even hate. Fire people – angry protesters who literally burn with outrage – basically want to tear up the nation and begin again. This is a different level of being from the dissenters of Air, who seek to talk things through. Fire is the precursor to direct action, be that constructive and worthwhile, or otherwise.

Parties left and right, movements, pressure groups and lobbyists, whether popular or elitist, are often involved in scorched earth policies – the taking of Fire unto the Land, metaphorically or even literally. Many will cheer if the Houses of Parliament ever go up in flames, yet the entire nation would be laid waste as a result of it.

Fire is the domain of heat, urgency and passion and human beings have not always held these things well. Too often and too easily has passion become hatred and anger. It takes a great deal to successfully control Fire. These Gods emerge from the South, powered by the Notus Wind, supported by the Angel Michael and exemplified in the world city of London.

The Exceptional Case of London

In some ways London must be treated almost as a different country. It is a product of the Fire Gods and a place that forges upwards and onwards with focus and speed, where dreams are made and with an energy that can literally catch people alight, or burn them out. It is a place with its own microclimate, always one or two degrees warmer than the rest of the South of England. It is the place of rush and hurry, urgency and impatience. It is no place for the faint hearted. Multi–dimensionally gleaming in some parts, filthy beyond measure in others it is the powerhouse and driving force of the British economy and the cockpit of the nation. Its diversity and energy might be a model for other parts of the country, yet every village, town and city must identify what makes it unique.

In Numerology the presence of Master Numbers indicates that something exceptional is taking place. Such is the case here, where the compound number of the names and regions of London frequently sum to 11, 22 and 33. Here then is the presence of the remarkable, the outstanding and the extreme.

22, in the positive, is the number of financial and material mastery. Its appearance in GREATER LONDON is bound therefore to assist its Secret Desire to be a prosperous area of the country, particularly considering that **there exists no other settlement of sizeable population in the entire British Isles whose name reduces to 22.** In the land of the 22 everything is bigger, badder, and bolder. Possibilities are extended and heightened and human mastery of life becomes possible. It is the number of transformation and will take whatever other numbers are shown from the name and try to paint them on a bigger canvas. We see this in DALSTON and its Secret Desire of 6 (for community, diversity and togetherness) writ large by its 22.

Place	Expression	Soul Urge	Secret Desire	First Letter	Repeating Letters/Numbers
London	11	3	8	L (3)	N, O (5, 6)
Greater London	22	5	8	G (7)	E, N (5)
Camden	22	6	7	C (3)	M, D (4) E, N (5)
Dalston	22	7	6	D (4)	A, S (1)
Greenwich	11	1	1	G (7)	E, N, W (5)
Harrow	11	7	4	H (8)	R (9)
Hampstead	33	7	8	H (8)	A, S (1)
Hoxton	33	3	3	H (8)	O, X (6)
Islington	11	6	5	I (9)	N, I (5, 9)
Kensington	11	2	9	K (2)	E, N (5)
City of London	8	9	8	C (3)	O (6)
Westminster	3	1	11	W (5)	(W, E, N) 5

11 is the number of thought–leadership. It is the number where ideas, beliefs and values are formed, take hold and spread outwards. In this light the popular characterisation of ISLINGTON as home of the commentariat and intelligentsia is correct. The 11 from its Expression seeks to build intellectually upon its Soul Urge of community and society (6). It does all this alongside its friend HAMPSTEAD (33), who seeks to take the ideals of community into a much larger sphere.

These many Master Numbers in and around LONDON (11) make the place unique within the UNITED KINGDOM (11) and thus a place of extremes. Everything that is bad about Britain – extremism, delusion, impracticality, financial mismanagement, and poverty are exemplified in London. London contains the kindest, wisest, and most open–hearted folk side by side with the biggest crooks in the nation. It is the magnet for pioneers and lost souls alike and so long as it is named thus it will forever be so.

There are very few places in the world that can match London's numerological energy, and it could lay strong claim, if there were ever invented such a thing, for the title of Capital City of the World. Among the prominent cities of the world only Sydney, Delhi, Vienna and Beijing sum to 11 (although these are the English versions of the names, and different spellings such as Wien 6, and Peking 8, do not come close). The international cities of Boston, Auckland and Athens come in at 22, while only Berlin surpasses them all, summing to 33. But London (11) within the United Kingdom (11) is strong and special indeed, a city and nation of world thought–leaders and visionary pioneers.

Interestingly we should also note the numerical energy of the CITY OF LONDON (8). Its semi–autonomous special legal structure makes it an inviolable entity that focuses itself almost exclusively on power and money. (In fact the powers of the Lord Mayor of London are extensive, far from ceremonial and pre–date many of those of Parliament and the Crown itself). As such, we diminish the City of London at the nation's peril, yet like all good 8–ness it ought to be the place of probity and exactitude, not corruption and crime. The City of London (8) connects very directly to the energy of the entire nation, the United Kingdom of Great Britain and Northern Ireland (8). It is little wonder that conspiracy theorists think the nation is ruled from the Square Mile.

Lastly the number of WESTMINSTER (3) is very much in harmony with the names England, Wales and Northern Ireland, but not with Scotland. It is a wonder how it has managed to be the parliament of the four nations for so long. Parliament is of course the place 'to parley'; to speak and discuss, an essential characteristic of 3. But that does suggest that the real *business of governing* (rather than talking about it) might be (or already is) more effectively done elsewhere.

For all these reasons and more London will always be special and treated differently from the rest of the nation. The Regency poet William Blake recognised this in his re–imagining of London as Golgonooza, the City of Imagination and home of great art and science. Blake leaned heavily upon his own interpretation of fourness in conjuring up his vision of Utopia, extending the mystical influences of four beyond London and out across the whole nation. There are many other examples of 'the London Difference', told in such books as *The Aquarian Guide to Legendary London,* by John Matthews and Chesca Potter. These include fascinating occult stories such as that of The London Stone, and the significance of the Church of the Knights Templar, just off Fleet Street.

Returning to the nation as a whole, Fire is the mother of invention and inspiration. This occurs in Fire at a level beyond that of the fleeting ideas of Air. In Fire we are subject to a burning vision and enlivened by a mission that we undertake with zeal, passion, and, maybe sometimes, irritation.

Too much Fire, however, and we are defeated, extinguished and exhausted. Our energies spent with no fight left. Although we may win the battle we will, in this state, lose the war. Intolerance, envy, and frustration may then take root. Yet the presence of Fire – and its symbiotic relationship to Light – always ultimately reveals a purpose and brings clarity. Fire controlled and harnessed brings a buccaneering spirit, vibrancy and new life. But this is not often the Britain of today.

In mundane life Fire used to be accessed by smoking and drinking. As many pubs have closed and legislation changed, so the Fire of choice is now coffee (a roasted bean) and in an often cold and wet land we have historically sought a better connection with Fire through holidays in the sun, even if that means going abroad.

The Gods of Fire may be harnessed literally through the fusion reactions inside nuclear power stations and intercontinental ballistic missiles, but mankind had better be sure that he has these Gods in a tight hold if disaster is to be averted. In the more basic way Fire can be harnessed by setting up a business, building an invention or pursuing a creative passion with nothing more than interest and enthusiasm. But the enemy when working with the Gods of Fire is always the same – no man or woman can successfully and safely wield Fire until they can successfully and safely manage their own being. Temper, impatience or intolerance in the heart of the user will only be increased under any invocation of Fire.

Drawing It All Together

Together the Forgotten Lands are 4 in number – Earth, Water, Air and Fire. (These are actually informed by a fifth, Akasha, which we will come to in the next chapter). These 4 are key to understanding the true nature of Great Britain, its geographical form, its behaviour, appearance and character. On another level we simply have 4 nations – Scotland, Wales, Northern Ireland, and England (directed by a fifth, London.)

The Numbers of Britain are 12 – 1, 2, 3, 4, 5, 6, 7, 8, 9, 11, 22 and 33. These are present (as well as sometimes noticeably absent) in all the faces of the nation. These represent the ideals of Britain, the energies we seek to embody, over–compensate for, and forget about.

The sum of the Lands and the Numbers is 16, illustrated in The Tarot as The Tower. The compound number of GREAT BRITAIN is also 16, and its root 7. These are then the key numbers of the nation, demonstrated repeatedly in the coming chapters. When the Tower of the Nation is built in harmony with its Numbers, on stable foundations and in co–operation with its 4 Lands (under the guidance of the fifth) then the people prosper. But when the British themselves forget the power of the Forgotten Lands and reject the Ideals of the Numbers then all they may construct are Towers of Wrongness, from which ruin is the only possible outcome. It should be noted that it is only the British themselves who wreak this fate upon the nation. No external force has succeeded in its attempts at destruction in 1000 years.

"I think I can save the British Empire from anything, except the British"– Winston Churchill.

Merlin, one of the key figures of the Matter of Britain, is supposed, according to Arthurian scholar R J Stewart, to have spent much of his life pondering the question, "how is it that the seasons are not all alike?" He was referring to the reasons why the day must cede to night, the summer to the winter, and the warm to the cold. Why could we not bask in warm daylight all the time? We might now re–frame his question for modern times. "how is it that people are not all the same, with common views, approaches, behaviours and attitudes?" In other words, why cannot everyone just be nice and get along?

The passing of the seasons, Merlin finally observed, was the very thing that caused the crops and plants to grow. And so it is today, where the different sections of society and diverse types of individual cause the life of the nation to expand. We must embrace, as Merlin did, the notion of AND, not OR. Differences in skin, belief, appearance and wealth are both the triggers of division and the causes of progress. Peoples are not all the same in order that they might grow. Homogeneity is death and 'right thinking' the preserve only of the fearful. Great Britain could be a microcosm of the entire World where diversity means what it was intended to; variance of thought, appearance, practice and belief, without exclusion of thoughts deemed uncomfortable, or practices seemingly unattractive. In this sense there is no right kind of diversity, just diversity that must include *every* possibility.

Great Britain once was, and again could be, a nation that holds the 4 Lands perfectly in balance in this way. This would not bring Utopia, but it would bring great progress. But this will not be achieved by sectarianism or segregation. No one who is biased, in any way at all, can possibly assist in this task, for the Forgotten Lands will sweep away or swallow up that person in an instant. To give merely one example, the class warrior who endures success and failure along his Road to Jerusalem must sooner or later realise that he and his cause are merely one incomplete aspect of the whole and, although he is bound to believe that he and his kind hold the keys to national salvation, he is also bound to be wrong about this. He cannot, of course, free himself from this wrongness until he liberates himself from his conviction of rightness.

The Deep Matter of Britain is therefore the story of how we connect to these 16 forces – the Gods and the Numbers together – and harness them toward the goal of evolution, which is the only clause in the Contract of Life that the Gods will sign. This may now seem an extraordinary, even impossible undertaking, yet we are at the same time one millimetre away from achieving it. The Forgotten Lands of Earth are discovered by the industrious, of whatever belief, appearance, or intelligence. The Lands Of Water are accessed by the sensitive and empathic, and Air by those willing to expand their knowledge and change their minds. The Kingdom of Fire belongs to the curious and the passionate, no matter what the objects of their curiosity or passion. And if those who would take these Four Kingdoms also possess self–knowledge – an idea of who they are and what they are for – then they will find themselves invincible, regardless of their physicality, race, religion, age or gender.

So who can provide the necessary leadership to bring these changes about? If the country has moved away from the Gods then who is to reverse the course?

Parliament. The Control Room of the Nation

Maybe it is the way that Parliament is presented on television, maybe it is the off–putting nature of the symbol of Parliament, the Portcullis, maybe it is simply MPs' bad behaviour? Whatever the reasons the disconnection between Parliament and the People has never been greater. But this need not be so.

The Palace of Westminster itself (housing the Lords, Commons, and everything in between) is full of occult significance. Its whole footprint is based on the four points of the compass. The Central Lobby, the meeting place between the four sections, has square tiles, forming a larger pattern of two interlocking squares. This octagonal hall leads off in four different directions, roughly (though not quite exactly) corresponding to the four points of the compass.

The 4–ness and the recognition of the Forgotten Lands, continues deep inside the building. To the East, with a fresco of Saint Andrew of Scotland over the doorway a corridor leads through to offices and hospitality. To the West the archway is presided over by Saint Patrick of Ireland and leads through to the exit. The North – South axis is governed by the Houses of Commons and House of Lords. The Commons is accessed through the North doorway, watched over by Saint David, and the South is watched over by Saint George leading to the Lords. The Four Forgotten Lands are deeply stitched into this place, as is our old friend Merlin for in the direction of the Lords is the robing room of the Monarch. This is elaborately and prominently decorated by artwork based upon the stories of King Arthur, Merlin and the Knights of the Round Table.

One of the prominent features of the House of Lords itself is the woolsack, a large red backless couch, containing wool from many of the nations of the Empire. This is the seat of the Lords Speaker. Wool is an attribute of Earth. The Lords chamber, empty at my last visit, also possessed a light atmosphere and a sense of high mindedness which I had not expected.

The House of Commons, directly down the other end of the corridor, is much, much smaller than it appears on the television and in photographs. The distance between dispatch boxes must be little more than eight feet and the overall proximity of other members is striking. It has not at all a highbrow atmosphere and its decoration is maybe even borderline shabby. It is easy to see how a strong personality could command this house, so near together is everyone seated. This closeness generates a great deal of heat and Fire, those necessary brothers of Light. This is simply not demonstrated on television, even with the recently improved camera angles, but it explains the combustibility of the atmosphere and to some extent the shouting and screaming. It is certainly no place for the shy, retiring and unconfident. Though the ceiling is high, allowing for an expansion of Air, it is no place for independent voices, which makes it all the more admirable when such a voice does surface. The whole process of voting is done with the feet, by the physical trooping through the division lobbies. It must take great courage to vote against the government whip, for with the proximity of members in the chamber there is no place to hide. Physical presence (Earth) is everything here.

After the bombing of the chamber in World War Two it was apparently Churchill who insisted that it be reconstructed, unchanged. We might consider the sense of this, and not fall so easily for the line regularly trotted out, of the chamber's irrelevancy and outdated ways. Although rightly maligned in some ways, the House of Commons is the ultimate location of truth. As an MP, so long as you take the opportunity to speak then you are speaking to the nation – energetically at least. Even if the debate is poorly attended the control room of the nation can be enlivened by any speaker's words. Getting elected and then deciding how much to obey the government whips are both things of concern, but the members are not impotent so long as they can get their voices heard. That, of course, begs the question of whether they really have anything to say.

The creative power of 3 is abundant in WESTMINSTER. It is this hub of creativity, at least potentially, which contains within it the greatest of all laws, the Formula of Pythagoras, $1+2+3+4=10$. The government (or lone MP) initiates a motion. This is an action of 1 and Fire. The opposition challenges it. This is 2, Water. The matter is then debated, 3, Air. The interaction of Fire, Water and Air is messy, noisy and unclear. Each MP lives in one of the stations, they bring Fire, or Water or Air to the debate and cannot see outside of their station. This process is derided as knock–about Punch and Judy stuff, but it is the creative process, which always brings forth a result (though that result may not always be the intended one). Every meal requires ingredients and preparation time before it can be eaten, every relationship involves back and forth. Whilst we are human there is no other way, and neither should there be. The process is perfectly adequate, if its component people are adequate.

The quality of Parliament, and thus the government, is a function of the quality of individually elected MPs. When an impactful individual, with a strong personality, a clear voice, and a timely vision arrives then the House opens its arms in welcome. If that Member recognises the sacred, magical, nature of the House, and the power of their own creative speech then much might be achieved. But until then, the place is a reflection of its people. If it is divided, then it is because the people are divided. If lacking it is because the people are lacking. The British Parliament is the national psychodrama made real, and if it is weak, sick, or corrupted then it is because the British people are. The simple yet distasteful fact is that the disaster of the Iraq War (the thing most cited as the root of distrust of today's parliament) is a direct product of the landslide election of New Labour in 1997. While Blair may have pulled the trigger, we loaded the gun and handed it to him without reservation or condition, often simply driven by hatred of the Tories. We, as the people, share in the responsibility and cannot in all truth offload it on to politicians.

An accusation commonly levelled is that Parliament is unrepresentative. Yet this is demonstrably untrue. I analysed the 2015 Parliament extensively by names and dates of birth. The date of birth could be reliably established for 523 of the 623 members. Of those 523 the Destiny Number (addition and reduction of the date of birth) was calculated.

	1	2	3	4	5	6	7	8	9	11	22*	Average with an even distribution of 1–22
No. of MPs	65	53	51	43	74	60	51	53	67	6	43	48
% of total	13	10	10	8	14	11	10	10	13	1	8	9

* The 43 MPs with Destiny 22 also appear in the 4 column, because a compound 22 always reduces to a root 4. The 6 MPs with Destiny 11 are treated separately, however, and are not included in the 2 column.

The figures are astonishingly balanced, indicating that the British Parliament elected in 2015 is directly reflective of the Destiny Numbers of the Nation. The only number that is significantly deficient is 11, the most extreme number of all. The parliament contains more humanitarians (9) than it does self–publicists (3) or theorists (7) and even contains a heartening amount of big thinkers and big doers (22). It is balanced, even, and totally representative of the country at large. Of course in this I am talking only about one factor of the individual character. A humanitarian 9 may still refuse their Destiny or act in inhumane ways due to external circumstances. But the point here is that the composition of the Parliament is not set up to fail or to biased in one direction or another. Contrary to the biased commentary, it *is* reflective of what is going on outside its walls. It has become far too easy to claim that Westminster is the home of self–serving fools, and whenever I hear that claim all I can see before that speaker is a mirror.

It is also often said that the South of Britain advances at the expense of the rest. Yet as a place of Fire it would always burn more brightly than the others. This is a necessary difference, not a superiority. The Southern Fire of passion and creativity needs the Northern Earth of practicality and consistency. Both in turn need the Eastern Air of movement and optimism, which relies upon the Western Water of compassion and empathy. Each needs the other, to inform it and to provide what it is not. A great deal of work, behind the scenes in parliament, addresses these very matters. We might then reflect upon the destructive role played by those reporting upon parliament. Notice in all news reports how the presenters move seamlessly from a reporting of the facts of what was actually said to an interpretation of what they heard. The reality of the interaction of the Forgotten Lands in the British Parliament is not only denied and ignored but actively twisted and distorted through the narrow lenses of the media. More on that later.

It is often said that Parliament has been emasculated by the controlling whips and spin–doctors, and has lost a lot of its powers to the EU. All this may be true, yet Parliament could exert itself if it wished to, though it no longer understands it own nature and has forgotten its words of power, which are 'I Create As I Speak'. In Aramaic this translates as ABRACADABRA (7). (The British occultist Aleister Crowley re–framed this as ABRAHADABRA, (3), with an H). MPs need not intone that particular word during debates, but they could do a great deal more to restore their own power and with it the people's respect.

Lastly, the nature of PARLIAMENT (1), and especially the HOUSE OF COMMONS (1), is to lead, where the nature of the HOUSE OF LORDS (4) is to oppose, instil reality and practicality, and, if necessary, block. It seems to me that the Lords continue to work with these numbers magnificently.

The Magic of Britain

Every nation on Earth possesses the connections necessary to access the Four Forgotten Lands. Every country, even the most barren and land locked, has a route whereby it may connect with each element, to however small a degree. Great Britain has, on and off over time, successfully managed this task. Thus it has an intimate experience of, and long standing relationship to, magic.

But one other factor looms large. Maybe this is even the dominant factor in the fate of any nation. It is the most invisible, intangible and powerful of them all – the fifth element, Akasha.

AKASHA

Simply another word for Spirit or Ether, the Akasha of a nation is the force that colours and drives the Four Forgotten Lands. In deciding whether the Earth is leaden, dense and dark, or supportive, nourishing and bountiful, it is Akasha that plays the governing role. The choice between an emotional expression or repression in Water is dictated by Akasha. Same for Air, to what degree do we value learning and education, and likewise for Fire, are we passionate about invention and creation or angry and hateful toward those who rock the boat? All these things are formed and directed by Akasha.

Akasha is impure. It contains the Karmic record of what the British – as an old, historic nation – have done, and thus what they now need to do in order for balance to be restored and completion to be attained. We will cover this Karmic aspect in detail later on.

Akasha is also formed by our current intentions, our thoughts, our feelings and our efforts. Those who constantly run the country down may well find that they get – by way of personal experience – exactly what they desire. This is reflected in the very visible reality that when it comes to general elections the nation gets exactly the result it deserves. An indecisive and divided nation cannot expect to be granted clear leadership. Indeed it might be said that such a nation would not deserve anything other than a reflection of itself. In such circumstances it falls to the Magicians to create change.

Occult Britain

Britain has a long history of association with magic, mysticism and the occult. From Merlin, the Knights Templar, and John Dee, through Francis Barrett, the Golden Dawn of late Victorian England – Crowley, Mathers and Waite – onwards to Dion Fortune, Gerald Gardner, Doreen Valiente and Alex Sanders to the current profusion of moots, gatherings and circles, Britain is and remains a place of magic.

Much has been done to document Britain's long association with magic and the occult, and this is not the place to replicate others's work. Suffice to say that all Brits might consider how deeply interwoven magic has become with the fabric of the nation at large so as to not mistakenly ignore it or wrongly believe that it is the same the world over. It simply is not. Although the open and enlightened Dutch have made significant contributions to the philosophy of magic, and there is a great deal of evidence for its widespread practice in Germany we have to look very hard to find anywhere on the planet where the topic is so deeply ingrained. Many will point to the witch doctors of Africa or indigenous shamans of Australia or America, but the truth is that there is no-one else on the planet who has taken the practical application and study of magic and mysticism so far and has embedded it so deeply, or for so long, as the British.

Modern Witchcraft, now so prominent in our culture through the success of US television programmes like Charmed, owes its origins to Great Britain. The global popularity of Tarot can be attributed to four people – the vision of two British men, Aleister Crowley and Arthur Edward Waite, and the execution and inspiration of two British women, Lady Frieda Harris and Pamela Colman Smith – in the first half of the twentieth century. This is not to degrade the efforts of others, particularly the farsighted and enterprising Americans who lifted the whole thing up a notch in the sixties. But it was born in Britain, and not by accident. British-ness enabled it to flourish, and in turn it shaped the development of the nation.

Similarly the old British Cunning Man and Wise Woman tradition continues to this day. Still now, as centuries ago, virtually every settlement in Britain contains a healer, a sorcerer, a psychic or a herbalist. Their skills vary, and they continue to operate unseen to those without the appropriate eyes to see.

The land of Britain is replete with occultism. Stonehenge, Avebury, the Rollright Stones, Rosslyn Chapel, and Glastonbury have become places of pilgrimage and ritual. But there are smaller versions of these things going on all over the country, maybe two doors down from you, though no one else in the street would ever know.

The greatest modern day contribution to British Magic however is fictional, yet no less powerful. The global impact of Harry Potter has entrenched across the world the notion that magic and sorcery happen in Britain. In her writings JK Rowling has performed an enormous service to the nation.

Everyday Magicians

Every healthy society possesses many thousands of non–occult Magicians, people who, without any conscious mystical understanding, are somehow able to harness the forces of nature to make things happen. Richard Branson is to all intents and purposes a Magician, able to create something out of nothing. Likewise for Simon Cowell and Chris Evans, to name but two.

44

Many business people are Magicians, but so are artists and writers. William Shakespeare was undoubtedly so, as was Edward Elgar and even Stock, Aitken and Waterman. David Hockney, Damian Hirst, Jamie Oliver, even Gordon Ramsay – all these people create something from nothing and use the concentrated forces of Earth, Water, Air and Fire toward a specific end in order that it may become so. They get up early and physically place themselves where they need to be (Earth); they generate flow, human interaction and emotional involvement (Water). They converse, think, research and learn (Air) and they apply passion to all that they do (Fire). Conversely if they do not have passion they do not do it. And, perhaps more importantly, they hear the spirit of the times.

Magical Leaders

Transformational leaders are the ones able to tap into the spirit of the times. Not the spirit of yesteryear, or the world to come – these are quite different things – for leadership is a function of the now. This requires sensitivity and awareness on the part of the leader to tune into the Akasha and discern what is needed (as distinct, possibly, from what is wanted). Today's world of focus groups and 24/7 media commentary has distorted things, but a Magical Leader will still be able to move beyond this and speak directly to the National Spirit. Tony Blair did this in 1997, while Margaret Thatcher did it in 1979, and to a lesser extent in 1983 and 1987. To disagree with or dislike these individuals should not lead us into denial of their power, influence and connection.

Not all leaders are magical leaders of course. It is doubtful whether every Prime Minister can be judged to have been in communion with the National Spirit, although to some limited extent controversialists like Enoch Powell and Tony Benn clearly were. When the leaders of the nation are successful, or effect real change, they do so informed by, or in harmony with, the Akasha. They can hear what the nation is crying out for, even if no one else can, and through their life experience they are able to bring the call to fruition. The most powerful example of this is Winston Churchill.

Occult Winston

It is only possible to make sense of Churchill's life and career if we look at it from an occult perspective. In ordinary human and political terms he was a walking disaster zone – intemperate, intolerant, untrustworthy, neither Conservative nor Liberal, or maybe Conservative and Liberal. He made a succession of shockingly bad decisions throughout his career, was rightly accused of being a warmonger and correctly heaved out of office following his war victory in 1945.

Yet for all this, and for the myth making that has grown up around him, he was the nearest thing to a national saviour we have ever known. To accept this fully we must move beyond judgement and revisionist history and into simple recognition. Occult significance is accrued to something that is necessary and transformative. It might not itself be a model of good behaviour.

Churchill was born on 30th November 1874 (30+11+1874 = 1915. 1+9+1+5 = 16 = 7). He therefore possesses the Key Number of Britain, 16, enabling him to connect to all of the Lands and all of the Numbers. He also possesses 7, enabling him to understand the name of Great Britain. He came of age during the explosion of spiritualism and occultism of Peak Empire in late Victorian and Edwardian Britain. This was a country where the upper classes displayed no shame in exploring all things magical and mysterious. Edwardian Prime Minister Arthur Balfour attended spiritualist evenings on more than one occasion and, a little later on, the Head of RAF Fighter Command during the Battle of Britain, Sir Hugh Dowding, was a committed spiritualist, writing a series of books on the subject after the war. Apocryphal stories swirl around Churchill himself and his possible direct involvement with spiritualism, druidry and the occult. I myself have experienced one of these when after receiving some occult instruction from a very old lady in Gloucestershire the remark was made to me that "this is what we used to do with Mr. Churchill." Of course we will never know the full story, but there can be little doubt that however he did it, he heard the voice of the nation like no other. Winston's significance therefore is that by his actions he allowed us, today, to continue to work within the occult realms. For how long do we think this would have been tolerated in Nazi Britain?

The relevance of Churchill's controversial life becomes all the more clear if we think about Anthony Eden, Churchill's long anointed successor, who possessed almost identical numerology to the old man himself, yet lacked utterly the experiences of Winston, and had failed to cultivate the appetite necessary to go beyond himself. This demonstrates that whatever numbers we might have, we must ultimately be the ones to do something with them and rise to their challenge. Or not.

The War of the Flags

It is the easiest thing in the world to rally a nation behind a flag. Nothing has changed in this regard in all human history. Witness the fervour of revived Scottish nationalism behind the blue and white Saltire to see this in action. It is always successful because – so long as the flag is designed by one connected with the soul of the nation – the flag becomes the repository of history, desire and regret. At the point of its adoption by the nation the flag will then be made the recipient of the people's hopes, dreams and fears. This becomes true even for those who shun the flag; such can be its power. In short, a national flag is a powerful occult symbol of the Akasha made visible.

The United Kingdom possesses a unique national structure; a country of four countries under one flag. This is without compare in the world, all the more powerful when we realise that four is the number of earthly mastery, depicted clearly in the Tarot by The Emperor.

Among the flags of the current 196 countries of the world, very few are based upon this number four. The French tricolor of Liberté, Égalité, Fraternité, for example, is a product of three, as are, in their own ways, the Belgian, Dutch, Italian and German flags. The Polish flag is a function of two. Even where there is some four–ness it is often only geometrical and aesthetic, or if it is meaningful – such as the flags of Jamaica and Mauritius – then it cannot be classed as influential. Even when a national flag contains a four legged cross it cannot necessarily be asserted that the home nation has balanced the four lands. The cross of the crucifixion, for example, is an unequal representation of four and appears on all Scandinavian flags, turned sideways through ninety degrees. The only possible exception to this – where a country outside of the UK possesses a flag of balanced four–ness and exerts influence in the world – is Switzerland.

To fly a flag is to make a visible assertion of belonging, to claim unto oneself an understanding and appreciation of what it means to be part of something and what such a belonging enables you to do and be. Those who do not fly the flag, either metaphorically or actually, through ignorance or refusal, cut themselves off from a current of energy, knowledge and sustenance. Patriotism such as this is not a function of narrow mindedness or nationalist bigotry, but the ultimate energetic expression of belonging, affirming one's own existence as part of something bigger as well as recognising the rightness of where and when you were born and live. Nationality matters viscerally, invisibly, and energetically. It matters when and where the flag is flown, when it is at half–mast, and what other flags are flown alongside it. It is consistently astonishing to me that those who step into an awareness of subtle energies are often the first to renounce the subtlest yet strongest energy of all – nationhood.

Looking around the world we see the European Union working with the number twelve from the number of stars on its flag. The US Stars and Stripes has fifty stars and thirteen stripes ($50 + 13 = 63$. $6+3 = 9$, the highest single number) providing fullness and completion. The Peoples Republic of China has a very powerful flag, consisting of four small stars alongside a fifth larger one. This was designed as recently as 1949 and is a direct representation (intended or not) of the Four Forgotten Lands under the guidance of the fifth, Akasha. This five–ness is repeated in the national emblem of China, as well as being reflected in the flags of the Special Administrative Regions of Hong Kong and Macau. Five is powerful in our Western model of the elements, as well as the Chinese variant, Wu Xing, where it presents as Metal, Wood, Fire, Water, Earth. China then extends its five–ness further through the establishment of semi–autonomous government for its Five National Central Cities – Beijing, Guangzhou, Shanghai, Chongqing and Tianjin. The Chinese take these kinds of associations – though they view them through their own lens – very seriously. Of course it is not sensible to ascribe cause and effect here, but it is worth noting that the Chinese are at the same time both keepers of a powerful occult flag and a global economic, political and military power.

In light of this we can now recognise the power of the Union Jack, and see it for the powerful occult symbol that it is – a perfectly balanced and visible depiction of the four nations (Wales shares the Cross of St George with England) and the Four Lands, before they were forgotten. It contains both a horizontal/vertical cross (+) and a diagonal cross (x) signifying how the component nations add up to 4, yet when multiplied together come to 16, the sum of the Lands and the Numbers of Britain. Its geometric form holds all forces in balance – good and evil, mercy and severity, Tories and Labour, the people and the land, the Crown and the people – and produces strength from balance. To see this clearly we must look far beyond many of those who wield and adhere to the flag, so that we may see its inherent power and energy, which will out-live all who try to mis-appropriate it. Historically there has never been a flag anywhere in the world that contained a comparable degree of power. Except one. The flag of Nazi Germany.

The four legged swastika is an ancient and enormously powerful occult symbol, long pre–dating the Nazis and used traditionally in the Hindu world as a representation of the Sun. Hitler co–opted this power, distorted its image and harnessed its four–ness toward his own ends, kicking off what many believe was an occult war.

The German blitzkrieg across Europe in 1939–40 defied military or political logic, with Hitler over–ruling his generals as he marshalled forces – based around the swastika – they could not understand. Later on these same forces would come to overwhelm him, but in the meantime it was Churchill alone who stood firm, overruling the British establishment's desire for a peace settlement. This was a war of the focused mind, a war between the Nazi control of the Elements and British control of the Four Lands. It was maybe an inevitable war between BERLIN (33) and LONDON (11). Who could access and control the greater occult power?

The Magical Battle of Britain

Most people now accept that during the summer of 1940 a series of witches' gatherings took place in the New Forest in the south of England. Their task was, through magic and ritual, to imprint upon the minds of Hitler and his generals the belief that they could not possibly cross the English Channel. Various older members of the coven died as a result their efforts, from a mixture of exhaustion and pneumonia, though it is said that they willingly sacrificed themselves in order to make the ritual more effective. This, in conjunction with the protective workings of Dion Fortune's occult group in London, is believed by some to have played a decisive role in the RAF's victory over the Luftwaffe in the Battle of Britain, Hitler's decision not to invade and the eventual turning of the tide. At that time, prior to America's entry into the war, Britain was hopelessly outnumbered. The Dad's Army that might have resisted Hitler's invasion forces would have been like a pinprick on an elephant. Without magic against them the Nazis would almost certainly have prevailed.

A great deal of folklore and speculation has grown up around these New Forest Coven stories, but whatever happened there also gave rise to the revival of paganism and the birth of modern witchcraft, primarily through the work of Gerald Gardner. But to what extent were Dion Fortune and the New Forest Coven really responsible for the survival of Great Britain? We can no sooner answer that than to know fully of Merlin's involvement with King Arthur, or John Dee's with Queen Elizabeth I in the subsequent formation of the British Empire (though interestingly Dee did invoke the number 7 – BRITISH EMPIRE – during his extensive workings). But whatever the truth, it seems that all Great British leaders and movements have had the power of Akasha – channelled and focused by a Mage or not – firmly at their backs. All those today who would profess interest and involvement in magic owe the Britons of those days a great debt. For in a Nazi Britain there could be no room for any Magus or Priestess outside the black halls of the SS.

Magic and Today's National Akasha

The occult tradition lives on in Britain, but we ought not underestimate the forces ranged against it. The EU, for example, is implacably opposed to folk remedies of all kinds, including herbalism. Its directives are always anti–small trader and pro–regulation, and its religion is always a form of Catholic Science. The upsurge in environmentalism, pro–green, anti–fracking movements in the UK might on one hand be seen as a reconnection with the Earth. But in my experience not all of these groups possess knowledge or interest in the thread of an anciently old Britain, instead preferring to claim for themselves a degree of righteousness that would not feel out of place in an American evangelical church. In the mainstream the triumph of marketing that is the New Age movement, singing songs of Love, Light and Happiness, bears no relationship to the reality of the Forgotten Lands or the Numbers.

Those interested in the continued existence and development of Great Britain must sooner or later call upon that which is most British – Merlin, in all his guises – to confront the many false religions that pervade the nation today. The group mind (as Dion Fortune referred to it), or the National Akasha, has now become so polluted by contrary influences that some might consider it fractured beyond repair. The Americanisation of much of British life only distorts the language and connects the British to things that do not actually matter to them. The globalisation of business and finance has been a treasure trove for London, but a disaster for parts of the rest of the country. Rolling international media has been a similar catastrophe for the British, plugging them into impossible situations on the other side of the planet that cause them to disregard causal and relevant events on their own doorstep.

Magic, though often practiced in dark corners, has never really been about superstition or quaint folklore. It's practitioners have always been deeply involved in the business of human progress. Magic requires inventive minds and always brings forth new thought. Technology now purports to do this for us, though in due course it may simply enslave us. The qualities of magic are the qualities of Britain, a country dressed up in old-fashioned garb but historically full of independent free thinkers. Where others promote or develop, Britain, through magic, originates. It always has, which is why magic has lived here so long.

But our modern day ignorance of the British connection to magic is the cause of a great deal of national trauma. Whenever we openly refute magic the Gods hear us and are bound to reply. When restrictions were imposed on herbalists in the 2008 Consumer Protection from Unfair Trading Regulations disaster followed. In the same year that magical herbalists were regulated by the Muggle State the UK financial system fell off a cliff.

The Holy Grail

There is much folklore about mystical and magical items, which move from nation to nation dictating where the power of the world truly lies. From Indiana Jones' capture of the Ark of the Covenant to legends about the Spear of Destiny, the lance that supposedly pierced Christ's side on the cross, the story is always about the transfer of power that has become imbued within an object. If you hold the object then you hold the power, they say. Except this is not the whole story, for another level of power is found in ideas and their application.

Great Britain is an idea now, much more than it is a thing. That idea manifested, once upon a time, a Global Empire, and then as the idea was forgotten so the Empire was lost. Yet the possibility of coherent four–ness, a true and clear expression and invocation of the Four Forgotten Lands, in tune with the Numbers, guided by and in turn influencing the National Akasha, lives on. Much of this may be embellished, romanced or distorted, but the secret key is an ideal, not a thing. It may be that once a nation understands and wields that secret they are forever destined to then lose sight of it. This way they may experience what it is like to have and to have lost, and to live with all the highs of glory and the lows of poverty, haunted by the tiniest chance that the sunny days may come once more.

It is only when the British learn what Great Britain *really was*, will they be ready to create everything that it might yet be. This process will not about invoking Britannia, Minerva or Boudicca. It will not be about socialism or conservatism. It will be informed by the past, but not constrained by it. This creation will be an act of magic, but not one confined to ritual. It will take place every day of the week, indeed it already is, in every facet of human experience across the nation. Great Britain is already once more a place of Magic, full of Magicians.

Merlin: Lord of the Dragon

A great deal of magic and meaning is obscured within simple stories. Tales of creatures and forces beyond the understanding of ordinary man are woven through the history of Britain. The tales of Merlin's work with Dragons is one such instance.

50

Depending on which myths you access, Merlin, the Chief Sorcerer of Britain, gained mastery over the most powerful force in the Land, the Dragon, dispatching the destructive Dragon and harnessing the power of its creative twin. He placed the attendant powers under his control, but under the direction of the King, whose surname was Pendragon. This, however, was not a family name but more likely a title, Head of the Dragon. But what is a Dragon?

Quite simply the planet Earth is the Dragon. An enormous and continuous backbone of mountains runs down the centre of every ocean on the planet, spewing fire into the water and creating new rock underneath. The whole planet, the Dragon, is breathing in this way as it flies through the air (or in reality, space). The Dragon contains within it the Four Forgotten Lands. Earth in its rocks, stones and precious metals, Water in its oceans, Air in its atmosphere, and Fire in its volcanic explosions. The Dragon is the embodiment of the Four Forgotten Lands in one awesome being, the control of which makes all things possible.

The Incredible Numbers of the British Monarchy

Much like Churchill, nothing can really be understood about the British Monarchy without taking an occult perspective. Such a point of view always awards us with the freedom to move beyond fashion, prejudice and deference. We might then see that presence in the Royal Family does not occur by accident of birth but through the Akasha, and that their enormous wealth and privilege sits hand in hand with an enormous karmic responsibility.

While not the oldest continuous monarchy in the world – that title goes to the Imperial House of Japan which can trace its line back to 660BC – the British Monarchy has been one of the most influential and long lasting that the world has known, providing the thread by which all present Brits are strung together in sympathy with all previous Brits, going back centuries. The downsides of this are very real – the greater the force of the past, the weaker the force of the future. But this does not prevent the realisation that the King or Queen is to all intents and purposes the singular, energetic embodiment of the Nation.

This process takes hold through the occult rite known as the Coronation, where any ordinary man or woman becomes the Monarch through *proclamation in ritual*. Though anachronistic to all Muggles the power of such a ritual should not be underestimated. Witness a similar ritual, in lite–form, at the Royal Wedding of Prince William and Kate, and the way that it drew the most cynical Brits into its arms. The same will happen again at the next Coronation, where a whole new generation will be incanted upon and their resentments of Charles drowned out, at least for the day.

Ritual, of any kind, is all about performing a deliberate series of manoeuvres and actions with intention, in a holy, revered or cleansed setting, using items held to be sacred. The more energy that can be drawn in the better, the longer the ritual (so long as the energy can be maintained) the better and the more otherworldly and extra–mundane the proceedings the more effective they will be. This is where the power of the Coronation Throne, used continuously for coronations over 800 years, the incomparable Crown Jewels, dedicated holy oil, special incense, soaring music, and unique robing all come together to create belief and acceptance in a monarch where none previously existed. The ritual itself is held to be sacred, and any attempt to interfere with it, or its components, is as destructive as a wrecking ball. The government of John Major might therefore wish to reflect upon the revival of Scottish nationalism in light of their decision in 1996 to return The Stone of Scone – the ancient stone that is supposed to have resided within the Coronation Throne since the 1300's – to Scottish custody. There are contrary stories that the Stone was in fact removed and broken in 1950, and thus never returned, the current one being a fake, but either occurrence constitutes an interference with the Magic of the Coronation. It is little wonder the Scots are so restive, having regained stewardship of an ancient artefact purportedly used in the coronation of Scottish and Irish Kings for a thousand years before Edward I, and prior to that by the biblical Jacob in his founding of the 12 Tribes of Israel.

As we have seen, the words GREAT BRITAIN sum to 7. Since 1066 Britain has had 41 monarchs. This does not include the two Cromwells or the 'Queen for Nine Days' Lady Jane Grey, but does include the uncrowned Edward VIII. 18 of these have had a name which sums to 7. Four Williams, eight Henrys, two Richards, two Elizabeths, one Anne, and one Victoria. These were some of the longest serving, most revered – and sometimes reviled – monarchs in history. They all connected intimately with the notion of GREAT BRITAIN, even before the name itself had come into use. To understand this further we must step out of time and from the loop of cause and effect. To speak a word is to associate with all other words of that same number. To repeat those words, and thus numbers, is to call them forth even more strongly. The spiritual power invested in the monarchy – even to this day – allows them to call forth with a greater degree of force than less powerful mortals. Therefore to be Queen Elizabeth II is to be plugged in to all the experiences related to Queen Elizabeth I, as well as all those of the other Monarchs of 7.

There are then a further 11 monarchs whose names sum to 3. Two Marys, two Jameses, two Charleses, six Georges. One glance at history confirms these monarchs reigning through difficult times for the Kingdom, or in unpopular ways.

When the current Prince Charles ascends to the throne he will either become King Charles III (3), or as he himself has suggested, King George VII (3) Either way, it would seem that there is trouble ahead, for him and/or the nation. Naturally there is no certainty that a regal name of 7 brings goodness, just that it is more connected to the spirit of the nation and more in harmony with the necessary thread of monarchy. (As an interesting aside we also see the presence of both these numbers in the fire at Windsor Castle on 20th November 1992. 20+11+1992 = 2023 = 7, and 1992 = 21 = 3. 1992 (3) was later classed by the Queen as her Annus Horribilis). Looking at the line of succession beyond Charles the pattern continues, with William (7), George (3), Charlotte (3) and

Henry (7). There have been hardly any exceptions to these names of 3 and 7, and very few of them recent. Edward, of which there were eight, sums to 1 and Stephen (1135–1154) sums to 6.

Finally, the compound number of the UNITED KINGDOM is 11, and only one ruler has possessed this number in their name – Oliver Cromwell. His rulership was marked by the assumption of the title LORD PROTECTOR (8), similar in numerological power to QUEEN (8), and one of the very necessary numbers of the nation, rather than KING (5). To be Queen seems to demand something different than to be King. In the Tarot card number is 8 is mostly named as Strength (though sometimes as Justice). Both Tarot figures are personalised female representatives of power. The King, card 5, is the Hierophant, a teacher and a preacher as much as a ruler. It remains to be seen to what degree Prince Charles, should he ascend, is able to embody this aspect of Kingship.

The Places of Britain

Wherever the British are born, and live now, dictates how they interact with and experience the energy of the nation. Those who live in a city like Manchester or Glasgow have different daily visions and encounters from those who live at the end of a rural track in the middle of Shropshire. Photographs of these places tell us precisely nothing about what it is actually like to live there day in, day out. Thought processes, emotions, energy levels and enthusiasm are all influenced by where we live. The causes of this are sometimes attributed to ancient ley lines or geopathic stress, but in truth the explanations are much simpler.

As the aura of human energy expands and contracts, depending, in part, on that which surrounds it, so does the mind and the heart. City dwellers react faster to problems because they are in an environment that encourages such, yet they are easier to persuade into community–minded thinking due to their daily need to be tightly packed together with others. In the less crowded places the mind and spirit are able to run freer. As independent thought always flourished far away from Ancient Rome, so it does again far away from London. The human being can energetically expand where there is literal space to do so. In Central London, for example, the space is only ever upwards, where the whole skyline draws your gaze ever higher. Necessarily here the vista is rarely wide, whereas in the countryside it is much more so. Sunday afternoon access to panoramic views across the Thames, or the expanse of such places as Hampstead Heath or Hyde Park, should not be taken as being in any way comparable to daily life in the Yorkshire Moors or the Cotswolds. Although Londoners may hold claim to being more sophisticated and intelligent than their country cousins, what actually matters is not the amount of information and stimulus (which Londoners are drowning in) but the depth of awareness that is available. Countryside living facilitates perspective, while city living enables involvement.

Britain is a country with varied terrain and therefore we can develop this a little further. Generally speaking those who live with higher vantage points develop (or prefer) detachment and aloofness, while those living next to the sea, especially if in low lying basins, can find themselves experiencing ever changing moods, while enclosed and land locked areas can breed narrow mindedness. All islanders, of whatever kind, tend toward separation. Most places of course exist in a goldilocks zone containing some of each characteristic.

It is naturally not as simple as this, but in my travels to many different parts of Britain there is no doubt that different places possess a different energy, which is not determined by population, road or rail connectivity, history, or the presence (or even absence) of industry or universities. The prime determinant of the conditions of these places is their name.

The Numbers of the Places of Britain

Once we have named something – a place, thing or person – we attach to it a vibration that wishes to be fulfilled. In effect, to name something is to bring it alive, causing it to demand matching vibrations. Every appearance of a letter or number (or element) does this, bringing forth a continuum, running positive to negative, over which we, the subjects, are guided to operate. This explains why certain people – for no logical or material reason – feel at home in certain places. Their own vibration sits in harmony with that of the name of the place.

However, once we have named a place we must remember what that place demands of us. If we somehow forget the message of a place name, and omit to give it what it energetically needs then that place will fall into disrepair and exhibit what we might call 'bad energy'. It is not that the energy is bad per se, simply that we have failed to nourish the place in the way it demands.

That is not to say that everywhere else possesses 'good energy'. All place names vibrate in polarity, sometimes positively and sometimes negatively, along the spectrum pre–assigned by the name and its numbers. The success of a settlement is really just a matter of letting it do what its name wants it to do. Any sensitive, on arrival in any British town, will immediately sense this, although they may not be able to explain why. Here is why.

We calculate the numbers in the same way as we did with the component nations, though for ease we will simply now use the Expression (all of the letters of the whole name) and note the first letter of the first word, along with any repeating letters. All these three factors must be weighted together to provide an interpretation. So, for example:

O	X	F	O	R	D				Compound		Root
6	6	6	6	9	4	=	37	=	10	=	1

Oxford's Expression – the way that it meets the world – is 1. This is coloured by its repeating letter (given more strength because it is also the first letter) of 6. 1 is the number of invention, independence of spirit as well as narrow–mindedness and selfishness. 6 is the number of community, togetherness and co–operation. These accord perfectly with the essential vibration of the city, which seems in a constant tug of war between the demands of the individual and the demands of the community. The presence of the four 6's means that community often wins. This is the Oxford that I know.

Within every settlement there is another level of detail. To live on MAIN STREET (7) is energetically similar to living on PALL MALL (7), but very different to living on CHURCH ROAD (9). To live in CAMBRIDGE (8) is not dissimilar from living in CHELTENHAM (8), but very different to living in ST HELENS (3), while DORSET (9) is again very different to MERSEYSIDE (5) though similar to RUTLAND (9). These differences are first energetic, from the name, and *then become* cultural and economic. The name vibration of a place, over time, attracts what it needs and repels what it does not.

During interpretation the name of the country takes precedence, determining the overall shade of what is possible. The next most important name is that which is given when asked the question 'where do you live?' This varies from person to person but usually the closest city or town is given, rather than the county. The bigger the population of the place the more weight and influence it will carry, and where a small settlement possesses a powerful or historic name energy we must place its potential in context with the surrounding larger population centres.

What Places Want. What They Really, Really Want.

In addition to the meanings listed earlier, here are some more positive and negative expressions for each of the numbers, together with some indications of how each numerical energy might form in a settlement. For each there is listed some actual towns and cities of Britain that sum to those numbers, as well as some fictitious and mystical place names. A fuller list is available in Appendix A: The Places of Britain.

1.

Independence, invention, innovation, insularity, exceptionalism. A leadership role.
CANTERBURY (lead place of the Church of England). OXFORD (leading home of global education).

2.

Sensitivity, beauty, harmony, peace, tranquillity, and its opposites of division, segregation, fear.
BELFAST. There are very few '2' places in the UK, and Belfast is a perfect example of how the continuum works. BELFAST energetically demands peace and harmony, yet through human frailty it must pass through division into order to reach that peace. Humans are the determinant of how the name and number reach fruition. There are many places in the UK that do not appear to express their number yet, deep down, eventually they all do.

3.

The arts, culture, creativity, design, performance, self–expression.
SALFORD (the new home of BBC and ITV). BRIGHTON (long time capital of self–expression in the form of gay rights and alternative lifestyles). GLASGOW.

4.

Manufacturing, materials technology, restrictive practices, order and tradition.
PLYMOUTH. SUNDERLAND. NOTTINGHAM. BIRMINGHAM. BATH. Also, ALBERT SQUARE, CORONATION STREET and EMMERDALE. Further, AVEBURY and STONEHENGE.

As the number of Forgotten Lands, all these places might provide doorways to their re–discovery.

5.

Connectivity, diversity, a travel destination or a passing through place. A place that changes its mind and composition.
GRAVESEND. FOLKESTONE. BIRKENHEAD.
Also, AMBRIDGE.

6.

Family, community, and society orientated.
PETERBOROUGH. BOLTON. YORK. SOUTH SHIELDS.
Also, CAMELOT.

7.

The British Number. Non–conformist, an outlier, isolationist. Home of science and technology, as well as mysticism and nature. Very connected to the past. Eccentricity, the place of dreams, and nightmares
LIVERPOOL. MANCHESTER. NEWCASTLE UPON TYNE. ORKNEY.
Also, WALFORD.

8.

Money, business and finance. Wealth generation and preservation. Insurance and banking. High quality shops and restaurants. Prizes reputation and self–image.
CHELTENHAM. ROYAL TUNBRIDGE WELLS. SUTTON COLDFIELD. BRENTWOOD. The importance in the national psyche, of somewhere like BRENTWOOD should not be overlooked. The town is the home of the much maligned, though it seems necessary, television programme 'The Only Way Is Essex'. It is through seemingly silly things like this that we can think afresh about why many things in Great Britain exist at all. Answer: because on some level they are needed.

9.

A self–contained place, complete within itself. Somewhere with its own character and history.
NORWICH. SOUTHAMPTON. MILTON KEYNES. LEEDS.
Also, ROYSTON VASEY.

11.

A place of extremes. Division. High achievement vs. low failures. A place suitable for thought leadership and innovation.
CARDIFF. AYLESBURY. SHEFFIELD. DURHAM. CIRENCESTER.
Also, CAMBERWICK GREEN, TRUMPTON and WALMINGTON ON SEA. Interestingly, there were 7 Trumpton Firemen and 7 members of Captain Mainwaring's Dad's Army. Both these programmes touched GREAT BRITAIN (7) very deeply.

22.

All things become possible.

There are no significant centres of population that sum to 22 outside London.

33.

A black hole. Or a very special place.

CHESTER. PAISLEY. BARNSLEY. WATFORD. BRACKNELL.

Foreign Relations

The British must be forever mindful that there is a world beyond the English Channel. They may understand this world a little more using the Numbers, which can say a lot about national sympathies as well as rivalries. The drawback though, is language.

To numerate GERMANY (11) is to attain a very different answer than numerating DEUTSCHLAND (3). Yet the nation is received to the British as Germany, though projected outwards as Deutschland by the Germans. Thus the name of a nation, in its host language, is touched by the inhabitants themselves, while the translation of the name of a nation is what those outside of it see, or project onto it. GREAT BRITAIN (7) thus becomes GROSSBRITANNIEN (4) to the Germans and transforms from an awkward eccentric with grand ideas, but ramshackle methods (7) into a well–organised and powerful obstacle (4).

This is, in fact, the basic reason for war, the misunderstanding through language of the national energy. Deutschland is trying to show its character and intentions through demonstrative expressions (3), yet the British see this as a tendency toward extreme behaviour and intransigent obsessiveness (11). As such an entire nation's honest endeavours along their own personal path are misinterpreted. This is not to say that a nation always means well (particularly when its essential energy is overthrown and the nation renamed in some way), but the limitation of language, where a translation can never be 100% accurate, is the root of many global problems.

Supranational bodies such as the European Union are attempts to resolve this, but they are flawed for the British EUROPEAN UNION (6, society and community) is the Dutch EUROPESE UNIE (9, enlightened humanity), and the German EUROPAISCHE UNION (4, a place of security and order). And those differences are without considering the influence of accents (acutes, graves, circumflexes etc) or additional letters, all of which would potentially numerate differently. As such, the European Union is a different thing depending on what language you use. These differences of host language vs. foreign perception will continue as long as there are different languages in the world. No language can be considered the 'truthful' one, though we might consider that the numerology of the nation in the host language would provide the most powerful influence.

Through transliteration – the replacement letter by letter of the host language with its Roman Latin equivalents – we may come to understand a little more about the energies of Arabic, Greek and Cyrillic words, but even this is limited. All language is formed of symbolic alphabets, all of which are trying to say different things. Different languages *do not* seek to describe the world around us in the same way using different characters. No, that is by definition impossible. They each seek to describe the same things in different ways. For that is how they see them. Much more data on the numbers of Britain's overseas friends and foes can be found in Appendix B: Foreign Relations.

Finally it might be noted that significant relations seem to occur between GREAT BRITAIN (7) and other countries with like numbers, such as POLAND (the trigger for British entry into World War Two and the subject of much modern day debate about immigration) and GREECE (fellow democrats and travellers in the who–will–leave–the–EU–first project).

The Old Colonies

Names that numerate to odd numbers (1, 3, 5, 7, 9) tend to develop harmonious relationships with other names of odd numbers. GREAT BRITAIN (7) resonates with the UNITED STATES OF AMERICA (3) and SAUDI ARABIA (5) for example. Even numbers on the other hand (2, 4, 6, 8) tend to get on with other even numbers. CHINA (8) and RUSSIA (6) seem co–operate well, at least from the outside. Odd and even together is complementary, but different, which in international relations might mean conflict.

Like numbers however – 7 and 7 for example – either get on famously or clash vigorously. Either path is a result of a close intertwining, one being very much like the other. This has happened with one ex–colony and one current overseas territory.

RHODESIA (7) was an economically flourishing part of the BRITISH EMPIRE (7) until it went its own way with a unilateral declaration of independence (UDI) in 1965. It did so in order to preserve its difference from its neighbours and its historic colonial way of life. The fact that the overwhelming black majority of the country was ruled by a small band of white British proved secondary to the power of the letters and their numbers in shaping the thoughts of the decision makers. This is not to excuse the actions of the white supremacists, but to throw light upon the driving forces behind their decisions. Similarly GIBRALTAR (7) now performs a similar, though less racist role, as an outpost of Empire on the edge of Spain. 7 is always the number that does not wish to belong (except to itself). Taking this issue wider we see both GREECE (7) and SWITZERLAND (7) in the English language as outliers or outsiders in the European Union.

Two further locations that have caused the British great trouble were NORTHERN IRELAND (4) and the FALKLAND ISLANDS (4). Both were places where the British Army was involved in order to preserve the British way of life. This 4 is shared by SARK and the ISLE OF MAN.

The Karma of The British: War, Politics and Leadership

"The present is like the past, the past like the present"
"They are the same, it is said"
Four Finger Wu and Ian Dunross, both with important decisions to make in
British Hong Kong
From The Noble House by James Clavell.

Great Britain's footprint on humanity, especially in the last three hundred years, is vast. Varyingly good and bad, it shows us that the success of any nation is sometimes the inevitable product of war and conquest. But even one glance at history demonstrates that victory in battle never endures, that the victor is always, at some point later on, the vanquished. Therefore lasting national progress can never be secured by war alone. Other matters must play their part. Sooner or later any nation must discover that its worth is determined primarily by what it can generate by itself for itself. Trade and exchange may follow, increasing the prosperity of the nation. But if there is nothing of worth in a nation there will be no trade, for trade is essentially an exchange of surplus to compensate for lack. And whatever is lacking in the nation is revealed by the Letters and the Numbers.

In Numerology a name always reveals its Karma by the letters, and thus numbers, that it is missing. The arising issues and scenarios then require additional effort to correct, in which the holder of the name may or may not succeed, quickly or slowly. The perfected nation will possess, in the English or host language, some of every number. Such nations are rare.

Lack of	Brings issues with	In possible scenarios
1	Innovation, identity	Difficulty with self–image and sovereignty.
2	Compromises, co–operation	Splendid isolation or constant conflict.
3	Communication, expression	Draws attention to self, breeds resentment and disapproval. Shies away from co–operation.
4	Structure, order, work	Regimented and unimaginative. Or skilled builders.
5	Travel, diversity, discernment	Disconnection. Revolution. Isolation.
6	Society, community, love	No social provisions. No community or folklore. Family problems.
7	Science, education, spirituality	History appreciated more than progress. Irreligious or dogmatically worshipful.
8	Money, power	Wealth, poverty. Power, weakness.
9	Humanity	Invasion, subjugation.

As before the lack of a number brings forth a spectrum over which those who connect to the nation can operate, in order to resolve, positively or negatively, the national Karma.

Great Britain's Karmic Trail

The old country of ENGLAND that existed before the Acts of Union in 1707 lacked the letters that correspond to 2, 6, 8 and 9. Thus we see a nation almost perpetually in conflict with itself or others (2), with virtually no social provision or community spirit (6), frequently on the verge of bankruptcy (8) and busily engaged in subjugating foreign hordes, as well as sections of its own people (9). The ENGLAND of today, when it refers to itself by such a name, all too often continues these traits, though the lack of community and society may be partially ameliorated by the Secret Desire of the name (addition of the consonants) summing to 6. This reflects the ongoing and unfinished battle within the English over all things socialist and communitarian.

The country of GREAT BRITAIN that followed from the Acts of the Union in 1707 lacked 3, 4, 6 and 8. This was then a nation that flamboyantly drew attention to itself by foreign adventures (3), was a place of regimented behaviour and class structure (4), still lacked any kind of social provision (6) and was financially bereft or near to it (8). This country no longer possessed the lack of 9, indicating somewhere that it was on the road to becoming a more humane, less oppressive nation. Any removal of lacking letters indicates karmic progress.

In 1801 the UNITED KINGDOM OF GREAT BRITAIN AND IRELAND was born. This nation lacked only one number – 8 – and she spent the following 120 years attempting to resolve this by amassing the greatest collection of military hardware and economic muscle the world had probably ever known. She did this under the auspices of the BRITISH EMPIRE, which lacked 3 and 6 connecting back to the long running issue of England and showing as disparity in social conditions and the inevitable dislike that others had always taken to it. The overall expression number of the UNITED KINGDOM OF GREAT BRITAIN AND IRELAND (22) made for global dominance and grand achievement, manifesting through the prism of 8 as money, power, poverty and weakness. With LONDON (11) as the capital of the nation the power of the numbers radiated around the world.

In 1922 the loss of Southern Ireland caused the name of the nation to be changed to the UNITED KINGDOM OF GREAT BRITAIN AND NORTHERN IRELAND, which now lacked no numbers at all. The Karma of the nation, on one level, had been resolved, but the ultimate price had been paid – the loss of Ireland, the fracturing of the Forgotten Lands and the disappearance of the Master Number 22. The Empire was finished.

Today's nation is confused in its identity, due to its various names. Within the world community it is often known as just the UNITED KINGDOM, which lacks 1 and 8 – bringing troubles with identity, sovereignty, power and money.

In this respect the UNITED KINGDOM is a very different nation from anything that existed pre–1922. As GREAT BRITAIN the nation is diminished further, becoming an 18th century relic in a 21st century world. And should the nation fracture into pieces then none of the four component nations will fare well.

The common factor in mostly all of the individual, shortened and component names of the nation is the lack of 8, which speaks to our essential poverty, and our continued – and incomplete – quest for wealth and power. This is perhaps one of the most important insights of all for it really defines the nation on multiple levels. It contributed to the establishment of Empire, the two world wars, post 1945 economic crisis, the Thatcher obsession with inflation, the Banking Crisis of 2008 and the surprise re–election of Conservative governments in 1992 and 2015.

With an Expression and a Secret Desire of 8, plus its absence from the letters of the component nations we have too many 8–based issues. This reveals why foreign interests now own much of the nation's industry, and how the national wealth is not spread around. As a nation the British remain fundamentally lacking in the necessary power, financial or otherwise, to do their will. They miss the 22 of the Days of Empire and have an on going problem with authority. Tony Benn saw this clearly "democracy, to the British, means a deep loathing of power." Those who established the early police force knew that the people would only be policed by consent, and today the Nanny State and the EU are the manifestations of George Orwell's Big Brother. The nation's difficulty with all these things is connected to its imbalanced 8. This could be partly healed by the consistent use of the correct name of the whole nation – the UNITED KINGDOM OF GREAT BRITAIN AND NORTHERN IRELAND – yet such a mouthful appears only on official documentation.

The Karmic Progress of Germany

The relationship between Germany and Great Britain defined the twentieth century. Germans are the people with whom the British have the most – and least – in common. They have both been civilizing, as well as destructive, forces in the world, as well as the homes of great inventions and advancements. Both have nurtured spiritual and magical thought. The British magical Hermetic Order of The Golden Dawn was, in fact, German inspired. Like Great Britain, Germany has moved through many incarnations and name changes in its evolution. Both have experienced disputed borders and debates about national identity, attempts at Empire and a succession of strong, and weak, leaders. But it seems much harder, even for the Germans themselves, to identify the essence of Germany. Unfortunately, all attempts to look at the occult history of Germany run up against a group of people who plundered all things magical for their own ends – the Nazis. But the Nazis did not invent magic, nor do they own it.

The Numbers of Germany

From the Roman historian Tacitus and his account, around 98AD, of The Germania, through medieval personalities like Charlemagne, and onwards past Wagner and Hitler, the story of Germany is of ever-changing forms and identities, all somehow involving the marshalling of mystical forces to the ends of power and truth.

With Emperor Charlemagne's purported use of magical texts (he was supposedly gifted a rare and powerful grimoire by Pope Leo III) and Hitler's distortion of the ancient symbol of the Fylfot Cross into the crooked cross of the Nazi Swastika we see just two examples of a land deeply connected to magic.

But the forces within the Forgotten Lands are blind, and can be wielded positively or negatively. The Nazi Swastika was an inversion, an anti-clockwise interference with the motion of the Forgotten Lands. Although Hitler and the Nazis evoked these powers very effectively they soon lost control of them.

The modern story begins with the establishment of the German Confederation in 1815. This was an alignment of small German speaking states that were a hangover from the old Holy Roman Empire. This association, the DEUTSCHER BUND (9) possessed big ideas yet lacked 6 and 7 in its letters. There was thus no sense of belonging to a collective (6), and a hankering after a mythical past (7). This gave way, in 1867, to the development of a more formalised country, which no longer lacked 6, the NORDDEUTSCHER BUND (6). A sense of community had been gained.

The work of the first German Chancellor, Otto von Bismarck, was instrumental in the creation of Germany's next incarnation, the DEUTSCHES KAISERREICH (3), which endured from 1871 until the end of the First World War. This nation too was lacking 6 and 7, though with its Secret Desire and Soul Urge both as 6 great efforts were made during this time to address social issues (6) with the founding of the world's first Welfare State and great advancements in technology and science (7). This was a country that would not be ignored (3).

At the end of the First World War the name of the nation was changed once more, but to no significant numerological effect. The new nation, DEUTSCHES REICH (3) persisted through the post war Weimar Republic and into the Nazi period carrying the same lack (6 and 7) and the same excess (3). The nation demanded to be recognised yet still possessed at its heart no sense of society or togetherness (6) and no spiritual connection (7). The name of this nation persisted until 1943 and it is through this lens that we might understand the appeal, to the Germans of the time, of Hitler.

Central to Hitler's offer to Germany was the promise of *Volksgemeinschaft*, the establishment of a people's community, whereby individual efforts and desires would be suborned to the good of the whole. This is a very 6 concept. The fact that the whole only included those of Aryan blood is of course a perversion of the core idea by the Nazis, but nonetheless, alongside the offer of a mystical/spiritual connection to something bigger (7), depression ravaged Germans were offered a compelling narrative that addressed the century–old wounds of the nation. Through this prism we might come to understand that Nazism and Hitler were not a European wide phenomena (except by invasion). They were particularly and uniquely German, speaking directly to the deficiencies shown by its Numbers and Letters.

The final shape of the German nation, before its utter destruction, took place in 1943 when Hitler's expanded territory was incorporated under the title GROSSDEUTSCHES REICH (9). Finally the nation possessed a name without any missing numbers, and thus it had repaid and rebalanced all its previous Karma. But how can this be? How can a nation simultaneously balance its Karma and become the most murderous regime in history?

The answer to this takes us directly to the heart of what it means to be alive. Many people suggest that happiness is the only purpose of living, and without happiness there is no point. Yet even a superficial involvement in magic, mysticism and spirituality reveals that great things can be realised and gained in the midst of pain and misery. This suggests that the ultimate realisation and repayment of Karma may be discovered through ruin, rather than success. It is also interesting to note that by the end of World War Two the main enemies, the UNITED KINGDOM OF GREAT BRITAIN AND NORTHERN IRELAND and the GROSSDEUTSCHES REICH were both free of Karmic Lessons, possessing within their names some of each possible number energy. Through catastrophic conflict with each other the Letters and the Numbers of the nations had gained what they needed, learned what they must, and could – following mutual destruction – begin again. This may be hard to accept but none of what is said here should be taken as suggestive of justification for what occurred during this time, except in the sense that everything is to learn from, including pain, horror, and suffering.

Post war Germany became effectively Day Zero. The nation was split into the magic number of four administrative regions and then in 1949 East Germany formally split off as the DEUTSCHE DEMOKRATISCHE REPUBLIK (4). This nation too was karmically clear, with no missing numbers whatsoever. But it was a stagnant and monolithic entity, without desire for growth or development in any way (4), and a salutary lesson to those who believe that karmic resolution must always deliver joy and happiness. It is much more likely that karma generates the conditions for life, development and progress. Of course many of its population did possess the desire to grow and it was they, ultimately, who led the way toward re–unification.

And so we arrive in the present, only to miraculously discover that the wheel has turned again, yet almost in exactly the same way as before. The current BUNDESREPUBLIK DEUTSCHLAND (9) now lacks, as Germany so frequently has, the number 6. Its preferred method of filling the void of community this time around is through its position as an expansive force at the heart of the community of Europe. We will see if this proves any more successful than previous attempts.

The Multi–Dimensional Language of Tarot

The Tarot is a living alphabet. It contains 22 letters, 4 Lands and 10 numbers.

Each of the 22 Letters refers to a mode of expression, the creative desire of that energy to manifest itself in the Four Forgotten Lands. These energies are visualised and personalised by the artist in their depictions of each card, and join together with other letters to form names and words. These words are thus manifestations of the Cosmos – Akasha – in the world.

Each of the 4 Lands is represented externally through the four suits, and then is personified in each of the four courts (King, Queen, Knight and Page). Earth is shown through Pentacles, Water through Cups, Air through Swords and Fire through Wands. Some of the terminology (and attribution) differs between decks. The 10 Numbers appear straightforwardly in each of the Suits, beginning with Aces.

Thus, every single name or word, written or spoken, appears in the four lands of Earth, Water, Air and Fire. Words appear first in Fire as a spark or flash, then in Air as a thought, then in Water as a feeling and finally in Earth as a mundane reality. All words are not created equal, nor are all speakers or writers of those words. The failure to write or speak a word convincingly, resonantly or clearly results in a failure of that word to manifest in any or all of the four lands. But when a word is successfully pronounced, enunciated and vibrated then it resounds through the lands and is ultimately made flesh. This is but a tiny introduction to one of the most hidden secrets of all – Creative Speech. Much more is said about these principles and techniques in *Emergence Book Three: Creation*.

For any word to manifest – which means that the principles behind the word are given life – the speaker or writer must deliver them with conviction, from within themselves. This is what all successful writers and orators do. Both Churchill and Hitler, with or without knowing it, spoke in this way, and thus the world became exactly as they commanded.

The Tarot then enables us to understand what is actually being created when words are spoken. We simply numerate all the letters of a word and match them up to their Tarot counterparts. The details of the entire process belong elsewhere, but basically operate on five levels. Let us take an example word – ENGLAND (3) – which is ruled overall by The Empress (III), whose energy seeps out into the world every time the word is spoken.

Momentarily we can see that by using the cards of the Tarot to replace the letters of the Roman alphabet we have stepped into a much more open and comprehensive language, a form of communication much more akin to hieroglyphics than to graphical letters. The word now provides direct imagery, and thus clues, as to how the word desires to be made flesh. This connects us more deeply with an understanding that *'the word is the thing, and the thing is the word'*.

	E	N	G	L	A	N	D
Akasha	Hierophant	Temperance	Chariot	Hanged Man	Magician	Temperance	Emperor
Fire	Five of Wands	Five of Wands	Seven of Wands	Three of Wands	Ace of Wands	Five of Wands	Four of Wands
Air	Five of Swords	Five of Swords	Seven of Swords	Three of Swords	Ace of Swords	Five of Swords	Four of Swords
Water	Five of Cups	Five of Cups	Seven of Cups	Three of Cups	Ace of Cups	Five of Cups	Four of Cups
Earth	Five of Pentacles	Five of Pentacles	Seven of Pentacles	Three of Pentacles	Ace of Pentacles	Five of Pentacles	Four of Pentacles

The presence of The Empress (III), whether she shows herself as Boudicca, Queen Elizabeth I, Victoria, Elizabeth II, Princess Diana, Mrs. Peel in The Avengers, or Peggy Mitchell behind the bar of the Queen Vic, reveals the female nurturer as a strong force at the heart of the nation.

The Hierophant (V) is always the preacher, who in England often commands as much influence as the Monarch or Prime Minister. Today's Hierophants are the media talking heads, the Imams and the gurus who pronounce upon everything, and the evangelists of the past (rather than doers) like Tony Blair, Tony Benn and William Gladstone. England often comes to resent such people, but always finds replacements when the old doctrines are discredited.

The many Fives throughout the name all reveal a miserable picture of the stress and conflict endemic in the nation, whose fate is to live in perpetual conflict with its neighbours and itself. We may take this as a warning that if Scotland does break away then the rift will be not be peaceful.

Resonant Numbers

Every event – be it from the formation of a word, name or appearance of a key date – projects its energy outwards like a radiating Sun, touching everything that it possibly can. The sum total consequences of any event are impossible to calculate, though we may, through the methods contained here, understand the direction and shape they may take, as well as their real meanings and lessons. But every event also seeks to perpetuate itself, to live on and then live again for another cycle.

This is tracked primarily by dates. These generate numbers, which seek to draw unto themselves like numbers, and repel unlike numbers. This is seen in normal everyday scenarios, where we work in places where we feel positive and purposeful and live where we feel welcomed. Those kinds of feelings inside us are often simply a function of the numerical energies that are present within us, and our surroundings.

We can understand this in the context of Britain by examining the numerology of some of the institutions of the nation and the history they have taken part in forming. Please bear in mind that the formation of these features of British life can in no way be deemed accidental.

The Numerology of the Conservative Party

The British Conservative Party is one of the most successful political parties in history, forming the overwhelming majority of governments in the last two hundred years. Part of its success must be attributed to its role in addressing the national karma, the imbalanced 8 within many of the names of the nation.

It all began with the appointment of Lord Liverpool as Prime Minster on 8th June 1812 (8th, and 8+6+1812 = 1826 = 17 = 8). Though at that time technically a Tory (rather than a Conservative, for the two things are not the same) he went on to become Britain's longest serving Prime Minister and his government is often credited with laying down the foundations for the later growth and prosperity of the Empire.

The Conservative Party (CONSERVATIVE PARTY = 17 = 8) grew out of the modernising efforts of Sir Robert Peel (he of police 'bobbies' fame) and his statement of Conservative values in The Tamworth Manifesto released in 1834 (1+8+3+4 = 16 = 7). This confluence of one of the national numbers, 16/7, with the nation's karmic number 8, was to prove powerful.

Only two Conservative Prime Ministers were born on an 8 date – Lord Salisbury on 3rd February 1830, and Arthur Balfour on 25th July 1848 – but numerous successes for the party have occurred where 8 has been prominent. The election successes of Anthony Eden in 1955 (26/5/1955. 26 = 8) and Harold Macmillan in 1959 (8/10/1959. 8th = 8) are two examples of this.

On 11th February 1975 (11+2+1975 = 1988 = 26 = 8) Margaret Thatcher was elected leader of the Conservative Party, and then assumed the role of Prime Minister on 4th May 1979 (4+5+1979 = 1988 = 26 = 8). She went on to govern the country throughout the 1980's, presiding over a decade defined by money and power. Interestingly the two pivotal events of her time in office were the Argentinian invasion of the Falkland Islands on 2nd April 1982 (2+4+1982 = 1988 = 26 = 8), which made her, and the Poll Tax Riots in London on 31st March 1990 (31+3+1990 = 2024 = 8), which effectively finished her.

Lastly on the matter of 8 we can recognise the evisceration of the old Conservative Party at the hands of Tony Blair's New Labour in 1997 (1+9+9+7 = 26 = 8). The numbers show us how organisations both rise and fall, and how when the negative traits of a number are too apparent – and in 8 it's bullying, hectoring and domineering – the energy turns on itself.

We might conclude from all this 8–ness that the Conservative Party was and is a necessary thing so long as the British seek to resolve their national karma. We might say that Lord Salisbury, Arthur Balfour, Eden, Macmillan and even people like Enoch Powell, born 16th June 1912 (16+6+1912 = 1934 = 17 = 8) were all essential, that they had to happen. It might be that as soon as Margaret Thatcher was elected party leader it was *necessary* that she be elected Prime Minister, and *necessary* that she served so long. Once this course was set then it would always result in conflict, rebellion and ultimately the defeat of the party. For *necessary* we might even read desirable, that all these things could be seen as good, right, and in tune with what the nation needed, for its growth if not its universal happiness. Whether sectional interests supported or opposed all this is secondary to the essential playing out of the national karma. As Thatcher was elected so she would be eventually swept away, as sure as night follows day.

To some degree it is fair to say that the Conservative Party is the party of money and power (key 8 traits). Many people hate the party and its leaders for that precise reason, yet this data causes us to ask why, if the party is not somehow needed (as opposed to simply wanted), has it been so successful? This question looms larger than ever in the aftermath of its shock election victory in 2015 (2015 = 8). Maybe the current Conservative Party is a direct manifestation of our unresolved relationship with matters of money and power (8)?

The absence of any discussion of Winston Churchill, in relation to the Conservative Party, is interesting and deliberate for he possesses not one scrap of 8 anywhere in his name or date of birth. Indeed, at one time he was a member of the Liberal Party, and in 1924 he was elected as a Constitutionalist, neither a Conservative nor Liberal. Numerologically Churchill is much more connected to the nation, than to any one party.

We will shortly see that this profusion of 8–ness, though it does appear to a small degree in the history of the old Liberal Party, does not appear in any way at all in the names or people of the Labour Party.

The Conservative Party has two other prominent and repeated numbers. These are the two connected numbers, 4 and 22.

22 is the number of extremity, mastery, dominance and great transformative achievements, while its lower counterpart 4, as well as being the number of the Forgotten Lands, is also the number of repressive traditions, negativity and darkness. 4 generates a box of security and order, whilst 22 is capable of applying those foundations on a much larger canvas. 22 can be the number of material greatness, informed by spiritual principles. 22 expands and seeks more, but 4 sometimes contracts and seeks less, or attempts to exert tight control over what it has. Let us not forget that it was the number of the nation of Peak Empire, the UNITED KINGDOM OF GREAT BRITAIN AND IRELAND, from 1801–1922.

Sir Robert Peel, the unofficial founder of the modern Conservative party, was born on 5th February 1788 (5+2+1788 = 1795 = 22). The Earl of Derby, the longest serving leader of the party from 1846 to 1868, was born on 29th March 1799 (29+3+1799 = 1831 = 13 = 4). The full name of Victorian Prime Minister Lord Salisbury (birth date 8) was Robert Arthur Talbot Gascoyne–Cecil, which sums to 4. He reflected his own 4–ness perfectly when he said, of his attitude to government that, "whatever happens will be for the worse, and therefore it is in our interests that as little should happen as possible." A grim approach to life, some might say, yet perhaps desirable and necessary, and certainly extremely 4–like, in its lower vibration at least.

The 1922 Committee is the seat of backbench power within the party and was formed and named as a result of the Conservative victory on 15th November 1922 (15+11+1922 = 1948 = 22). Harold Macmillan was appointed as the leader of the Conservative Party on 22nd January 1957 (22nd. 1957 = 22) and his successor Alec Douglas–Home was born on 2nd July 1903 (2+7+1903 = 13 = 4). Then it gets really interesting.

Margaret Thatcher was born on 13th October 1925 (M = 13th letter of the alphabet. 13th = 4. Also 13+10+1925 = 1948 = 22) and was elected leader in 1975 (22). Her Chancellor Geoffrey Howe's resignation, which triggered hers, took place on 1st November 1990 (1+11+1990 = 2002 = 22/4) and she resigned later that month on 28th November 1990 (28+11+1990 = 2029 = 13 = 4).

Her successor John Major was born on 29th March 1943 (29+3+1943 = 1975 = 22) and was almost forced to resign by a rebellion of his backbenchers in the Maastricht debate on 22nd July 1993 (22nd. 1993 = 22). While Margaret Thatcher's nemesis was Michael Heseltine, born 21st March 1933 (21+3+1933 = 1957 = 22), John Major's nemesis became Michael Portillo, born on 26th May 1953 (26+5+1953 = 1984 = 22). Note here also the profusion of the 13th letter of the alphabet, M.

This repetition of 22/4 does not take place in the Labour Party, nor do the Conservatives possess the numerical repetitions that Labour do. This is not something that is common to all politicians. These are energetically two very different organisations, the Conservative Party being successful and productive when vibrating as 22 – enabling transformation, and a grand vision of substantial material change – but all too often sinks into the closed–mindedness of 4. The late Thatcher–Major period of the party might be characterised by the common trait of 22, self–destruction, and even after many wilderness years and the shock victory of 2015 it remains to be seen what legacy David Cameron (David = 22, born in 1966 = 22) manages to bequeath the party, for in the same way that their rise and dominance seemed both necessary and inevitable, so its continued existence cannot be guaranteed by anything other than a deep national need. To some extent its final success in the economic deliverance of the nation might also be the party's final death warrant. Its whole raison d'etre seems to revolve around money and power, it is almost as if it needs economic crisis in order to function.

David Cameron might have accrued more power to himself and his cause had he not asked people to call him Dave. Though DAVE produces 5, a powerful number as well as his own Destiny Number (born 9th October 1966, 9+10+1966 = 1985 = 23 = 5), it is a far less effective and more reactive number than 22.

We might get a clue about the future from the current party logo, the Tree, reflecting a connection with the EARTH. This replaced the Flaming Torch (FIRE) in 2006, demonstrating a movement of focus from a burning light to roots and stability. The 2015 election campaign saw the dressing of that tree with the occult power of the Union flag, but it remains to be seen to what degree the party can fulfil its purpose, renew itself in office and stave off the fate that it has visited upon itself so many times before.

Opponents of the Conservative Party might feel a little more optimistic if they recognised the degree to which the party seems to be karmically needed (as opposed to wanted). They may further gather strength to their cause if they actually addressed the party by its true name. To continue to assert malice to the TORY PARTY (5) is to aim and miss the CONSERVATIVE PARTY (8). The party derives its essential strength and purpose from its name. Very few people in the Conservative Party refer to themselves as Tories. It is little wonder that the party keeps springing back to life, when all those years of attack have been focused on the wrong target.

The Numerology of the Labour Party

Both Conservative and Labour possess a good mixture of the two national numbers, 16 and 7. This must be so for their influence upon the nation is so great. In this regard the last Old Labour Prime Minister Jim Callaghan, born on 27th March 1912 (27+3+1912 = 1942 = 16 = 7) is as significant and necessary to the up and down development of the national life as Churchill, born 30th November 1874 (30+11+1874 = 1915 = 16 = 7).

The Scottish Labour Party (the forerunner of the modern national party) was founded on 25th August 1888 (25th = 7) and the Independent Labour Party was founded on 16th January 1893 (16th = 7). As well as Jim Callaghan, we also have the founder Keir Hardie, born 15th August 1856 (15+8+1856 = 1879 = 25 = 7), the first Labour Prime Minister, Ramsay Macdonald, born 12th October 1866 (12+10+1866 = 1888 = 25 = 7) and the leaders who were never to become PM, John Smith, born 13th September 1938 (13+9+1938 = 1960 = 16 = 7) and Ed Miliband, born 24th December 1969 (24+12+1969 = 2005 = 7). All these were pivotal figures in the life of the nation, experts at muddling through in the Great British tradition. The winners among them had to win, while the losers had to lose. Each played their part in the grand story.

The Labour Party itself was formed in 1906 (6 in the 1900's). The letters of the word LABOUR sum to 6, as do separately the consonants and the vowels of NEW LABOUR. Keir Hardie, the founder was born on the 15th (6) and the

1923 General Election, which led to the first Labour Prime Minister, took place on 6th December 1923 (6th = 6. 6+12+1923 = 15 = 6). The year 1923 also sums to 6.

Clement Attlee, who led the party to its 1945 landslide, was born on 3rd January 1883 (3+1+1883 = 1887 = 24 = 6). Harold Wilson's election in 1964 occurred on the 15th (6) October, and his landslide two years later in 1966 (6 in the 60's). Although he was defeated in 1970, Wilson was re–elected on 28th February 1974 (28+2+1974 = 2004 = 6). The name HAROLD WILSON also sums to 6.

The three most famous Labour firebrands of modern times were Nye Bevan, born on 15th November 1897 (15th = 6. 15+11+1897 = 1923 = 15 = 6), Tony Benn, born 3rd April 1925 (3+4+1925 = 1932 = 15 = 6) and, outside parliament, Arthur Scargill, born 11th January 1938 (11+1+1938 = 1950 = 15 = 6).

Tony Blair was elected leader of the party on 21st July 1994 (21+7+1994 = 2022 = 6). He himself was born on 6th May (6th = 6). It is interesting to note that both Ed Miliband (24th December 1969) and David Miliband (15th July 1965) share this 6–ness in their day of birth.

The Labour Party seems able, over time, to tap into the number of the nation (16/7) but also brings its own 6–ness to bear. 6 is the number of togetherness, community, society (indeed the word SOCIETY = 33 = 6), family, love, care and responsibility. Negatively it is an unthinking and over–emotional number that is unable to cut apron strings or take responsibility for its actions. The Tarot card of 6 is The Lovers. This is why the party speaks and acts almost exclusively in terms of unity, compassion, cohesion and community. Their concern for these things is heartfelt, but the party's passion can blind it to economic aspiration and financial management and cause it to believe that its values – of 6 – are somehow universal values. They are not.

All things of 6 are subject to the Law of Equalisation. A symbolic representation of 6 occurs in the Seal of Solomon – two interwoven triangles, one upward pointing, one downward. This represents the bias and desire of 6 toward equilibrium and harmony and shows an obsession with the concepts of excess and lack. The Labour Party has been enormously successful in framing much of the debate in modern society around these ideas – that *they* have too much, *they* don't have enough, *this* happened for too long, *this* didn't happen long enough, people are too exposed to *this* and not exposed enough to *that*. Their inability to accept the presence of excess and lack leads to the generation of all sorts of Utopian ideas where excess and lack – of money, welfare, education, love and happiness – are rubbed out in favour of equalisation. Yet this New Jerusalem craved by the Labour Party can never, ever be achieved. The TV programme has to end in order for the next episode to begin; the meal has to be eaten in order for the next one to be prepared. If we lay too much in the sun we burn, too much in the water and we wrinkle, too much in our bed and we ache. This is the essential nature of life and whilst there are human beings on a material plane there is nothing that can be done about it. And neither should there be for difference equals change. No difference means no change and no growth.

Attempts at any form of equalisation – of moods, of trying to make the days all the same, or the weather all the same, or employees' conduct all the same – always wind up in reality as attempts at oppression where the 'up' is smoothed out in favour of a constant but equal 'down'.

This principle manifests in the hard left 'purity wing' of the Party, and always becomes an intolerance of those with differing points of view, an inability to accept that nothing lasts forever, and a belief in the malignancy of those who do not see, feel or think the same as they do. This is the rot in the Loving Labour garden, and the root of the nation's estrangement from the Forgotten Lands. The compound number in the cases of Bevan, Benn, and Scargill is 15, which is attributable to The Devil in the Tarot. 666 is also reputed as the Number of the Beast. We might also reflect that US Republican President George W Bush was born on 6th July 1946 (6+7+1946 = 1959 = 24 = 6), which might explain his closeness to Blair (born on the 6th, within the Labour fold of 6), peas in a pod as they clearly were.

Additionally the Labour Party itself was born on 12th February 1906. (12+2+1906 = 1920 = 12 = 3). In certain circumstances the number generated by the whole date of birth may be combined (rather than added) to the number of the day of birth, in this case 3 and 3 giving the rare and unusual Master Number 33.

33 is a number that almost defies human manifestation. All Master Numbers are higher vibrations of their roots. Where 2 is sensitivity and deep feelings, 11 is unbounded awareness and genius level insight. Where 4 is the builder, 22 is the architect. And where 6 is love, compassion and care, 33 says 'We Are One.' However, as the Labour Party has a little pinch of this, and by co–opting the word SOCIETY (33) it might get more, so its aims become ever more unworldly, for the number contains great positive, but also great negative. Wherever, in individuals, we see a 33 we find a person of great love and compassion, but with the potential for great irresponsibility and recklessness. It is revealing that the words CRECHE (without the acute e) and POLICE both sum to 33. Is it really an unfair slight on the Labour Party to accuse them of wanting an authoritarian, nannying state?

The Labour Party therefore operates along the spectrum of 6 –15 –33, and its success or failure, survival or death, is dictated by its position along this spectrum. When it is 6 – The Lovers – it is caring and compassionate, the founder of the NHS and the supporter of the poor and unemployed. When it is 15 – The Devil – it is the enslaver of the people to doctrine, dogma, fear and welfare dependency, as well as being flat out destructive of all that gets in its way. When it is 33 it is the reflection and prime mover of society, almost literally as Blair said, the political wing of the British people. But these 33 goals are too high, too ungrounded, for the party has not yet fully understood and exorcised its own evil – its tendency to involve itself in everyone else's lives (for their own good of course) even when unwanted and unwarranted. Therefore for everyone's safety, there should be no successful Labour Party until its Dark Side is resolved. The 2015 general election forced the party to look deep into its very heart. If from the ashes of its defeat there emerges a force capable of truly channelling the 33 then nothing but good will have come from the trauma.

The result of the post–defeat Labour leadership contest was announced on 12th September 2015 (12+9+2015 = 2036 = 11). This keys in directly to the number of the United Kingdom, showing its significance for the nation as a whole. The new leader Jeremy Corbyn was born on 26th May 1949 (26+5+1949 = 1980 = 18 = 9). The last Prime Minister of the UK who possessed a 9 from his date of birth was Neville Chamberlain, though the very first official Prime Minister, Robert Walpole, some three hundred years ago, was also a 9.

By looking at the letters of his full name JEREMY BERNARD CORBYN we see that they sum to 8, though they also lack 8 within them as does the more commonly used JEREMY CORBYN. Couple this with a Soul Urge for JEREMY BERNARD CORBYN of 22 (or for JEREMY CORBYN of 16/7), together with his birth on the 26th of the month and we have an individual perfectly in alignment with all that is British, but aligned in precisely no ways to all that is Labour. Is this the genuine end of the Labour Party as a national force? Can he become Prime Minister? The numbers cannot say. But they very clearly state that it is essential that he try, for his candidature has really nothing to do with the Labour Party and everything to do with the wider country. Numerologically he seems significant, though the numbers around his election as leader resound with unrealistic dreams and impossible hopes.

Numerologically Corbyn possesses shades of Nelson Mandela (born 18th July 1918, thus two 9's), and the ANC (9). More interestingly still Corbyn's support base, his party-within-a-party MOMENTUM sums to 33. But how can such an energy be usefully channelled without its idealistic members descending into splits and faction fights, or alienating the millions of moderate people who are more concerned with their daily life of 6 (family and responsibilities) than with the high-minded principles of 33?

Returning to the general numerology of Labour it is important to note that the numbers we have revealed are all the more powerful because they are generated using the same rules as the Conservatives, bringing data from four different locations –the names of individuals, the names of organisations and the dates of birth of individuals and organisations. The frequency of repetition of these numbers is beyond anything that can be produced by chance. The frequency of the number 6, as demonstrated here, does not manifest in either the Conservative or Liberal parties. It does however manifest in other British institutions, as we will shortly discover.

The last point to make is about the party logo. The colour red offers a potential link to FIRE, passion and energy, and the modern emblem of the Rose – far from being a soft, feeble thing –can be interpreted as a further link to FIRE through its scent, and AIR through its upward growth. Recent years have seen attempts by the party to co–opt the occult power of the Union Jack but without much enthusiasm or success, for the party must resolve its position along the spectrum of 6 – 15 – 33 before matters of presentation can have any significant effect.

The Numerology of the Liberal Party

Here we will look at various incarnations; the old Liberal Party, the SDP/Liberal Alliance and the modern Liberal Democrats.

The word LIBERAL sums to 5. This is the prime number of change. Within a 3 x 3 grid, into which the numbers 1 to 9 are placed, starting at the bottom left and working upwards and along, the central position is always occupied by 5. (This is also the position of 5 if the numbers are placed in the same grid but in the ancient Chinese Lo Shu arrangement). This number can therefore go anywhere and do anything for it is the only number capable of touching any of the other numbers directly. It is capable of change in multiple directions and is always invested in the business of revolution and expansion. However, this 5 must have a direction, a clear overall goal. It cannot simply react to everything around it for without clear direction the polarity of the number reverses and the 5 is overwhelmed and torn apart by the other numbers. This speaks to a point broader than Britain. To be a LIBERAL, anywhere in the world, is to be an agent of progress and change, yet if the LIBERAL (5) loses sight of himself then he is almost certainly destroyed by those who wish to change him. Sectional interests thus come to infiltrate and transform the host LIBERAL (5) if he does not know precisely who he is and specifically what he is for. This has been the consistent failure of the LIBERAL throughout the decades – to be overtaken by narrow external interests.

The National Liberation Federation was formed on 31st May 1877 (31+5+1877 = 1913 = 14 = 5). The old Liberal Party was led and influenced by Lord Palmerston, born 20th October 1784 (20+10+1784 = 1814 = 14 = 5), William Gladstone, born 29th December 1809 (29+12+1809 = 1850 = 14 = 5), the Marquis of Hartington, born 23rd July 1833 (23rd = 5) and Lord Rosebery, born 7th May 1847 (7+5+1847 = 1859 = 23 = 5). Throughout this period the Liberals were the agents of progress and improvement in society. From 1895 (1895 = 23 = 5) onwards none of their party leaders, in name or date of birth, or any of its key dates bore any relationship to 5. This corresponded with the decline of the party and its steady replacement by Labour as the opposition to the Conservatives.

Decades later the party tried out various leaders in an attempt to recapture its distinctiveness. Archibald Sinclair, born on 22nd October 1890 (22+10+1890 = 1922 = 14 = 5) was leader from 1935–1945, as well as playing a key part in

World War Two as Secretary of State for Air under Churchill. The party later tried Jo Grimond, born 29th July 1913 (29+7+1913 = 1949 = 23 = 5) and successfully experienced a Liberal mini–revival during the late 50's and early 60's. But it was not to last. Even the electoral successes of the 1970's under the Master Numbers of Jeremy Thorpe were to be short lived. Interestingly Thorpe possessed both 11 and 33. That is too much for one man and was proved as such in his spectacular fall from grace.

Moving forward, the Social and Liberal Democratic Party (forerunner of the modern Lib Dems) was founded on 3rd March 1988 (3+3+1988 = 1994 = 23 = 5) and the newly re-badged Liberal Democrats experienced advances at both the 1997 election, on 1st May (1+5+1997 = 2003 = 5) and again notably in 2010 (6th May 2010, 6+5+2010 = 2021 = 5) where Liberals took part in government for the first time in over 80 years. We might also note the two 3's formed by the modern Lib Dem date of birth. We last saw this 3 and 3 combination in the Labour Party, which is not present in the Conservatives. Maybe this is why so many people have yearned for a re–alignment on the left of the Lib Dems and Labour, in opposition to the Conservatives?

Alas the party could not resist the backlash generated by its decision to abandon the pursuit of real change in favour of simply a slightly different form of management and the party was all but wiped out, mainly by its previous coalition partners, at the 2015 General Election. It then replaced its one time successful leader Nick Clegg, born 7th January 1967 (7+1+1967 = 1975 = 22/4) with Tim Farron, born 27th May 1970 (27+5+1970 = 2002 = 22/4). Plus ça change!

The current logo of the party is a yellow bird. Yellow is the colour of expression and communication, and the Bird elementally connects to AIR.

A brief look at the SDP/Liberal Alliance is instructive if we wish to distinguish signs of real change from the noise generated merely by a desire for change. In 1982, just before the invasion of the Falkland Islands, it seemed that Britain was stood on the edge of a new political age. The SDP – led by the four Labour MPs who had broken away from the increasingly Tony Benn dominated Labour Party – were polling 50% and more, while Thatcher's Conservatives were roundly hated and Labour's hard left increasingly marginalised. This time, they said, it was going to be different. Of course, a little over 18 months later the game was up when the SDP failed to make any kind of breakthrough and Margaret Thatcher was re–elected by a landslide.

The SDP was formed on 26th March 1981 (26+3+1981 = 2010 = 21 = 3) the letters of which sum to 3. The party was founded by The Gang of Four, which might have been enormously powerful but for the vanity of one man. Dr David Owen was born on 2nd July 1938 (2+7+1938 = 1947 = 21 = 3). 3 is the number of attention, recognition and expression. The number of writers, journalists, and public speakers; it is little wonder that the party was celebrated by a media naturally composed of the same. One wonders, therefore, whether the SDP was ever really more than a vehicle for the expression of frustration, initially by its founders at the direction of the Labour Party, and subsequently by its supporters at the direction of modern life. Either way the fate of the SDP and the subsequent demise of the Liberal Democrats is informative to everyone who wishes to effect lasting change in Great Britain, in five key ways:

1. Political parties have distinct souls, revealed by their numbers.
2. Individuals who become significant (through success or failure) in those parties are the ones who share or connect with that soul.
3. History takes the individuals and the parties through a series of necessary steps in their life cycle. In other words, sometimes defeat and decline is inevitable and right.
4. When a party forgets what it is, is overtaken by people who do not share or understand its soul or is touched in some way by karmic individuals, possessors either of the numbers of the nation, or holders of Master Numbers (for example, Lloyd George, Churchill, Thatcher, Blair), then extreme things happen to the party and thus the country.
5. The greatest force in Great Britain is the invisible desire to fulfil its numbers and to resolve all traces of the national karma. This is the force that determines who is elected and who is turfed out of office. The only thing that political parties can do is to align with this.

Some Recent Attempts at Karmic Resolution

The exponential growth of the City of London as a world financial centre is an attempt – albeit unbalanced and unwitting – to resolve the national karma and fulfil the national destiny of 8. There are many consequential issues arising from this, not least the question of whether the money generated in the City generates as much tax revenue for the nation as it should or might. This is not a matter of evasion, but globalisation, and might take decades to work through, as will the general economic efficiency of the nation; who pays the bills and from where the money comes.

An imbalanced 8 will always produce boom and bust, recession and growth, inflation and stagnation, and economic disparity. Historical obsession over economic and financial matters such as the Corn Laws and Tariff Protectionism in the Victorian/Edwardian times, the Gold Standard in the 1930's, the strength of Sterling in the 1960's, Prices and Incomes Policy in the 1970's, monetarism in the 1980's, the ERM and the Euro in the 1990's, and the national debt burden since 2008 are all attempts to manage 8. None of these things are functions of politics or class. They are a function of our language, which is a product of the numbers.

Karma can be resolved by mistakes, as much as it can by success, and Karma in 8 is as much to do with power as it is money. The parliamentary approval to invade Iraq, taken on 18th March 2003 ($18+3+2003 = 2024 = 8$), is a case in point. This has proven to be a complete disaster, but it should not blind us to the awareness that Britain is always likely to play out its karma on the global stage, because its footprint is everywhere.

The British created Iraq and attempted (along with the Americans) to control it for many years. Does the British adventure in Iraq draw a line under future serious military excursions? There was certainly reluctance to go anywhere or do anything in the ten years that followed. But was this a good thing, or was it appeasement and cowardice of the worst sort? Are British values worth fighting and, if necessary, killing for or not? The answers here are not at all clear and we should separate the decision to go into Iraq from the subsequent mis–management of the war. Have the Lessons of 8 been resolved, by a realisation that the British should not be in the business of projecting power across the world? And if so, are the British prepared to deal with those who would project their power in the vacuum that remains? All these things are unresolved questions of 8.

When parliament voted against military action in Syria on 29th August 2013 (29+7+2013 = 2050 = 7) it was the first time a British Prime Minister had lost a vote on war since 1782. This was profoundly significant and did not occur on a day of 8 as we might expect, but of 7, one of the national numbers. This suggests the lessons of 8 have further to play out, but more information is needed here for it is the manner of military intervention that is also key in 8. The British have always tended to exert their military power disproportionately. At times they are hopelessly unnumbered or outgunned, as seen at the death of General Gordon, the Charge of the Light Brigade, and the Massacre at the Somme. At other times though small in number they manage to overcome enormous opposition, for example at The Siege of Mafeking, the Battle of Britain, and the retaking of the Falklands. The British lesson of 8 gifts them with military inappropriateness – snatch landrovers in IED country being but the latest fiasco. Sometimes British power is applied well, as other times badly, but it's rarely applied in balance. This must also be resolved, so that it is not just a matter of where British forces go, but in what strength and what manner. In this, as usual, Britain is hamstrung by its history. From the defeat of the Armada to the Battle of Britain, the nation has grown used to performing above itself. But this is no way to balance an 8.

The Language of 8

In an attempt to master the nature of 8 we subconsciously create names and words that provide fuller 8–ness. These words then become emotive, reminding everyone what is lacking, whether that be by filling the gap, or making it bigger and more apparent.

CHELSEA, CAMBRIDGE, TEMPLE and STATION all sum to 8. As does MANCHESTER UNITED, ASTON VILLA and TOTTENHAM HOTSPUR. COMIC RELIEF does the same, as does QUEEN (be it the band or the monarch). KARAOKE, FISH AND CHIPS, SEASIDE, BOXING and UNDERCLASS also create 8. All these names are woven prominently into the fabric of the nation.

Both TESCO and FORTNUM AND MASON are 8, as was BRITISH RAIL. MARKS AND SPENCER and BOOTS give us 8, as do, ironically, MONETARIST and SOCIALIST. The CHANCELLOR OF THE EXCHEQUER, FOREIGN SECRETARY and MINISTER vibrate to 8. As does POLICE STATE. But let's not dwell on that one.

Vicariously we access the realm of 8 by visiting WEATHERFIELD, BROOKSIDE and HOLBY, but the biggest appearance of 8 in British daily life is through its national newspapers.

The Numerology of Tabloids & Broadsheets

The UK's print media is awash with the influence of 8. Any pretence that these publications are impartial is therefore laughable. But it is not an editorial conspiracy or owner interference that causes the bias. These newspapers cannot do anything other than project and reflect the issues associated with their numbers. And when their numbers, which are primarily 8, are the very same numbers lacking in the nation then we can see that their agendas, distortions and commentary are necessary and will continue until the national karma has been resolved. Although print media itself has been in recent decline the website reach of many of these publications continues to grow and their influence, if anything, extends.

The Times was born on 1st January 1788 (1+1+1788 = 1790 = 17 = 8). The People was launched on 16th October 1881 (16+10+1881 = 1907 = 17 = 8) and the Daily Mirror on 2nd November 1903 (2+11+1903 = 1916 = 17 = 8). The Sun was launched on 15th September 1964 (15+9+1964 = 1988 = 26 = 8) and, after a faltering start, was re–launched by Rupert Murdoch on 17th November 1969 (17th = 8, and 17+11+1969 = 1997 = 26 = 8). The Daily Mail, though founded in 1896, was re–launched in tabloid format on 3rd May 1971 (3+5+1971 = 1979 = 26 = 8).

Additionally The Sun's first Page 3 was on 17th November 1970 (17th = 8), The Herald (previously The Glasgow Herald) was re–launched on 3rd February 1992 (3+2+1992 = 1997 = 26 = 8) and the Daily Star Sunday on 15th September 2002 (15+9+2002 – 2026 – 8). And just in case anyone was thinking that this applied only to old media, The Huffington Post UK was launched on 6th July 2011 (6+7+2011 = 2024 = 8).

Names of 8 are less frequent, but modern publications THE INDEPENDENT, CITY AM and METRO all individually sum to 8. No other numbers appear with such frequency.

The role of national newspapers in British life is therefore key. They exist as a mirror, to provide – through comment, opinion, news, features, investigations, campaigns, witch hunts, and propaganda – that which we lack. It is not our print media that makes us gossipy and salacious. It is our weakness of character and our imbalanced 8's that give rise to and feed the print media.

The BBC's Karmic Role in the Life of the Nation

The BBC is as near to integral to the modern national identity as it is possible to get, and through it we can observe many of the issues troubling Great Britain. We will not see these things, however, through the BBC's supposedly balanced news reporting, but through their biases, especially where they intersect with other organisations and aspects of the nation.

6, 7 and 8

There are three numbers that appear prominently and repeatedly in the BBC. First we see the national number 16/7. The numbers of the letters BBC (2+2+3 = 7) reveal this, as do the popular programme titles LITTLE BRITAIN, THIS LIFE and NEWSROUND. The first licence was granted to the BBC on 18th January 1923 (18+1+1923 = 1942 = 16 = 7) and the first royal broadcast took place on 23rd April 1924 (23+4+1924 = 1951 = 16 = 7). The first edition of the flagship programme Grandstand took place on 10th October 1958 (10+10+1958 = 1978 = 25 = 7) and Blue Peter was first aired on 16th October that year (16th = 7). All these things plug the organisation into the very soul of the nation.

Next we can see the presence of 8, from the birth of the founder himself, Lord Reith, on 20th July 1889 (20+7+1889 = 1916 = 17 = 8), to the opening of Broadcasting House on 15th May 1932 (15+5+1932 = 1952 = 17 = 8), and the first episodes of Doctor Who on 23rd November 1963 (23+11+1963 = 1997 = 26 = 8) and EastEnders on 19th February 1985 (19+2+1985 = 2006 = 8).

BBC Radios One, Two, Three, and Four were all launched on 30th September 1967 (30+9+1967 = 2006 = 8), while CBBC and CBeebies first aired on 11th February 2002 (11+2+2002 = 2015 = 8). An important point in the BBC's recent history was marked by the publication of the Hutton Report (H = 8th letter of the alphabet). This heavily criticised the BBC's role in the row surrounding the Iraq 'Dodgy Dossier' and the subsequent death of Dr David Kelly. It was released on 28th January 2004 (28+1+2004 = 2033 = 8) and triggered a point of perfect intersection between the BBC and the nation, as both attempted to resolve, play out, or simply further understand the national issues of 8, which in this case referred to questions surrounding the projection of military power. The subsequent reorganisation of the BBC post–Hutton has produced two out of the three BBC Trust Chairs as 8's – Chris Patten, born 12th May 1944 (12+5+1944 = 1861 = 17 = 8) and Rona Fairhead, born 28th August 1961 (28+8+1961 = 1997 = 26 = 8). From all this we might infer the BBC, right from its inception has been engaged in a sincere attempt to assist in resolving the karma of the nation.

Moving on to 6, the BBC was founded on 18th October 1922 (18+10+1922 = 1950 = 15 = 6), and Broadcasting House was opened on 15th May 1932 (15th = 15 = 6). The very first Reith Lecture was given on 26th December 1948 (26+12+1948 = 1986 = 24 = 6), and BBC1 in colour was launched on 15th

November 1969 (15th = 15 = 6). There are many other appearances of 6 in its history, which include no less than six out of its eighteen Director Generals being either Destiny 6 or Day of Birth 6, with four of the five most recent ones having that distinction. This may be no real surprise, given that 6 is the number of service. However we have already seen that the Labour Party possesses a large amount of 6, and the Conservative Party does not. In essence therefore the two organisations – BBC and Labour – are intrinsically in sympathy with one another. The BBC, at least recently, has been a Labour thing, and Labour is a BBC thing. Even if this is not the whole story and each organisation possesses strands of other energies then it is most certainly true that the BBC is not, energetically or in its heart Conservative or Liberal. Although 8 features strongly in both the Conservative Party and the BBC it should not be inferred that they are therefore connected to each other, as much as they are separately connected to the far bigger and independent picture of the karma of the nation.

The BBC is thus, almost certainly, biased towards certain viewpoints and approaches. Even when the Corporation employs journalists and presenters who themselves possess very little number 6, if those individuals wish to get on within the organisation they will, inevitably and over time, absorb the invisible values and world view of the organisation into themselves. It can be no other way. It is not a conspiracy, but the issue becomes starker if we take a comparative glance at other television stations.

The words ITV, INDEPENDENT TELEVISION and the lesser used CHANNEL 3 each, individually, sum to 6, with the organisation itself founded on 22nd September 1955 (22+9+1955 = 1986 = 24 = 6). Channel 4 followed later, first broadcasting on 2nd November 1982 (2+11+1982 = 1995 = 24 = 6).

ITV switched to a colour broadcast on 15th November 1969 (15th = 6, also 15+11+1969 = 1995 = 24 = 6), TV–AM was launched on 1st February 1983 (1+2+1983 = 1986 = 24 = 6) and ITV launched its most recent rebrand on 28th October 2002 (28+10+2002 = 2040 = 6). As an interesting aside the opening credits for the Good Morning Britain segment of TV–AM prominently featured – though hidden in plain sight – the Four Forgotten Lands. First there was a visual of the rising Sun (Fire), then a skydiver and a flock of birds (Air), then a naval warship (Water), and finally a shot of the ground (Earth). Each of these Elements contained life, be it people or animals. Powerful stuff, for seven o'clock in the morning! More interestingly still, the one time boss of the company Bruce Gyngell, was supposedly an avowed practitioner of numerology, and was even rumoured to have based many executive decisions upon it.

By coming right up to date with shows like the X FACTOR (6) we see that much British television programming is propagandistic – promoting things of 6, a 'togetherness' vibration, with values of family, society, community, support, love, trust and all things co–operative. Sky TV has been an exception to this, and certainly much of its news, sport and entertainment programming feels different. The only presence of 6 that I can find anywhere in its names, key dates or personnel is the day (though not whole date) of birth of Sky News former political editor Adam Boulton, born on 15th February 1959 (15th = 6). Sky TV broadcast first on 5th February 1989 (5+2+1989 = 1996 = 25 = 7), but SKY SPORTS sums to 9, while SKY NEWS gives us 8 and SKY MOVIES is 3. These are all very different channels from the old fare of the BBC, ITV and Channel 4.

Sky TV seems now, numerologically, as British as a cup of tea (7) and Sky News seems to fulfill something deep within the psyche (8), while the traditional terrestrial channels seem to have headed down a sectional route, biased toward the number 6. But as we saw with the Labour Party, 6 (The Lovers) quickly connects to 15 (The Devil). The numbers of the BBC show this and we might wonder if the organisation is not concealing more up to date variants of Savile within its midst?

It is clear to see that the BBC (and to some extent ITV and Channel 4) constantly present sectional issues of 6 – care, family, society, and welfare – as universal issues. There is not so much overt bias in party-politics, as there is in tone, culture and values. The BBC is now quite far away from being a balanced organisation and we should not find it impossible to consider life after it, or at least after it moves into balance. When an organisation serves a nation, through addressing its lack, or supporting its nature then that organisation may thrive. But when these core principles are neglected in favour of a narrow stream of 'correct thinking' then it becomes an organisation that grows ever more alien to its viewers and listeners. A widespread awareness of this has already begun.

The Judgement of the British

The Rider Waite Smith Tarot is one of the best selling and certainly most widely known Tarot decks in the world. Conceived and executed at the peak of the Empire in Edwardian Britain, its artwork captures a particular English–ness with some of the work inspired by the artist's time in the small town of Winchelsea on the Sussex/Kent border.

Let us focus on card number 20, Judgement. This depicts two families – man, woman and child in each – rising up to the call of a trumpet, issued from the Archangel Michael. From the trumpet is hung a flag, the Cross of St George, the flag of England, and the banner of the City of London. What does all this mean?

When I first noticed these details (though they had always been there, hidden in plain sight) I realised immediately that the number 20 corresponded to the current century, the 2000's. The imagery was then suggestive of the British waking up, wising up, and rising up. Could this be the century of karmic resolution for Britain, or merely England? I also realised there were 6 people in the scene, with one additional being – the Archangel – making 7, the number of the nation. It struck me like a bolt of lightning – this century may bring the Judgement of the Nation, on the people, by the people.

But what form will this Judgement take? In the Hebrew Kabbalah the card is sometimes associated with the letter Shin, which brings forth Fire. Additionally the Archangel Michael is connected to compass South, again Fire. Aleister Crowley, through his reinvention and reimaging of the card extended this to include a world drowned by Fire. If we look further into the Kabbalah the number 20 is sometimes referred to as The Breaker of The Elements, highlighting two possible outcomes – the collapse and abandonment of the Forgotten Lands in order that we might rediscover and reconstitute them, or their final dissipation following our loss of control, leading to inevitable ruin.

We may look beyond this Tarot, to the old French seer Nostradamus, for further insight as to the fate of the nation. Mario Reading's modern interpretation predicts the separation of Scotland from England during this century, an English exit from the EU, A King Harry – not William – and a global nuclear war and famine wherein England manages somehow to hold itself above the global fray as Europe withers and collapses.

Can we really believe any of these wild suggestions? The only thing we may say with certainty is that any of them *might* come true – but none of them *need* to. The Judgement to which I refer is ultimately no more than self–realisation and personal awakening which is available, at all times, to everyone. But in order to self–realise the British must know much more about where they have come from, what they have done, and what they are yet to do.

Strength VIII & The Time of the Feminine

Card 8 in the Rider Waite Smith Tarot shows a woman holding in check a Lion. The suggestion is not of coercion or exertion by any physical force, but of the Lion being indicative of a woman's inner nature as well as the external forces that act upon her. The telling thing is that it is the female to whom the card speaks, and the woman – not the man – who is connected to the number 8.

The history of Britain has been deeply influenced by women. The land itself is mostly referred to in the female. Britannia and her ancestor Minerva are female. During the days of Empire the homeland was referred to as the Mother Country (as opposed to the German Fatherland) and that land has been ruled throughout history by assertive and influential female monarchs –from Boudicca, to Queen Elizabeth I, Victoria, Queen Elizabeth II and, though not a monarch, Margaret Thatcher. Under the aegis of the feminine the nation has always pursued its destiny, but when the nation has faltered it is because women have faltered. The connecting line between the female and the nation cannot be clearer, yet paradoxically this makes it hard for most to see.

As we have seen, our lessons of 8 give us a distorted idea of money and power. There is too much, and then there is too little. We have not enough here, but too much there. In attempting to solve this we might raise taxes to 100% of earnings, and find that there would never be enough money to do the things we wanted. Or we might abandon taxation altogether and disband the state, so that nothing is held in common. We would then find that our sudden personal wealth is insufficient for our needs. These are dynamics that can be *explained* by economics but are not generated by economics. In certain parts we are already much poorer than we are prepared to recognise, and in others much richer than we are ready to see. It might even be possible to change the appearance of the nation wholesale, but without resolving this issue of 8 in any way at all, such is its depth. Today it is money, tomorrow it will be power, next week it will be different forms of money and power. Whether the discussion is about Pounds Sterling, Euros, Bitcoin or Bristol Pounds the underlying question remains the same. Who can control the Lion that roars? The suggestion is that it is only women that can do this now.

Election Judgements

There has not yet been invented a better way for the British people to pass judgement upon their rulers than democratic elections. Whilst not perfect by any stretch the system of parliamentary democracy enjoyed in the UK seems preferable to anything else that has so far been suggested. Even if that is too much to accept election results present a great opportunity for the British to look upon themselves and see what they have become. From every angle, an election is a Day of Judgement.

But many now wonder why we have government at all, especially in its current form? The answer is straightforward, but unpalatable. Government exists in order to create the right conditions for human development – nothing more and nothing less. It does this by acting as a remedy for our individual failings, so that we always get the government we deserve. Government is our light and our shadow, sometimes delivering what we want, at other times what we need – often in the form of a bitter medicine. The belief that government is self–serving is an emotional mis–reading. We are one, are we not? If we are interconnected, then isn't the government us, regardless of party? If we will not or cannot check ourselves then that other aspect of us – the government, through law – will do it for us. Thus the behaviour, attitude, tone and policy of any particular government depends entirely upon what we as a people have become and what we need to learn. Government exists to take decisions so that we do not have to. In a world of Dark and Light someone has to deal with the Darkness. Within a democracy the people have an opportunity to control themselves, yet if they do not take this then, as night follows day, the system will morph into a dictatorship so that control is exerted upon them. Democratic government cannot be taken for granted, yet it is, every day, by millions of people.

Up until quite recently British General Elections took place over the course of several days, and sometimes, as in the case of 1945, several weeks. This is again the case today where postal voting begins up to two weeks before the official Polling Day. Other equally important dates might then include the date the new government assumes office (often the day after polling day, though not always), the date of the first Cabinet, or the date of the first Queen's speech. All might be revealing, but for all this Polling Day remains significant as a focus of candidates' and voters' energy, so we will look at patterns generated by those, as well as the overall – Universal – year in which the election took place.

Universal Years

The Universal Year is arrived at by the addition of all the numbers of the year in question, without reference to the day or month. Thus, 1966 = 22 = 4. 2010 = 21 = 3. The Universal Year tells us a lot about the mood of the nation and the spirit of the times, the backdrop against which the election is fought.

Elections were fought at the close of both World Wars, in 1918 and 1945. 1918 = 19 = 1. 1945 = 19 = 1. No other election years since have produced this 19/1, the number of independence and self–determination, new beginnings and fresh starts. Both these elections produced landslides against the parties dominant in the wartime coalition and each signalled a different turn of the page for the nation.

Four elections since 1918 have been fought when the Universal Year has been 8 – 1970, 1979, 1997 and 2015. Each produced larger movements between parties than expected, a change of government, and were key years in the national attempt at resolving the 8 of money and power. The result in 1970 was a rejection of Harold Wilson's economic policies and was interpreted as heralding a return to Conservative competence and efficiency. This was soon scuppered by Edward

Heath's power struggles with the Unions. The new Thatcher government of 1979 sought to finish what Heath had left undone, yet was coloured by strife and power plays from Day One, while the Blair landslide of 1997 was expected to provide a new deal for the nation and a re–balancing of power away from the old interests, but in fact resulted in numerous overseas military adventures. The Conservative's surprise victory in 2015 so far seems to be a defining moment in the nature of British interaction with the world, its financial condition, and internal power structures.

Seeded Years

Every day projects itself forward through time, seeding consequences deep into the future. This happens every day of every month of every year, but is noteworthy when something important happens on that day, for the seeded year that is created then becomes a focus of further important and connected events. There is no certainty that any seeded year will be recognised or grasped by the people of the future, but it is there for the taking and when it is then we witness the creation of permanently memorable history, for good or ill. The Seeded Year is derived from the first result in the addition of day, month and year. For example, 28th July 1914, the outbreak of the First World War, $(28+7+1914 = 1949)$ seeded ahead to 1949, its issues unresolved until then.

Polling Day on 30th May 1929 was fought against the backdrop of a government that was widely seen to be past its sell by date. It produced a close result in terms of number of votes (Labour 8.05 million, Conservative 8.25 million), and resulted, through a disproportionate spread of votes, in a Labour government. It was then only two years until the next election. This polling day seeded forward to 1964 $(30+5+1929 = 1964)$, which was another election year.

Polling Day on 15th October 1964 was again fought against the backdrop of the government out of time and energy. It produced a close result in terms of the number of votes (Labour 12.2 million, Conservative 12.0 million), which resulted in the Labour government of Harold Wilson, who lasted two years before calling another election in 1966.

This is what some might call a meaningful coincidence. However, I suggest that the correct energetic conditions for the second event were seeded by the first. It is then worth noting the timespan between the original event and its seeded year. In the first case of 1929 to 1964 the period was 35 years, but in the second example 1964 seeded forward to 1989, a shorter period of 25 years. Since 1918 to the present day the trend has been for the timespan between origin and seed to become significantly shorter.

Obviously, every single date is seeded by a previous one, as well as seeding ahead another. Thus everything is a consequence of something that has happened before, even if we cannot numerologically trace the whole picture. We can however see that the election of Edward Heath on 18th June 1970 projected itself forward in time to 1994, which saw the election of Tony Blair as leader of the Labour Party. These two events are not as unrelated as they might first appear. It is not, of course, that one creates the other, but that one gives rise to the chance and necessity of the other. The Heath government of 1970 was beset by issues around nationalisation and was ultimately felled by the trades unions. Blair, from 1994, completed the trades unions' marginalisation in public life and abandoned the Labour Party's historic commitment to public ownership. It was Blair who exorcised the ghost of the Heath government, not Thatcher.

Seeded Years also allow us to understand how current matters may continue to remain unresolved. Tony Blair was elected leader of the Labour Party on 21st July 1994. This produces a seed year of 2022. The reasons for his leadership, together with its subsequent failings, are likely to remain unresolved until that time. The 9/11 attacks in New York, which so changed the world, produced a seed year of 2021, the 7/7 London bombings produced a seed year of 2019, while the parliamentary approval for war in Iraq, given on 18th March 2003, projects forward to 2024. All this sets Britain up for a tumultuous period as these matters all come to fruition.

Two more examples will give us a sense of an occasional time dilation that also takes place.

Margaret Thatcher's landslide election on 3rd May 1979 projected forward a mere 8 years to 1987, two elections into the future. The actions and results of her government would therefore be plain to see, very quickly. Similarly, the Blair landslide of 1st May 1997 projected forward only 6 years to 2003, the year of the start of the Iraq War, at which Blair signalled that defeat in the parliamentary vote would lead to the fall of his government. How quickly do some chickens come home to roost?

The fragmentation of the electoral map in the 2015 General Election may be traced back to its root – Polling Day 5th May 2005 at which the topic of immigration was prominent – and in turn projected forward to its seed, 2027. Through all these numbers we can see one thing very clearly; that although news cycles and scandals last a few days, the actions of electors and governments have long–term consequences. Sometimes matters can be healed and resolved within years, at other times it takes decades. Either way, our judgement always has ramifications, the unfolding of which can be seen through the Numbers.

How Do Elections Touch the Nations?

We know that each nation of the Union possesses controlling numbers. 7 is the prime number of Scotland. It is 6 for Wales, 3 for England and 22/4 for Northern Ireland. Great Britain, like Scotland, has 7 (reminding us that Scotland sits at the very heart of the Union) and the United Kingdom operates along the 2–11 spectrum. All of these are touched additionally by the expression of 8 and its historic lack within the letters. So, whenever any of these numbers appear at General Election time we know where the nation(s) will be touched deeply.

Take the election of the first Labour Prime Minister, Ramsay Macdonald, on 6th December 1923. The day was a 6, the sum of the whole date comes to 6 (6+12+1923 = 1941 = 15 = 6) and the sum of the universal year came to 6 (1923 = 15 = 6). 6 is the number of togetherness, society and the Labour Party. At this election Ramsay Macdonald also happened to be standing for the constituency of ABERAVON (6) in WALES (6). Therefore, this event, on this date touched all these connected things profoundly.

There are many other confluences of numbers around leaders, parties and elections, and the national numbers are touched to some degree at all General Elections. But pivotal decisions take place where multiple numbers are placed in play. There is considerable data on this in Appendix C: British General Elections, but three more really significant things leap out.

The General Election of 1966 (31st March 1966) occurred on a 4 day, in a 4 Universal Year and the whole date summed to 2. This election, therefore, would touch Northern Ireland (4) particularly and the United Kingdom (11/2) as a whole. Following this election, in 1969, in the face of continued rioting the British Army was deployed in Belfast and Derry, heralding the start of The Troubles, which would continue for another thirty years, ending symbolically (if not actually) with the Good Friday Agreement in 1998. The Seeded Year of the original 1966 General Election was the year 2000.

More recently we can see that Polling Day 7th May 2015, was a special Karmic date for the nation, touching Scotland (7th = 7), the United Kingdom (7+5+2015 = 2027 = 11 = 2) and addressing the lack of 8 (2015 = 8). Though this system does not enable us to predict outcomes, it does allow us to observe what the election was really all about. Any campaign that can tap into what the date is asking of the nation is likely to be successful. Looking ahead, if the next election takes place on 7th May 2020, then the numbers generated will be 7, 7 and 22/4. It will therefore be an election, once again, all about Scotland (7) and the very existence of Great Britain (7), but for the first time since 1966, about Northern Ireland (4), and also potentially the future form and existence of the Conservative Party (lots of 22). It may be that these issues arise prior to the election and the vote becomes all about them, or that the result raises these issues to prominence. Either way let us hope that sufficient attention is being paid to events in the Northern Irish parliament at STORMONT (8).

The Judgement of Prime Ministers

The British Prime Minister is an influential, symbolic and powerful figure. It is through the holder of the office of Prime Minister that the nation gets to look directly upon itself. The role is second only to the Monarch in its mystical power and as such we must take note of the nature, attitude and condition of the person involved. In order for the Prime Minster to be taken seriously, to be supported and to be successful it is essential that he or she is seen to be – whether this is an illusion or not – one of the people. And if not one of the people, then on the peoples' side, or displaying qualities the people themselves would like to embody. All historic Prime Ministers can be observed in this way, either in the case of Thatcher (respected though not universally loved), Major (neither loved nor respected) and Blair (initially loved, then respected, then ultimately neither). To be PRIME MINISTER (15 The Devil, 6 The Lovers) is to be the object of a great deal of projection and thus to be intimately connected to SOCIETY (33, 6) and DEMOCRACY (6), although it is also to be part of an unholy alliance between CHIEF WHIP (15, 6) and MEMBER OF PARLIAMENT (15, 6). In this sense 666 – and its manifestation through the parliamentary whipping system – really does seem to be a Number of the Beast. In this sense we may also look upon our Prime Ministers as Shadow figures, performing duties and functions which we would rather not, but nonetheless need to be performed. A Prime Minister may be any one of these things described, but he or she will never be insignificant.

The various roles of government can be revealed further through their numbers. The DEPUTY PRIME MINISTER (16 The Tower, 7 The Chariot) is clearly the fall guy in any government with functions quite distinct from any other. The CHANCELLOR OF THE EXCHEQUER (8) provides the missing link to power and is one of the Four Great Offices of State, theoretically of equal importance to the Prime Minister (who is technically first among equals with the Foreign and Home Secretaries making up the Rule of Fourness). Interestingly the FOREIGN SECRETARY (8) and any MINISTER (8) actually serve the same duty – the acquisition, maintenance and exertion of power. While the AMBASSADOR (3) talks, the functions of balance and justice are maintained by the HOME SECRETARY (11 Justice, 2 High Priestess) and any SECRETARY OF STATE (11, 2).

There have been 52 holders of the office of Prime Minister, many of them serving multiple terms, sometimes returning to the post years after being defeated. Broken down by the addition of the numbers of their date of birth, they appear in the table overleaf.

The only number poorly represented in this distribution is 11. This is perhaps as it should be, for 11 is the number of spiritual and theoretical, rather than earthly or mundane power. The other relevant Master Number, 22, only appears three times, signalling the minimal amount of real transformation that the modern country has ever undergone. (A result of 33 from a date of birth is mathematically impossible, using the method DD+MM+YYYY, on our current calendar).

The most frequent number is of course, the number of the nation, 7. Appearing eight times, in governments of all parties, these are the Karmic people, the ones who had to be there in order for the nation to continue. From William Petty ending the American War of Independence, the Great Reform Act of 1832 and the abolition of slavery across the Empire under Charles Grey, Campbell–Bannerman's 1906 social reforms and Liberal landslide, Ramsay Macdonald as the first Labour Prime Minister and Churchill as the saviour of the nation to

Prime Ministers by Destiny Number	
Destiny Number 1	**Destiny Number 7**
William Cavendish-Bentinck (Duke of Portland) William Pitt 'The Younger' Henry Addington (Viscount Sidmouth) Spencer Perceval Lord Liverpool Benjamin Disraeli H H Asquith	William Petty (Marquis of Lansdowne) Charles (Earl) Grey Henry Campbell-Bannerman Ramsay MacDonald Winston Churchill Anthony Eden Harold MacMillan Jim Callaghan
Destiny Number 2	**Destiny Number 8**
Charles Watson-Wentworth (Marquis of Rockingham) Arthur Wellesley (Duke of Wellington) Andrew Bonar Law Tony Blair Gordon Brown	George Grenville Augustus FitzRoy (Duke of Grafton) Robert Gascoyne-Cecil (Lord Salisbury) Arthur Balfour
Destiny Number 3	**Destiny Number 9**
Frederick (Lord) North William (Baron) Grenville George Canning Frederick Robinson (Viscount Goderich)	Robert Walpole Henry Pelham Lord John Russell David Lloyd George Neville Chamberlain
Destiny Number 4	**Destiny Number 11**
Edward Smith-Stanley (Lord Derby) George Hamilton-Gordon (Earl of Aberdeen) Alec Douglas Home Harold Wilson	Thomas Pelham-Holles (Duke of Newcastle)
Destiny Number 5	**Destiny Number 22**
William Cavendish (Duke of Devonshire) Henry Temple (Lord Palmerston) William Gladstone Archibald Primrose (Lord Roseberry) David Cameron	Robert Peel Margaret Thatcher John Major
Destiny Number 6	
John Stuart (Earl of Bute) William Pitt 'The Elder' William Lamb (Lord Melbourne) Stanley Baldwin Clement Attlee Edward Heath	

Anthony Eden's ruin of the nation at Suez, Harold Macmillan's cry of 'You've Never Had It So Good' and accelerated retreat from Empire, to Jim Callaghan's cruelly necessary Winter of Discontent, which consigned Old Labour to the wilderness. Although almost all Prime Ministers can be seen as having an impact in some way, these kind of national events seem to be reserved for 7's.

Although many Prime Ministers of Britain can be said to have presided over losses of some kind (to paraphrase Enoch Powell, *"All political careers end in failure"*) these '7' Prime Ministers sat at the helm under the greatest losses of all. Petty lost the American colonies, Charles Grey lost interest in politics, even though he achieved more in one term than many achieved in three, Campbell–Bannerman lost key reform legislation in the Lords and had himself only a short time as PM, dying quickly after leaving office. Ramsay Macdonald presided over a split in his party and the economic crisis of 1931. Churchill, though victorious over Hitler, did not win the war without great cost. Eden was humiliated at Suez and Macmillan gleefully abandoned the colonies, leaving Callaghan to abandon prices and incomes control and any vestige of influence over the trades unions. One can only wonder what losses a Prime Minister Ed Miliband (7) would have inflicted on the nation.

78 Cards of the Tarot: 75 Prime Ministers, and counting.

The formal post of British Prime Minister is a relatively new invention. The first person officially titled as such was Henry Campbell–Bannerman in 1906, previous to which the lead person in government was officially referred to as the First Lord. Although it is now generally accepted that Sir Robert Walpole was the first 'Prime Minister' there is debate over the precise comings and goings within the office during the late 18th century. Some sources list William Pitt 'The Elder' as First Lord from 1766–1768, while others claim he also led the government briefly in 1757. Others debate whether the Duke of Wellington was in charge briefly during 1834 while the nominated man, Sir Robert Peel, was tracked down overseas and recalled to London. All this makes for typical British inaccuracy, but one that I have tried to clarify so that we may read each Prime Minister in relation to a Number and a Tarot card.

The core idea belongs to the American author Dusty Bunker, who proceeded to attribute individual Tarot cards, in a defined sequence, to the list of US Presidents. Her work is fascinating and, although any such insights are bound to be subjective, their value lies in how such an exercise brings forward a new perspective, where information appears that might not otherwise be available.

By my counting – detailed in the following pages – David Cameron is the 75th Prime Minister of the United Kingdom. By matching up each PM in sequence with the cards of the Tarot immediately shows that we must be, politically, at the end of days, there being only 78 cards in the deck. Let's step through this sequence, breaking it – like the cards themselves – into five sections.

The Time of the Founding Principles: 1721 – 1827

First we have the 22 Major Arcana cards, representing the founding principles of the modern nation, starting with Sir Robert Walpole in 1721. Taking office in the wake of the South Sea Bubble catastrophe his period would cover the musical composition of Rule, Britannia! By Thomas Arne in 1740. This was a great statement of intent during the phase of The Magician.

By the end of this Time, 106 years later, the foundations of the modern nation and the Empire had been firmly laid. Scottish revolutionaries had been subdued, The Seven Years War in Europe had been won, and though the American colonies had been lost the Union as we still know it today was set, with British influence extending into India by Clive, the first connections with Australia being made by Captain Cook, and the enormous forces generated by the unfolding Industrial Revolution starting to be unleashed upon the world. Victory at the Battle of Waterloo in 1815, during the term of the 22nd Prime Minister, Lord Liverpool, secured the foundations for ongoing British dominance. This period saw the Whigs increasingly lose ground to the Tories. William Pitt 'The Younger' appears in the influential positions of 16th (The Tower) and 18th (The Moon) and presides over the formation of the United Kingdom of Great Britain and Ireland in the Acts of Union in 1801. The only Prime Minister (so far) to have been assassinated was the 21st occupant of the office (The World), Spencer Percival.

The Major Arcana: The Founding Principles. 106 years

Number	Tarot	Prime Minister	Party	In Office	Date of Birth	Destiny	Approach
1	I	Robert Walpole	Whig	1721-1742	26 August 1676	9	8
2	II	Spencer Compton (Earl of Wilmington)	Whig	1742-1743	unknown		
3	III	Henry Pelham	Whig	1743-1754	25 September 1694	9	7
4	IV	Thomas Pelham-Holles (Duke of Newcastle)	Whig	1754-1756	21 July 1693	11	3
5	V	William Cavendish (Duke of Devonshire)	Whig	1756-1757	8 May 1720	5	8
6	VI	Thomas Pelham-Holles (Duke of Newcastle)	Whig	1757-1762	21 July 1693	11	3
7	VII	John Stuart (Earl of Bute)	Tory	1762-1763	25 May 1713	6	7
8	VIII	George Grenville	Whig	1763-1765	14 October 1712	8	5
9	IX	Charles Watson-Wentworth (Marquis of Rockingham)	Whig	1765-1766	13 May 1730	2	4
10	X	William Pitt "The Elder"	Whig	1766-1768	15 November 1708	6	6
11	XI	Augustus FitzRoy (Duke of Grafton)	Whig	1769-1770	28 September 1735	8	1
12	XII	Frederick (Lord) North	Tory	1770-1782	13 April 1732	3	4
13	XIII	Charles Watson-Wentworth (Marquis of Rockingham)	Whig	1782	13 May 1730	2	4
14	XIV	William Petty (Marquis of Lansdowne)	Whig	1782-1783	2 May 1737	7	2
15	XV	William Cavendish-Bentinck (Duke of Portland)	Whig	1783	14 April 1738	1	5
16	XVI	William Pitt "The Younger"	Tory	1783-1801	28 May 1759	1	1
17	XVII	Henry Addington (Viscount Sidmouth)	Tory	1801-1804	30 May 1757	1	3
18	XVIII	William Pitt "The Younger"	Tory	1804-1806	28 May 1759	1	1
19	XIX	William (Baron) Grenville	Whig	1806-1807	25 October 1759	3	7
20	XX	William Cavendish-Bentinck (Duke of Portland)	Tory	1807-1809	14 April 1738	1	5
21	XXI	Spencer Perceval	Tory	1809-1812	1 November 1762	1	1
22	0	Lord Liverpool	Tory	1812-1827	7 June 1770	1	7

The Time of Fire: 1827 – 1859

Next comes the unsheathing of the first of the four mundane elements, and the very beginning of the descent of ideals and principles into practical reality. It is during these years – from George Canning to Lord Derby – that the nation, as we truly know it now, is forged. All this was done by 14 Prime Ministers in 32 years, most of them Tory/Conservative, all corresponding to the Tarot suit of Wands. No Prime Ministers during this time possessed a Destiny Number 1 (invention and origination), while 8 out of 22 did in the previous Time of the Founding Principles. No Prime Minister during this time served for more than 6 years, whilst in the previous Time five of them had served for a decade or more. Matters moved fast during the Time of Fire.

This saw the rapid expansion of the Industrial Revolution (which itself was a product of Fire, through the application of heat to create steam), of the Empire (with the British taking even greater roles in India and Hong Kong), and a quickening of the pace of life itself. Although the Houses of Parliament suffered extensive fire damage during this time, the Light descended such that slavery was abolished and the Great Reform Act extended voting rights and reformed rotten boroughs, setting the stage for the democracy of today. In addition the controversial Corn Laws greatly affected both foreign trade and home food prices. Overseas the British fought the Crimean War, during which took place that ever–so–British exposition of hope over reality, The Charge of the Light Brigade. We might reflect that there can never really be light without fire.

The builders of this new world were the Tories – who, during the influential period of Sir Robert Peel (born 5th February 1788 = 22), rebranded themselves Conservative in the form we know them today – and the reforming Whigs who ruled for 19 out of the 32 years. But change was needed, such that at the very end of this Time the influential Whig reformer Lord Palmerston would smoothly create a bridge into the next Time by his founding of the Liberal Party.

Number	Tarot	Prime Minister	Party	In Office	Date of Birth	Destiny	Approach
		Wands: The Time of Fire: Action, Forging, Courage, Ambition, Drive. 32 years					
23	KW	George Canning	Tory	1827	11 April 1770	3	11
24	QW	Frederick Robinson (Viscount Goderich)	Tory	1827-1828	1 November 1782	3	1
25	KnW	Arthur Wellesley (Duke of Wellington)	Tory	1828-1830	1 May 1769	2	1
26	PgW	Charles (Earl) Grey	Whig	1830-1834	13 March 1764	8	4
27	AW	William Lamb (Lord Melbourne)	Whig	1834	15 March 1779	6	6
28	2W	Arthur Wellesley (Duke of Wellington)	Tory	1834	1 May 1769	2	1
29	3W	Robert Peel	Conservative	1834-1835	5 February 1788	22	5
30	4W	William Lamb (Lord Melbourne)	Whig	1835-1841	15 March 1779	6	6
31	5W	Robert Peel	Conservative	1841-1846	5 February 1788	22	5
32	6W	Lord John Russell	Whig	1846-1852	18 August 1792	9	9
33	7W	Edward Smith-Stanley (Lord Derby)	Conservative	1852	29 March 1799	4	11
34	8W	George Hamilton-Gordon (Earl of Aberdeen)	Peelite	1852-1855	28 January 1784	4	1
35	9W	Henry Temple (Lord Palmerston)	Whig	1855-1858	20 October 1784	5	2
36	10W	Edward Smith-Stanley (Lord Derby)	Conservative	1858-1859	29 March 1799	4	11

The Time of Water: 1859 – 1905

Lord Palmerston demonstrated the art of reinvention by ushering in the Suit of Cups at the height of Victoriana, marked by the adoption in 1861 of a black shroud by the melancholy Queen following the death of her beloved Albert. This was the time of feelings (repressed or otherwise), compassion, connection, and humanitarian impulses, as witnessed by Gladstone's reforms, Disraeli's literary flourishes and even Lord Salisbury's dour imperialism. At this time Britain really did rule the waves, with an unrivalled fleet. What mattered to governments of this period was what took place overseas – the Suez Canal was purchased and opened, while agitation for Irish Home Rule became greater and the Boer Wars continued on.

When Arthur Balfour succeeded his uncle, Lord Salisbury, in 1902 his designation as the Ten of Cups signified the height of Empire. This Time of Water had lasted longed than that of Fire – now 46 years had passed to cover 14 Prime Ministers, seven of whom were Liberal and seven of whom were Conservative. Over that period each party had ruled almost exactly, on and off, for 50% of the time.

Caps: The Time of Water: Humanity, separation and togetherness, compassion, understanding. 46 years

Number	Tarot	Prime Minister	Party	In Office	Date of Birth	Destiny	Approach
37	KC	Henry Temple (Lord Palmerston)	Liberal	1859-1865	20 October 1784	5	2
38	QC	Lord John Russell	Liberal	1865-1866	18 August 1792	9	9
39	KnC	Edward Smith-Stanley (Lord Derby)	Conservative	1866-1868	29 March 1799	4	11
40	PgC	Benjamin Disraeli	Conservative	1868	21 December 1804	1	3
41	AC	William Gladstone	Liberal	1868-1874	29 December 1809	5	11
42	2C	Benjamin Disraeli	Conservative	1874-1880	21 December 1804	1	3
43	3C	William Gladstone	Liberal	1880-1885	29 December 1809	5	11
44	4C	Robert Gascoyne-Cecil (Lord Salisbury)	Conservative	1885-1886	3 February 1830	8	3
45	5C	William Gladstone	Liberal	1886	29 December 1809	5	11
46	6C	Robert Gascoyne-Cecil (Lord Salisbury)	Conservative	1886-1892	3 February 1830	8	3
47	7C	William Gladstone	Liberal	1892-1894	29 December 1809	5	11
48	8C	Archibald Primrose (Lord Rosebery)	Liberal	1894 – 1895	7 May 1847	5	7
49	9C	Robert Gascoyne-Cecil (Lord Salisbury)	Conservative	1895-1902	3 February 1830	8	3
50	10C	Arthur Balfour	Conservative	1902-1905	25 July 1848	8	7

The Time of Air: 1905 –1957

The suit of Swords arrived shortly after the death of Queen Victoria. Could the Time of Water have been more expressive and enjoyable had the Queen not ruled it in one long sulk? We will never know, but as the tide turned so the music changed. Well before the First World War it was commonly accepted that knives hung in the air and that conflict was approaching. Little did anyone suspect that by the end of this Time the Empire would be all but gone, the economy wrecked, and the national spirit transformed.

Conflict was the name of the game during the Time of Air, and new ways were found of broadcasting anger and dissent. This was the time of radio, telegraph, television and air travel. Where during the Time of Fire, battles were won with cannon, and during the Time of Water by ships, now it was aircraft that dominated. Witness the devastating application of air power, the howl of the German Stuka dive–bombers, the evocative sounds of the Spitfire and heavy drone of the German bombers over London. This movement into the Air was accompanied by the creative speech of Hitler and Churchill resounding around the room, courtesy of that technological leap – the radio. To our modern sensibilities none of this is remarkable, but it was all very new, at the time

In politics the upper class reformers of the Liberal Party steadily lost ground to the more forthright Labour Party as debate became much more polarised along class war lines. Irish Home Rule was finally granted and the name of the nation changed in 1922 to the United Kingdom of Great Britain and Northern Ireland, but only after much bloodshed. Germany was confronted twice during this period, with the nation taken to the brink during the Blitz and the Battle of Britain.

The era began with the King of Swords, Henry Campbell Bannerman, elected in a decisive Liberal landslide with a clear mandate to enact change. The Conservative dominated House of Lords stood in the way of almost all of this. The Queen of Swords, Asquith, who tackled a restive suffragette movement and a belligerent Germany, followed him. After two years of disastrous war Asquith could not stand it any longer and gave way to a more active Knight of Swords, David Lloyd George, who vigorously prosecuted the war to its bloody conclusion.

Much of this Time was defined by stress and conflict including the General Strike of 1926, and the economic collapse in 1931. It could be said that many Prime Ministers recognised this and sought to heal the nation, for there were multiple coalition governments during this Time.

Swords: The Time of Air: Ideas, Conflict. 52 years

Number	Tarot	Prime Minister	Party	In Office	Date of Birth	Destiny	Approach
51	KS	Henry Campbell-Bannerman	Liberal	1905-1908	7 September 1836	7	7
52	QS	H H Asquith	Liberal/National	1908-1916	12 September 1852	1	3
53	KnS	David Lloyd George	Liberal/National	1916-1922	17 January 1863	9	8
54	PgS	Andrew Bonar Law	Conservative	1922-1923	16 September 1858	2	7
55	AS	Stanley Baldwin	Conservative	1923-1924	3 August 1867	6	3
56	2S	Ramsay MacDonald	Labour	1924	12 October 1866	7	3
57	3S	Stanley Baldwin	Conservative	1924-1929	3 August 1867	6	3
58	4S	Ramsay MacDonald	Labour/National	1929-1935	12 October 1866	7	3
59	5S	Stanley Baldwin	Conservative/National	1935-1937	3 August 1867	6	3
60	6S	Neville Chamberlain	Conservative/National	1937-1940	18 March 1869	9	9
61	7S	Winston Churchill	Conservative/National	1940-1945	30 November 1874	7	3
62	8S	Clement Attlee	Labour	1945-1951	3 January 1883	6	3
63	9S	Winston Churchill	Conservative	1951-1955	30 November 1874	7	3
64	10S	Anthony Eden	Conservative	1955-1957	12 June 1897	7	3

In the time of Air, the run up to and aftermath of the Second World War is worth examining in some depth, alongside some other interpretations of the cards.

The Five of Swords: Stanley Baldwin. 1935–37.
The German army builds, Churchill agitates for re–armament, Baldwin resists.
A E Waite said of the card: Destruction, infamy, dishonour, loss. And when reversed: The same.
Arthur Norris said of the card: You will fight a battle and lose it. Look for a new direction. And when reversed: Despair, loss, mourning.
Could Baldwin have sensed the inevitable outcome of any war and done his best to resist it? Or was he still mourning the dead of the Great War barely two decades previously?

The Six of Swords: Neville Chamberlain. 1937–40.
Appeasement. Outbreak of war.
A E Waite said: A journey, route, envoy. Reversed: A declaration, confession, publicity.
Arthur Norris said: Moving away from trouble, difficulties are overcome. Reversed: Someone is rocking the boat, interference and unwanted proposals.
Did Chamberlain believe he had really secured 'Peace for our time' when he landed back in Britain to give his famous speech, *"I have in my hands a piece of paper..."* Had Chamberlain in fact, secretly carved up the map to give Hitler a free hand in Europe so long as Britain could maintain her Empire unmolested? It would not have been the first time that a British leader had acted in such a way.
The card shows an image of someone in transit between one land and another, carrying a load.

The Seven of Swords: Winston Churchill. 1940–45.
War and survival.
A E Waite said: An attempt, a wish, hope and confidence. Reversed: Good advice, counsel, instruction.
Arthur Norris said: Sneakiness. Use your brain. Direct tactics are useless. Reversed: Get good advice and wisdom. Exercise prudence.
Did Churchill's faith in espionage and code breaking win the war? What role did his inspirational oratory play? The card suggests that both were decisive. Is the sneakiness referring to Hitler reneging on the Munich agreement?
The card depicts someone fleeing from a scene, taking some swords and leaving some behind. The British evacuation from Dunkirk, perhaps? Suppose Chamberlain and Hitler had secretly agreed a carve up between a Nazi Europe and a British Empire, but Churchill reneged on that knowing full well that Britain could either fight now, under the auspices of the Seven of Swords, or later under the auspices of the approaching Ten. We will never know, but already we can see how Tarot helps us to construct a narrative quite beyond anything we might have consciously formulated. That is its strength; its ability to stretch the mind beyond the normal.

The Eight of Swords: Clement Attlee. 1945–51.

Post war reconstruction. Establishment of the NHS. Financial crisis.

A E Waite said: Crisis, censure, conflict, sickness. Reversed: Disquiet and difficulty.

Arthur Norris said: Crisis, calamity and conflict will impose limits and restrictions. Reversed: Frustrations and despair. Hard work is done for little reward.

The Attlee government found itself beset on all sides in its reconstruction efforts, with a victorious but virtually bankrupt and broken nation.

The card shows a bandaged and blindfolded person, surrounded by swords that prevent her from moving. Was this the state of post war Britain? Was the NHS an attempt to fix this?

The Nine of Swords: Winston Churchill. 1951–55.

The start of the Cold War. Tetchy relations with America.

A E Waite said: Failure, delay, disappointment, despair. Reversed: Suspicion, doubt.

Arthur Norris said: Injustice, quarrelling, anxiety. Reversed: Doubt and suspicion. A shady character.

The card image shows someone sat up in bed at night, surrounded by worries and anxieties. Churchill was often supposed to have conducted his Prime Ministerial business from bed during this period in office. Was he worrying about the weakening Empire, the strengthening of America or his anointed successors' ability to do the job?

The Ten of Swords: Anthony Eden. 1955–57.

The Suez Crisis.

A E Waite said: Pain, affliction, tears, sadness, desolation. Reversed: Temporary success, profit, power and authority.

Arthur Norris said: Ruin, disaster. All plans and hopes fail. Trust no one. Reversed: A temporary improvement. Self–honesty required.

Universally accepted as Churchill's successor many years before, Eden presided over a catastrophic reversal of British fortunes. The total failure of support from the American President Eisenhower and his Secretary of State Foster Dulles in Eden's attempts to wrest the Suez Canal out of revolutionary hands, confirmed the end of British global influence.

The card shows a person, face down on the floor, pierced with all ten (the maximum number) of swords in his back. This was the fate of the Empire upon which the Sun was never supposed to set. And it was Britain's greatest ally, America, who ran home the blades.

The Time of Air thus came to a close after 52 years of Liberal, Conservative, Labour, Coalition and National governments, all of which had been powerless to prevent the Empire being torn limb from limb.

Although from differing parties, many of the Prime Ministers of this Time were numerologically very similar. Stanley Baldwin was Prime Minister three times between 1923 and 1937 and although a Conservative he possessed the same

Destiny Number (born 3rd August 1867 = 1878 = 24 = 6), as Labour's Clement Attlee (3rd January 1883 = 1887 = 24 = 6). No other Tory or Conservative Prime Minister before Baldwin possessed this, the energy of society and togetherness. He interchanged 10 Downing Street in the period 1924–35 with Labour's Ramsay Macdonald (born 12th October 1866 = 1888 = 25 = 7) and was followed (after the brief Chamberlain period) by Churchill (30th November 1874 = 1915 = 16 = 7), Eden (12th June 1897 = 1915 = 16 = 7) and then into the Time of Earth by Macmillan (10th February 1894 = 1906 = 16 = 7). Additionally 6 out of 10 of the Prime Ministers of this period, ruling for 39 out of the 52 years, were born on day numbering 3 (3rd, 12th, 30th), itself the number of Air. We will shortly see further examples of this, where the numerological energy of a leader lingers long after their departure. It seems that although we are able to readily change our Prime Minister we are not able to change the Prime Minister's energy so easily. This speaks to the old notion that it doesn't really matter who you vote for because the government always gets in. This does seem numerologically, energetically, and karmically, to be true.

The Time of Earth: 1957 –

At the time of writing, in 2016, this era is already 59 years old, with three more Prime Ministers to come. This makes it the longest of the four elemental Times, representing a coming down to earth of the nation.

We begin with the old King of Pentacles Harold Macmillan, author of the popular Premium Bonds scheme, mass builder of houses, and creator of wide prosperity under which most of the nation had 'Never had it so good.' With this new beginning the national narrative became ever more about money, business and the economy.

A shift in the national preference occurred in 1964 when Harold Wilson's Labour Party squeaked ahead of the Conservatives for the first time since 1945. Commentators presented this, as a 'change' election, where the forces of backward Conservatism were overcome by the white heat of progress. But this kind of narrative becomes illusory when we see that the defeated Conservative Prime Minister Alec Douglas Home (born 2nd July 1903 = 1912 = 13 = 4. 2nd = 2)) and Harold Wilson (born 11th March 1916 = 1930 = 13 = 4. 11th = 11 = 2) share the same numbers and are in fact much the same kind of man. Nonetheless Wilson was elected, as the Knight of Pentacles, to inject some vigour into the nation.

His successor, Edward Heath, was born on 9th July 1916 (9+7+1916 = 1932 = 15 = 6) and, although a Conservative, he demonstrated his love of community by signing Britain up to the EEC.

The nation dipped back into its national number for the last time (as of 2015) with Jim Callaghan (27th March 1912 = 1942 = 16 = 7) who only inherited the post and failed to win the pivotal 1979 election against Margaret Thatcher.
Numerologically, Margaret Thatcher was a remarkable individual. The first 22 Prime Minister since Sir Robert Peel, 145 years earlier, she was in many ways a throwback to that Time of Fire. This 22 stepped forward to the doorway of national transformation and permanent change, yet as the 71st Prime Minister she only corresponds to the Three of Pentacles. Only? Here's what some think about this card.

Aleister Crowley said: Material works.
The Golden Dawn said: Business, paid employment, commercial transactions.
Arthur Norris said: Constructive work is done, the building up of something. A favourable card for new undertakings, potential for further earnings.

The image itself shows the entrance to a building, with two people waiting outside. Is this reminiscent of the symbolic handing over of council house keys as thousands of tenants became owners? Her period was partly one of economic progress, as well as economic destruction. Therefore an alternative take on Margaret Thatcher might say that she was simply a staging post, a developmental

Pentacles: The Time of Earth: Structure, possessions, business and money. 59 years and counting

Number	Tarot	Prime Minister	Party	In Office	Date of Birth	Destiny	Approach
65	KP	Harold Macmillan	Conservative	1957-1963	10 February 1894	7	1
66	QP	Alec Douglas Home	Conservative	1963-1964	02 July 1903	4	2
67	KnP	Harold Wilson	Labour	1964-1970	11 March 1916	4	11
68	PgP	Edward Heath	Conservative	1970-1974	09 July 1916	6	9
69	AP	Harold Wilson	Labour	1974-1976	11 March 1916	4	11
70	2P	Jim Callaghan	Labour	1976-1979	27 March 1912	7	9
71	3P	Margaret Thatcher	Conservative	1979-1990	13 October 1925	22	4
72	4P	John Major	Conservative	1990-1997	29 March 1943	22	11
73	5P	Tony Blair	Labour	1997-2007	06 May 1953	2	6
74	6P	Gordon Brown	Labour	2007-2010	20 February 1951	2	2
75	7P	David Cameron	Con/Lib Coalition Conservative	2010-2015 2015-?	09 October 1966	5	9
76	8P						
77	9P						
78	10P						

step in the life of the nation, and a necessary transition through the Time of Earth shown in the suit of Pentacles.

She was followed by John Major, who, in contrast to his appearance, possessed the same 22 Master Number (29th March 1943 = 1975 = 22). This can be seen in his signing and ratification of the life–changing Treaty of Maastricht, establishing the primacy of the EU over the nation state. As the Prime Minister of the Four of Pentacles we may classify his time as 'consolidated material success, a safe and secure position, no desire to take any risks.' These words from Arthur Norris reflect Major's attitude to government and the approach of many people who initially supported him. But the card, too often for him, fell in the reversed position bringing 'opposition, uncertainty and delay.'

Part of the beauty of the structure of the Tarot is that it perfectly addresses the ever–presence of change. No sooner has one card been turned, than another very different one is made ready. And so it is with the 73rd Prime Minister, the man of the Five of Pentacles, Tony Blair.

Arthur Norris identified this card with 'strain and anxiety about money, the loss of money, or the loss of a job. Spiritual poverty.' The picture is of two sorrowful souls, one injured, both locked out from the bright lights. On one hand, from 1997–2007, the nation experienced, for a while, a vast increase in living standards and a transformation of social attitudes. But on the other hand the gap between rich and poor exploded, as did the national debt, as did spending on welfare and worklessness. And that's not to mention the destruction of private pension provision outside of the public sector and buckets full of blood and treasure lost in the catastrophic Iraq War. Many sane people now believe (though they did not at the time) that Tony Blair sought nothing less than to erase the soul of the nation, bringing forth the virtual ruination of the country into the bargain, getting himself out just before the bubble burst. It is hard to see this card in association with him and come to any other conclusion. His time was coloured by the shut-out effects of globalisation, technology and mass immigration, a ballooning benefits culture and the virtual erasure of national identity. We don't have to ascribe cause and effect to see the connections. The people in the image of the card can still be seen walking around provincial town centres, every day. The seeds of this nation of lost souls were sown in 1997.

Gordon Brown followed, adopting the mantle of the Six of Pentacles. This card depicts a man dispensing alms – money, presents, gifts, charity, and bailouts – to others. Witness the vast sums handed over to prevent the banking system from total collapse. Although Brown (born 20th February 1951 = 1973 = 20 = 2) often clashed with Blair (born 6th May 1953 = 1964 = 20 = 2) the two men were the same, same but different and equally responsible for the created mess. Except that it fell to Brown to oversee the clear up.

Therefore, whoever would follow Gordon Brown to become the 75th Prime Minister of the UK was never going to have it easy. Cast with the Seven of Pentacles around his neck he would find himself waiting for the green shoots of recovery, only to find that when they did arrive they did him only small and temporary good. David Cameron's Seven of Pentacles is the card of hard work for little reward, of disappointment, deferred success, and tight money management. This may be coloured by the reversal – worry and anxiety over money. Either way, it is quite clearly the card of austerity. And if we follow Aleister Crowley's card meanings, it is also the card of failure.

Today money dominates virtually every dimension of British life. Everything costs more than it used to, yet wages and savings interest have failed to keep up. Risky ventures such as stock market and property speculation have pushed up asset values and made a few people a lot of money, but to the general discontent of the masses. Yet, given the previous cards, how could it ever have been any different? It therefore falls to David Cameron to be the farmer tending the national crop, wondering why some shoots simply refuse to grow.

It is not just David Cameron who is coloured by this late stage of the Time of Earth. Four of the five main political parties now have logos which connect strongly with Earth – the Conservative Tree, the Labour Rose, the UKIP £ sign and the Green Planet. It falls to the Liberal Democrats alone to resist the trend with their emblem of the Air, and their outlook, after the 2015 election, seems not too bright. During this Time of Earth the entire political debate is framed by all things heavy and fixed; the structure of the nation, economic infrastructure, national security, finance and jobs. Even Green politics is a product, self–evidently, of the Time of the Earth. Not one part of the political discussion can now be inspirational for the entire national consciousness is directed down toward the fundamentals of life. Those who have money find that they are stuck on the treadmill of earning more, yet paradoxically needing to spend more on relaxation and self–medication in order to recover and be prepared to earn more tomorrow. This is not really wealth in the true sense, but oppression and slavery, yet the place where many of the so–called middle class now find themselves. Still, this may be preferable to the condition of virtual desolation that those without money might find themselves in. As such, the Time of Earth is no time for the implementation of a vision. It is, for the moment at least, simply about management of the mundane.

As we try to assimilate all this, our old friend Merlin may once again be invoked. His question, 'why is it that the seasons are not all the same?' can now be rephrased and updated. Why is that governments are not all the same? Why do we have to have boom and bust, growth and decline, and changes in policy? The answer is so that we might grow. We cannot attribute a sequence of 78 distinct and meaningful images to our count of Prime Ministers without accepting somewhere, somehow, that there are invisible forces at work in shaping the nation. Within this rubric we are mistaken to believe ourselves free deciders, unconstrained at each election to choose whomever we like. The truth, it seems, is that we are merely puppets on strings, controlled by higher forces yet. There is no reptilian conspiracy here, merely factors we do not yet understand. It might be that financial ruin and the emptying of the national soul was necessary under Blair, and that whatever was said or intended Blair was simply destined to do those things. As such it may now be necessary for the nation to re–discover its identity and purpose and to embrace either a time of unparalleled, miserable prosperity or drown in a sea of debt, taxes and oppression. All this must occur before the wheel can turn again.

What Happens Next?

To complete the 78–card Tarot sequence, we must experience three more Prime Ministers after David Cameron. Their cards will respectively be the Eight, Nine and Ten of Pentacles, signalling the potential for a process of economic rebirth, industrial retooling, infrastructure investment, retraining and up–skilling. This planting of the future (8 of Pentacles) could lead to a windfall or dividend of some description (9 of Pentacles) and the transformation of the economy into a global powerhouse, with asset price inflation and widespread prosperity (10 of Pentacles). Or, in the event of card reversals we should expect nothing less than a descent into abject, economic ruin through imprudent lending (reversed 8), punitive taxation and a shattering of the social contract (reversed 9) culminating in mass debt defaults and disastrous speculative bubbles (reversed 10). Either way, nothing but money will be deemed to matter, and there may exist unparalleled wealth side by side with unprecedented misery. All this must play itself out before Britain can be presented with an opportunity for national renewal, for the path downwards toward the 10 of Pentacles signals a fulfilment and expiration of all the elements, not just Earth. We therefore approach a tipping point in the affairs of the nation unseen for 300 years.

Success or failure may be determined through the relationship between industry and finance. Since abandoning the Gold Standard in 1922 the trend has been for the nation to develop all things financial at the expense of all things industrial. This, unfortunately, represents a misunderstanding of the nature of Earth and Pentacles, which are always things of substance and form, not pixels on a computer monitor. Wealth is a function of materiality, not zeros in an electronic bank account. It is generated by all kinds of industry and manufacture, which can then subsequently be traded. Though banking and insurance – the application of money to make more money – are very Earth bound things, speculation is not, and if the underpinning foundations of British industry rot away further then the Tower must collapse. During this time Britain will either draw deep and necessary lessons from the 2008 Financial Crisis, or it may repeat the experience to a factor of 10.

If each of the next three Prime Ministers lasts for just one full term then the turning point comes in 2035, though the issues may come to a head before then. This would make the Earth Time the longest since the Time of the Founding Principles. Any prospective candidate for Prime Minister must be in touch with this trend, albeit unconsciously, if they are to stand a chance of being elected. If any of the successors to David Cameron are re–elected then the timeline is extended further, and in the case of early resignations the timeline is shortened. The British really are waiting, in this end of days, for the return of King Arthur. And they know it, deep down. They feel the effects of the Time of Earth in sluggishness, depression, oppression and apathy. Everything is heavy, always about work and money and unless deliberate attempts are made otherwise, there is never time for anything else. The nation is a long way from the historic inspiration of Akasha and the energy of Fire yet once again cries out for those things. Change is coming, but not yet. Destiny beckons, but still remains unfulfilled. The Stone of Earth awaits the one who may draw the Sword of Clarity from it. Revolutionary voices of all sorts may flower and fade as we approach the point of no return. The initial popularity of Jeremy Corbyn and his prescription for the Labour Party taps into much of this, and in spite of the fact that he is cast as a throw back and a dinosaur he is in fact way ahead of his time, attempting to bring forward a new era – except that the old era has not yet played itself out. He may see the results of continuing on our current track, but the zeitgeist is not yet exhausted and the prime determinant of success is always timing. Nonetheless all today's loud and angry voices are a function of and reaction to matters of Pentacles – oppression, the heaviness of bureaucracy, helplessness, immovability, lack of light and hope, the tortoise–like pace of change in government, things of the ground and of the planet, things of food, materials, money and goods. Strip these matters from the national debate and we would have nothing left to talk about, so we must get all this out of our system before a real shift can become possible.

A Lesson from the Past: The South Sea Bubble

Although Sir Robert Walpole is now recognised as the first real Prime Minister, the role in fact precedes him, in turn deriving from the ancient office of Lord High Treasurer. The direct line through the holders of the office of Prime Minister immediately prior to Walpole is confused, but to look at it, even darkly, provides some insight into what we should expect to happen to the nation as we approach the end of this Time.

The First Lord of the Treasury Charles Howard, Earl of Carlisle, filled the role of The Seven of Pentacles in the previous cycle. During his time, in 1715, we had the latest in a series of Jacobite uprisings, involving swathes of rebellion across Scotland. Remarkably David Cameron's comparable time in 2015 witnessed the, thankfully bloodless, electoral rebellion by the SNP in the UK General Election.

The subsequent First Lords were Walpole (for the 8 of Pentacles and his first stint), James Stanhope (9 of Pentacles) and Charles Spencer the Earl of Sutherland (10 of Pentacles). This period was dominated by further Jacobite rebellion north of the border and growing concern about the national debt. Sound familiar?

Many of the questions facing the nation back then are relevant now. Earlier on in each sequence Britain became more closely involved with Europe. In the old sequence 1688 saw the Glorious Revolution and the welcoming by the British Establishment of a Dutch King and Queen to the English throne, while in this sequence 1973 saw British membership of the EEC, pushed through by the

Establishment. Upon the passing of Queen Anne in the middle period of the last Time of Earth governance from Europe was extended, at that time by a Hanoverian King. In the comparable period now the debate is over further involvement in the EU. The first Prime Minister of the new regime, post crisis, Robert Walpole, also had a go at the job pre–crisis. Who can remain untainted today so they may step forward tomorrow?

The public mood then, as now, was varyingly excitable and fearful, occupied by foreign intrigues, concerned about the breakup of the homeland, and busy with the disgracing and imprisonment of politicians left, right, and centre. Everything has changed, yet nothing has.

The national debt had risen fast following the country's involvement in two messy, multi–agency continental wars (the War of Spanish Succession 1701–1714, and the lesser known but significant Great Northern War 1700 – 1721). A proposed solution to all this was the formation of the South Sea Company in 1711.

The scheme granted the South Sea Company a monopoly over trade and exploration of the waters off South America in exchange for its adoption of the entire British national debt. After a slow start the company's shares rocketed, making fortunes for many of those involved – including Walpole himself, though initially he was the only senior voice to speak out against it, "this will divert the genius of the nation from trade and industry." But after much hype of the company's prospects, and what we today would know as insider trading, the realisation finally hit home that no kind of profit could ever be made by the company and its share price collapsed.

The fallout was catastrophic, significantly damaging the British economy. It was not just the wealthy that were affected, for like all good bubbles the average man in the street was tempted in too, right at the last minute. Many other bubbles were also inflated during this time. From Churchill's History of the English Speaking Peoples:

"there was no limit to the credulity of the public. One promoter floated a company to manufacture an invention known as Puckle's Machine Gun, 'which was to discharge round and square cannon balls and bullets and make a total revolution in the art of war' the round missiles for use against Christians, the square for use against the Turk. Other promoters invited subscribers for making salt water fresh, for constructing a wheel of perpetual motion, for importing large jackasses from Spain to improve the breed of English mules and the boldest of all was for an advertisement for 'a company carrying on an undertaking of Great Advantage, but no one to know what it is.' This amiable swindler set up shop in Cornhill to receive subscriptions. His office was besieged by eager investors and after collecting £2000 in cash he prudently absconded."

Much soul searching and scapegoating took place after the crash and the early part of Walpole's second ministry involved clearing up the aftermath. All this took place in the previous time of the Eight, Nine and Ten of Pentacles, which we now approach again. Therefore, where are today's Company of Great Advantage and the modern Puckle Machine Gun? Is it to be found in the latest web craze or app, or in today's property bubble, where a one hundred year old, one bedroom flat in London sells for £1million and brand new duplex apartments overlooking the Thames for £25million?

The South Sea Company of old was incorporated as a kind of public–private partnership, the same method of which has funded the building of most of today's new schools and hospitals. The British establishment of 1711 was involved up to its eyeballs in the project. Where are our members of governments heavily involved today? Many have property portfolios and after leaving office become part of the corporate lobbying industry. Maybe we need to look further afield into the role of the Euro and the unaudited accounts of the European Union? Global trade deals also need examination, and we might await the eventually unwinding of Quantitative Easing with trepidation. Everywhere that government has its hand is a suspected root of the next bubble which, if it bursts, will be a manifestation of the Nine and Ten of Pentacles reversed.

Bankrupt Britain: How Not To Lose Everything in the Next Financial Crisis

Debt is evil. What is borrowed must always be repaid. This is true of nations as well as individuals. In the event of a default or bankruptcy the repayment may take on an alternative non-monetary guise, but that simply changes the form of the debt, not the debt itself. Acceptance or recognition of this truth is not necessary in order for it to show itself in our life.

Debt is good. It enables the future to occur today and for the fruits of life to be tasted in advance of their payment. The path, therefore, must be of balance – a sustainable ability to pay our debt is the key, not our desire to obtain things, regardless of our sense of entitlement or attachment to them. Everyone who borrows money is potentially guilty of this; rich and poor, worker and owner, family and nation. Bankers may now be glorified salesmen, in some cases pushing credit like heroin. But the drug, once taken, will always extract payment from its host.

Debt is slavery. Debt, even if it is repaid on time and in full, requires an ongoing constriction of human and cosmic energy. Many debts are only finally paid off long after the usefulness of the original loan has been forgotten, and its purpose exhausted. We can legitimately complain about low wages, or high food prices, but the belief that we are entitled to anything at all – beyond a shot at life – is the commonest driver of debt, and thus slavery, for when money is owed then we are under the control of those to whom we owe it. Our life is no longer our own and our actions and life choices are restricted – sometimes in very large ways – by the very real need to repay.

Companies and governments are not immune to this. However laudable the desire for investment or construction, if it is done by debt then a price will be extracted. Economists will always point to the technical ability of nations with sovereign currencies to print more of their own money to enable payment of all bills, or to historically low interest rates screaming to us 'borrow to invest, borrow to invest'. But the price of borrowing is not always financial.

Life on the Debt Merry Go Round – national or individual – can very be pleasurable, until the music stops. Just so long as someone else owes more money than you, or owes you more than you owe them then all seems well for the longest time. Until the wheel of credit stops turning.

Awareness of this dynamic is high, but workable solutions are rare. Many people shun debt not for the reasons given above, but because they genuinely believe that it is not possible to get money without compromising their values in some way. So they grind on in noble poverty. This kind of poverty conscious-ness is the over–awareness of lack, and the focus upon it to the exclusion of all else. Over time it produces a depressed soul incapable of changing their circumstances for the better.

Poverty consciousness always eventually breeds its opposite when the sufferer wakes up and embarks on a quest for short cuts. Swinging from fear to greed with the ever–present thought that they are missing out on the goodies of life they search desperately for a resolution. They may even find one in the guise of the 'Deception of Advantage'. This will show itself as a belief (usually encour-aged in get–rich–quick–you–deserve–it workshops and books) that they can gain access (for a fee of course) to some kind of information that others cannot. Involvement in internet forums and niche social media groups exacerbates this, and the fast moving nature of this technology facilitates impatience and error along their path.

The truth is that material wealth is achieved in only two ways:

1.   It is your life path, encoded prior to birth. The purpose of your life is to be materially wealthy and to understand what that means.
2.   It is not your life path, but it becomes your life choice. Like everything, if enough energy is focused toward this goal, and the price for it is paid, then everything becomes possible. But a price will be extracted, in order that the Universe remains in balance. This price may be a lack of loving relationships, an inability to develop the mind, or an inability to relax. Wealth might produce superficial happiness and shiny distrac-tions, but for someone to gain riches in defiance of their true purpose is the fastest road to their misery.

Our relationship to debt and money is distorted further by the assertion that no business can thrive without borrowing money. This is not anywhere near the whole truth of how business and industry works, for the greater secret of business – as we mentioned earlier – is value added; the transformation via labour and skill of dross into gold.

But debt and finance are sexier than regular old business. Business is dour and slow, requiring meetings, agreed specifications, and documented procedures, and the often–endless revision of all three. It needs goals and deliverables and it takes time. Finance on the other hand is hot – it's 24 hour, fast, exciting and often instant. Much more money can be made, much more quickly, in finance than it can in business. And, of course, lost.

The democratisation of global financial markets (heavily orientated around the City of London) using the twin powers of technology and debt is a disaster waiting to happen. Often marketed as the solution to all anxiety the financial markets are the great leveller and the ultimate ego–buster, merciless, and offering no compassion or generosity to the naive investor. Any degree of success within them will only be granted to the investor with self–knowledge and self–control. Any attempt to deny, or tendency to ignore flaws in ones own character will be the method by which the investor gets burned. There is no room for emotion in this world, and any attempt to right wrongs or to be on a mission for good will backfire. The financial markets are the vehicles by which the greedy and impatient (even if they are poor) are separated from their money.

Financial markets will separate the innocent from their money by the most readily accessible or personally appropriate means. The markets have the ability to hone in on our Dark Side and wipe us out in a flash. Every investor must examine their own deep, personal weaknesses and address them. The markets are the great healer, but complaints about their treatment of us are akin to complaining about the rain when we refused to take an umbrella out with us.

Success in the financial market is not, as some say, simply a function of information. No human being possesses all the information possible and someone else will always know more than you. The markets cannot be gamed in any way, even by insiders for whom the price will be extracted afterwards, in a currency they lack.

Within a bull market or a bubble this cautionary tale is barely audible for the prevailing belief is that anything is possible. Here even bad choices yield good profits. But in a bear market nothing good is possible and even good choices yield poor results. And in a wild market – such as we increasingly now see – only the skilled hunters survive.

As well as self–knowledge, the financial markets require the ability to admit errors and learn from them, as well as calmness, thoughtfulness, intuition and time. They require patience, continual vigilance, and constant alertness; looking, waiting for something to leap out. It is a fool's path to believe that there is another way, or that through big data mathematics, infallible trading algorithms or complex technology that there is an easy way to riches.

Political Correctness & The Illusion of Modernity

We hope that no one today would be fooled by an advertisement proclaiming 'A Company of Great Advantage, but no one to know what it is' because we can see through the language of the past from a mile away. But we are far less able to see through the language that swirls around us in the present.

Those who control the language control the nation, through the power of the numbers. While the intentions of those who seek to redefine the language are in some cases honourable, without an understanding of the mechanics of numerology the intuition driving the changes will sometimes go astray. Consider for example, how we no longer use the word CRIPPLE (7), in favour of DISABLED (11), yet have also partially abandoned PARENT (11) for CAREGIVER (7). Without even knowing the meaning of the numbers it is obvious that the noble causes of inclusion cannot prosper if the meanings behind these two changes are working in opposite directions. 7 is a disassociated, private number that wishes to be left alone. If this was the appearance of the CRIPPLE do we really want it to become that of the CAREGIVER?

In certain cases changes to language are helpful. To be classed as a FAILURE (9) is to have yourself defined as having reached the end, the last number in the sequence. But if the experience can be reframed as DEFERRED SUCCESS (1) then we see new shoots and fresh starts immediately appear. Similarly SEX WORKER (3) must be more inclusive than PROSTITUTE (1), but the 1 is independent where the 3 often works with others, and the 1 goes its own way regardless, while the 3 always seeks attention. As a result, although there was never a successful 'Rights & Recognition for Prostitutes' movement, there absolutely will be one for Sex Workers. It can be no other way for the words and their users are dictated to by the numbers.

Sometimes, contrary to intentions, the change makes no difference. The FIREFIGHTER (3) is the FIREMAN (3) and your SEXUAL ORIENTATION (6) is your SEXUAL PREFERENCE (6), or at least they effect to the same thing. What is clear even from these brief examples is that POLITICAL CORRECTNESS (11) is both enlightening and divisive. The introduction of new words as we seek to re–interpret old ways may lead us to a greater understanding of what we have been doing and assist the inclusion and involvement of everybody in society, but when PC language is imposed and enforced – without the lessons of the old words being learned then – then resistance, friction and confusion is inevitable. And a belief that we have somehow perfected our understanding of life by ascribing new words to old situations leaves us vulnerable to being carried away in the next bubble.

Understanding the Language of Great Britain

The British cannot assert or propagate their values if they don't really know what they are. And they will never know that until the forces behind everyday

English words are understood. This information – the energies brought forth and unleashed by words – is gathered through Numbers.

Different words with like numbers are obviously not the same things, and do not possess the same meanings. But they do tend toward each other, are suggestive of one another, lead to one another, are attracted to one another and get confused between one another. The utterance and repetition of one word generates the conditions for words of the corresponding number. All Words of 1, for example, tend over time to associate with and take on the manifestation of other Words of 1. While personal associations to one or other words may be made with full knowledge of the true meaning of the word, they can equally be formed accidentally, by projection, extension, illusion and misunderstanding. Many people, for example, refuse to identify as Conservative yet when asked questions about policy they will take a Conservative position. These people may even vote Conservative, though they would never call themselves such. We can see by this and the following examples that the very aims we proclaim are often set back and lead to disastrous unforeseen consequences when we attach ourselves to a word unthinkingly, allowing that word – which we think we understand, but actually do not – to manifest within us. True intuitives and sensitives will somehow know what a word really brings with it, though these folk may not possess the self–confidence to believe what they suspect to be true. The educated person will maintain that they have control of the forces behind words, through their comprehensive knowledge of English language and literature. We might infer the precise opposite however, for once set in motion the forces of words move to control their host speaker before they have even realised it.

Words of 1: suggesting leadership, independence, entrepreneurship, innovation, one–pointedness, yet also selfishness, impatience and narrow–mindedness.
People: COMMUNIST, CORPORATIST, LIBERTARIAN, ATHEIST, CHAPLAIN and REVEREND.
Beliefs: LIBERALISM, MONETARISM, SOCIALISM, NATIONALISM.
Systems: CONSTITUTIONAL MONARCHY, the CROWN, REFERENDUM.
All these words actually sum to a compound of 10 (The Wheel of Fortune) and a root of 1 (The Magician). All are therefore narrow and limited in scope, serving individuals and creating new cycles of change. The question might be asked of all these words – what comes next? Once you are communist what then happens? Once you have implemented monetarism what happens next? Once you have had your referendum, then what? The answer in all cases, from the 1, is that either the system itself – like the constitutional monarchy – reinvents and changes itself, or it is superseded by other words. Without constant reinvention and innovation – which is hard under the narrow aegis of 1 – the words implode upon themselves. They are a beginning, but little more than that.
Notice how the communist always tends to be an irreligious preacher, and both the libertarian and communist – at opposite ends of the spectrum – tend toward becoming corporatist. Note also how a corporatist structure may hatch out in one of two ways – communist or libertarian.

The word referendum should be doubly noted though, for it does, under all uses of the word and regardless of the result, signify the essence of 1 – a fresh start.

Words of 2: suggesting balance and the desire for harmony, and 11 – bringing enlightenment and division, illumination and separation, progress and extremes. 11, particularly, tending to be enlightened yet divisive, idealistic and ungrounded.
People: CAPITALIST, REPUBLICAN, CHRISTIAN, JEW, JEWISH, HINDU, WHIG.
Beliefs: CENTRE, CHRISTIANITY.
Systems: LIBERAL DEMOCRACY, SOCIAL DEMOCRACY, DIRECT DEMOCRACY.
Notice how easy it is to be capitalist and religious, in some sense, and how in the USA, Christian and Republican go together like hand in glove. See how liberal and social democracy are, to some degree, based on and exist to perpetuate religious and capitalist principles. All these things together tend toward extremes – great achievement, success and wealth, as well as destruction, loss and poverty. Great things are always possible under the 11, yet confusion may well reign under the 2. It is interesting to note how liberal democracy may tend, over time, to transform into social democracy and maybe, ultimately into direct democracy.

Words of 3: suggestive of needing attention, recognition, self–expression, communication and creativity. Can tend toward being more show than action.
People: ENVIRONMENTALIST, MONARCHIST, ANARCHIST, RADICAL, LIBERAL DEMOCRAT, SOCIAL DEMOCRAT, LUDDITE.
Beliefs: COMMUNISM, CORPORATISM, ATHEISM.
Systems: EMPIRE, REPRESENTATIVE DEMOCRACY.
Notice how loud and shouty some of these people are. Notice how the birth of the SDP in the UK was little more than a cry for attention and expression of feelings. Notice how the anarchist and monarchist are tightly bound to one another. One wonders about the ability of these people to do anything other than talk? Is to be a radical any more, really, than an expression of feelings? Is an environmentalist today any different from a Luddite of yesteryear? It is true that 3 is a creative and formative number so these people may well be busy in the construction of something, but often noisily.
Notice also how both communism and corporatism tend, over time, toward empire, and how after the disestablishment of empire the British hardly made any change at all by sticking with a representative democracy, possibly now unfit for changing times.

Words of 4: bringing structure, order and rules. Supportive, restrictive and oppressive.
People: GREEN, UNIONIST.
Systems: CAPITALISM, the TRADE UNION.
There is nothing in the slightest bit revolutionary about the number 4. It always seeks to self–perpetuate, sometimes to the exclusion of everything else. It is always a restrictive and heavy energy, immersed in tradition, order, rules and systems.

It can be no surprise that Unionists find themselves so prominent in NORTHERN IRELAND (4) and that the Green and the Trade Union find themselves in sympathy with each other, but in a symbiotic relationship with and against filthy capitalism. The Trade Union is defined in opposition to capitalism, and wherever the Unionist is in the ascendancy the Green will oppose him. They each feed off each other.

A great deal of confabulation occurs in the usage of all of these words. One Green will behave, think and campaign differently to the next one, establishing for themselves different priorities. But all the time the inherent energy behind the word is trying to peek through. The word will successfully achieve this if its user – lacking self–awareness or knowledge – surrenders control to the word they have themselves conjured up. This happens far more than most are prepared to recognise or admit.

Words of 5: Revolution. Travel, movement, freedom. Often defined by what they are against, rather than what they are for. An extremely powerful number, able to influence all other numbers, yet, paradoxically, is easily influenced itself.
People: MARXIST, LIBERAL, LEFTY, JIHADI, FASCIST.
Beliefs: ENVIRONMENTALISM, JUDAISM, JIHAD.
Systems: REPUBLIC, FAR LEFT, TOTALITARIAN.
The jihadi is the fascist, or certainly one is suggestive of the other. The idea of the republic is bound up with the left and tends over time toward being totalitarian – witness the transitions of Rome, and to some extent, the USA and EU. Further see how the dots are connected from environmentalism to the fascist and the Marxist. Is it any wonder people are suspicious of one when the other is right there waiting behind?
The spiritual concept of jihad is one of personal liberation, and the nature of Judaism has always been bound up with freedom. These two things, like environmentalism, begin as freedom movements, yet are always one step away from totalitarian movements, where the freedom to rebel against the movement itself is squashed. It is not therefore too much of a numerological stretch to say that environmentalism is fascist and totalitarian. In the same way Marxists are liberals who want a far left, totalitarian republic. The numbers do not lie, although people often do.

Words of 6: Love (of self, another, or all), togetherness, community, the whole, the collective, responsibility (and irresponsibility). Smothering, controlling, over–bearing. Including Words of 33, which are all these things, but in a much bigger way.
People: FUNDAMENTALIST, TORY, MUSLIM.
Systems: DEMOCRACY, UNIONISM. FEDERAL.
Beliefs: LIBERTARIANISM (15), LABOUR, PARLIAMENTARY DEMOCRACY (15).
Muslim and fundamentalist go hand in hand, as do Tory and fundamentalist. All these things are a product of democracy and are deeply connected to Labour, which though it attempts to embody the values of society is always destined to fail, for SOCIETY (33) is bigger than both DEMOCRACY (6), LABOUR (6) or TORY (6).

Words of 7: The number that will not fit in, accord or go along with others. Isolation, theory rather than practice. A worship of the mind, rather than the heart. Sometimes denotes a separation from reality and a system that is never quite right when implemented.

People: EXTREMIST, DEMOCRAT, AGNOSTIC, TRADE UNIONIST.

Systems: MARXISM, MONARCHY, COMMUNITY, ANARCHY, GOVERNMENT, DICTATORSHIP, FASCISM.

These are all people in love with theory, yet who always fail to take one vital piece of information into account. Notice how government connects to community, yet also to fascism, which in turn links back to Marxism. See also how monarchy and anarchy again sit together, locked in some kind of death grip. With 7 as the number of privacy and secrecy do we see the first flaws in the ideology of community, where inclusion actually masks great secrets, swept under the carpet in the name of togetherness? Community is so often substituted for society, yet do the two actually have anything in common?

Words of 8: Power and might. Financial, monetary, economic. The lesson of the nation.

People: SOCIALIST, MONETARIST, NATIONALIST, JIHADIST, CATHOLIC.

Systems: RIGHT, OLIGARCHY, THEOCRACY, POLICE STATE, COALITION.

The socialist does not fight for equity and fairness, but for power and money, as does the Catholic, nationalist and jihadist. None of these movements are about anything other than money and power – who has it, and why don't we? Is it coincidence that the SNP are nationalist, socialist and have taken, some would say, significant steps along the road to a police state with the open arming of police officers on the streets? Would we expect a coalition to be about anything other than money, and indeed to produce any other consequence than increased socialist and nationalist sentiment?

Words of 9: The number of completion, humanity, the bigger picture, yet also weakness, selfishness, victimhood and martyrdom.

People: CENTRIST, MODERATE, PROGRESSIVE, CONSERVATIVE.

Beliefs: ISLAM.

9 is arguably the most powerful number, mathematically absorbing all of the others. The Hermit, card 9 in the Tarot, demonstrates this by carrying the accumulated wisdom of all the other numbers. Yet so often 9 cannot realise its own power and will sacrifice itself for a perceived greater good.

Is the progressive the reaction to the conservative, or is the progressive, deep down, rather conservative themselves, and the conservative actually quite progressive?

From the numerology of Islam (9) and Muslim (6) we might accept its claims to be the religion of peace. But the compound number of Islam is 18, the Moon in the Tarot, which is reflected in the crescent moon of the symbol of Islam. The Imam also presents as 18, and then 9. Is the Path of the Moon the way forward, or is it a dark path, full of uncertainty? These numbers are certainly emotional, not rational, and although in part loving and humanitarian, they are wide open to being incorrectly channelled, abused and misdirected.

Financial Schizophrenia

Two of the most despised professions in Great Britain today are two of the most necessary, given that we live in the Time of Earth. They are ESTATE AGENTS (1), and BANKERS (7). This hatred is an expression of the British problem with money. Unaware of the fact that MONEY (9) is the great uniter, the British have cultivated a bad attitude to both wealth creation and displays of consumption. Many Brits are too quick to demonise the rich and too ready to revere the nobility of the poor. This is nothing new, but after centuries these old attitudes are now hardwired. Unfortunately they are also destructive and hold the nation and its people back from higher and better things.

Many spiritual and esoteric minded folk take this even further. They purport to be utterly disinterested in money. Sometimes this is because they have moved beyond its attractions and limitations, or more commonly it is because they are not very good at earning it and do not want to learn how. I remember a brief conversation with a world famous Tarot deck creator where the cards in front of us were all Pentacles. 'Why do you worry so much about money?' I foolishly asked. The reply was dismissive 'I don't care about money,' they said, only to be seen later on haggling with the event organiser over their fee.

Money is not the root of all evil. It is the human desire for short cuts and an easy life that in fact causes the trouble. Money may bring nothing positive by itself – a pile of cash does not equal happiness. But it does facilitate health (either through a better diet or treatment), enables rest, brings a sense of worth and accomplishment, enables us to help others and, more importantly, means that others don't need to help us.

It is true that the desire for more and more money is a very negative thing, but that only happens if the individual lacks knowledge of what money is really for, and instead chooses to believe that it is an end in itself or the doorway to more flat screen TVs, gadgets or shoes.

Money, in reality, equals freedom, which brings closer the chance of personal fulfilment. But any more than enough is too much, and many Brits are on the wrong side of that line.

The desire to abolish money, or to diminish its role in society is born of irresponsibility and an expectation that life is meant to be easy. It is true that a lack of money is no joke, generating feelings way beyond the small two dimensional minus figures on your calculator. Lack of money, in the face of desire or need, generates great restriction, heaviness and depression. Yet these are all products of the Earth, which can be resolved by actions from the Earth.

Everybody in Britain can work in some way, but that work should play to an individual's strength. As technology advances so the human being risks being outsmarted in a number of key areas. It has therefore never been more important for human beings to find a way to earn a living – paid either through currency or some other kind of exchange.

The Thatcher revolution is often portrayed as a give-away to the greedy and a debasement of compassion, but the truth may be rather more complex. Although the privatisations of the 1980's (8) did give way to eventual ownership of large swathes of British industry by overseas interests, that was not what was intended. Thatcher's error was to assume that Sid (the everyman character of the British Gas privatisation adverts) would buy, hold and stay involved – that is, take his dividends and involve himself in the company, the wider markets and by extension strengthen civil society. This vision, alas, was never communicated or encouraged, but it could have been the nation's resolution of 8. Unfortunately, with market manipulation, investor naivety, anti–wealth propaganda and economic mismanagement it was never to be, and share ownership of the businesses of the nation has declined ever since, where those private investors who now do own shares often do not hold them for long.

The People Built for Good Judgement:
Harry, Quentin and Zac. Helen, Qadira and Zoe.

The 2010 Westminster parliament contained 650 MPs. Only 17 of those – 2.6% – had first names beginning with the letters H, Q or Z (8). There were ten from Labour, one Plaid Cymru and six Conservatives. The 2015 Parliament returned only 20 – 3.1% – nine Conservative, nine Labour, one Plaid Cymru, one SNP. Bearing in mind that not every letter of the alphabet has an equal chance of starting a name (see the amount of pages dedicated to each letter in a dictionary or phone book), and that names beginning H, Q and Z are not common in British society then the frequency seems about right. But these are the letters of power, and the British parliament, just as it has an over–representation of white men, needs an over–representation of H, Q and Z.

8–people (first names beginning with H, Q or Z) have innately higher standards than the rest of us. It sometimes makes them inflexible, intolerant and stubborn, but fundamentally they are the professionals, the ones who want 'it done right' They are generally more honest and certainly more committed than the rest of us. Yes, individuals vary and none are incorruptible, but H, Q and Z are the letters of strength of character and commitment to purpose. We need many more of these people in government and national leadership roles – almost regardless of party – for they are the ones who are able to lead and effect real change, and the ones most able to channel, handle and direct power. Think Horatio Nelson and Herbert (Lord) Kitchener, Henry VIII, Herbert Asquith, and Henry Temple (Lord Palmerston). Even, if it helps, Harry Potter and Zane Lowe. Yes, there is a Dark Side to the Letters of 8 if they appear too frequently in one place (think Hitler, Himmler, Hermann Goering, Hess and Heydrich) but in the necessary amount – within the rules of an open and democratic society – people of 8 *can* work wonders.

The Formation & Break Up of Britain

The rise, fall and dismemberment of Great Britain is a matter of global significance, for nothing in true alignment to its own nature and in co–operation with the Forgotten Lands, can ever be defeated from *outside*. Such a nation can only die by festering dissent amongst its own people. Barbarians always wait outside the gates until those inside open them willingly. So it was in Rome, so it is in Britain, and so it will be again, elsewhere.

The Break Up of Britain has already begun and is accelerating. The fragmentation of lawmaking out to the devolved parliaments and assemblies, the ceding of power to transnational corporations and quangos, and subservience to regulations from Brussels has created a confused picture of accountability where it is doubtful that many in government are totally clear on what authority lies where. Witness further the confusion and conflation of British for English, the increasingly separate identity of the Welsh and Scottish, yet the seemingly increased adherence of the Northern Irish to Britain. When the crowds at the Last Night of the Proms sing 'Land of Hope and Glory' to which land are they now referring?

The Method of The Four Roads

There are two levels of numerology. The first is to transfer words into numbers and interpret from there. But a purer form of numerology occurs when dealing with numbers only. We do this through calendar dates.

From any given day, month and year combination we can perform five calculations. These show us The Four Roads, together with a fifth, the Power Number. Although this method is a manifestation of four (plus one), it is of a different order to the Four Forgotten Lands, the four elements or the four component nations of the Union. This method is dynamic, providing a commentary on the subject's progress through life. Each number can then be corresponded to a card of the Tarot Major Arcana for additional visual stimulus.

From a selected important date:

First Road: This opens immediately, and is the dominant number throughout the life cycle.	DD+MM+YYYY = Four digit answer. Add the four digits of that answer together. Continue adding the digits of the answer until the result is 1–9, 11 or 22. Example: 14 October 1066. 14+10+1066 = 1090 = 10 = 1. (Note: Add 14 to 10 to 1066. Not 1+4+1+0+1+0+6+6. The compound number will be different in this case, though the root will always be the same).

122

Second Road: This opens very soon after the First Road. It shows how the first road is implemented.	DD. Add the digits of the day together until the result is 1–9, 11 or 22. Example: 14 October 1066. 14 = 5
Third Road: This opens much later on, presenting another stream of manifestation, but only when the first two roads have been mastered.	DD+MM = Two digit answer. Add those digits together until the result is 1–9, 11, 22 or 33. Example: 14 October 1066. 14+10 = 24 = 6
Fourth Road: This opens very late on and acts as the catalyst that finally brings the others together.	First Road + Third Road. Add the digits of these together until the result is 1–9, 11, 22 or 33. Example: 14 October 1066. First Road 1 + Second Road 6 = 7
The Power Number: The product of the fusion of the Four Roads. The thing into which the subject will develop.	All Four Roads added together and reduced down until the result is 1–9, 11, 22 or 33. In this example of the date of the Battle of Hastings: 1 + 5 + 6 + 7 = 19 = 1

The Formation of Great Britain

Great Britain has undergone many incarnations and passed through many turning points in its long existence. The key ones occur when the name of the nation is officially changed or some kind of notable inauguration takes place. Historians will naturally debate what constitutes notable, but the usefulness of numerology is not found in its ability to establish a perfectly defined and delineated continuum. It is simply that the repetition of numbers from multiple locations forms a pattern, which enables us to see and understand things we would otherwise not. We want to use the correct data and make sure that data is accurate, but we don't want to get lost in the data.

Equally we do not want to get lost in an argument about the calendar. Britain has used various calendars over the centuries, indeed the further back we go the less reliable our calendars probably are. But, and this is an important point, the dates we use are the dates they used, regardless of their 'rightness' So if an old tale from 700 years ago tells us that "a great storm visited these islands on 12th day of February in the year of our Lord 1327" then that is the date we use, not any rectification or modern adjustment of it.

The First Era of Britain: 1066 –1284

Coronation of William I		England	25 December 1066	Universal Year 4
First Road	*Second Road*	*Third Road*	*Fourth Road*	*Power Number*
5	7	1	6	19/1

The nation that we recognise today was born with the Norman invasion of England in 1066. Although the commonly referenced date for this is the Battle of Hastings, William did not in fact fully conquer the nation until a little later. Our first marker is therefore drawn at the date of his coronation as King of England, 25th December 1066. (It is interesting, however, that the four numbers generated from his invasion on 14th October 1066 are identical to this, simply appearing in a different order). Christmas Day is therefore not simply the day of Christian worship, but the birthday of the original nation in this cycle.

The 5, together with the two 1's mark this as a significant change and turn of the page. A new impetus has been formed and all that has gone before is passed. Everything was different now. The 5 shows itself in the coming years as wholesale and revolutionary adjustments in the life of the nation and a new expansive mode of operation. The 7 shows, even then, a link with nature and a connection with history. New techniques and inventions would bubble away here, under the 1, 5 and 7. The 6 would show itself as the establishment of, and attempts to order, a civil society. The 1, 5 and 7, however, set the foundations for a rebellious and awkward country that will not easily be controlled by others and was set to take a leadership role in the world. The Power Number of 19/1 further underlines the fierce current of independence in the country and foretells the extent to which that would be prosecuted.

The Second Era of Britain: 1284 –1603

Statute of Rhuddlan		E W	19 March 1284	Universal Year 6
First Road	*Second Road*	*Third Road*	*Fourth Road*	*Power Number*
1	19/1	22	5	11

King Edward I of England's defeat and annexation of Wales, and its official adoption unto the crown (with some regional variations of law, and a few independent remnants) was formalised in The Statute of Rhuddlan on 19 March 1284.

Here we have the continued prominence of 1 and 5, expanding further the potential of the nation to invent, create, revolt and conquer. Endowed now with two Master Numbers 11 and 22, the forces inside the nation set their sights on a higher vision still. This nation was going to become a special place; the 22 wanted to do things bigger and better, the 11 was drawn to illumination, progress and God. The successful expansion into what would ultimately be four lands started to take place through incursions to Ireland and Scotland, though neither were yet wholly successful.

The Third Era of Britain: 1603 –1649

Union of the Crowns		E W S (I)	24 March 1603	Universal Year 1
First Road	*Second Road*	*Third Road*	*Fourth Road*	*Power Number*
1	6	9	1	8

The Union of the Crowns – whereby James VI of Scotland also became James I of England – is the next marker, signifying the partial welcoming (9) of Scotland and Ireland (9), and the continuing appearance of the independent, buccaneering, non–conformist 1. The first appearance of the number 8 as the Power Number becomes notable, especially with all the names of the nations lacking it. The 8 showed what was missing and necessary; money, power, order and authority. These would appear very shortly.

This was the third era to contain a repetition of 1, and each of the three eras so far contained this number twice. This is unbalanced and manifested into a Monarch who believed himself subject to God alone, King Charles I.

The Fourth Era of Britain: 1649 –1661

Commonwealth/ Protectorate		E W S I	19 May 1649	Universal Year 2
First Road	*Second Road*	*Third Road*	*Fourth Road*	*Power Number*
8	19/1	6	5	2

I have chosen the fourth marker not as the execution of King Charles I, but the formal establishment a few months later of the Commonwealth of England (including Wales), Scotland and Ireland. This was the republic for which Cromwell and the Roundheads fought so hard, yet it was to prove short–lived. The parliamentary system became stuck and achieved very little, which is what we would expect during a 4 period, the purpose of which was simply to make strong that which was weak. The people of the nation had seized power, though they seemed to not know what to do with it. But Oliver Cromwell, born on 25th April 1599 (25+4+1599 = 1628 = 17 = 8) was the 8 of this new nation made flesh. He knew how to wield power, how to subdue the Scots and the Irish, and to bring the nation together, albeit by the sword.

The 1, 5 and 6 remained from before, providing continuity of national spirit all the way back to 1066. This was already an old country, with ways that had become deeply embedded. Cromwell's 8 must have seemed somehow alien and although his influence lives on, his Commonwealth (or Interregnum as some know it) barely survived him.

The Fifth Era of Britain: 1661 –1707

Coronation of Charles II		E W S I	23 April 1661	Universal Year 5
First Road	*Second Road*	*Third Road*	*Fourth Road*	*Power Number*
5	5	9	5	6

It was suddenly as if the Commonwealth and the Protectorate had never happened when it was asserted that Charles II had been the rightful King ever since the passing of his father, 11 years earlier. The Interregnum was thereafter classified as an aberration, a dour expression of heaviness of 4 and very un–British.

There are many important dates in the early months of the Restoration, but the most significant must surely be the placing of the Crown back on the head of the monarch, which occurred to King Charles II on 23rd April 1661.

The profusion of 5 in this date rethreads the nation all the way back to 1066, and the 9 back to the 1603 Union of the Crowns. The restored monarchy was therefore both modern and ancient, that perfect British mix. The many 5's (within the Era of Five) brought freedom, adventure and release; witness Charles II's own personal lifestyle as an embodiment of this. It was indeed an expansive time, and the Coronation Day seeded forward to another important milestone in the nation's history, 1688, the year of the Glorious Revolution. Numerologically Charles II's Restoration was far more important, revolutionary and longer lasting than anything that Cromwell ever did.

The Sixth Era of Britain: 1707 –1801

Kingdom of Great Britain		E W S (I)	1 May 1707	Universal Year 6
First Road	*Second Road*	*Third Road*	*Fourth Road*	*Power Number*
3	1	6	9	19/1

The Kingdom of Great Britain was born with the Acts of Union on 1st May 1707. Scotland abandoned their parliament, but IRELAND (9) would remain semi–detached for another hundred years. The First Road 3 gives the impression that ENGLAND (3) was the lead nation in this Kingdom. Maybe some Scots never got over the sense that it was a takeover or a stitch–up? In reality it was much closer to a bailout, following Scotland's financially ruinous attempt to establish a colony in Central America.

Three out of these four numbers had now appeared on and off since 1066, but for the 3 to take the lead opened a new door, and the nation embarked upon great explosions of creativity with the works of Daniel Defoe, William Hogarth and Jonathan Swift and the establishment of the Royal Academy of Arts, which endures to this day. The period incorporated further creativity (3) and invention (1) with the birth of the Industrial Revolution. This number 1 continues to appear so frequently in the dates of the nation, from the modern day all the way back to 1066, that we ought to talk about it, and its compound 19, in more depth.

19/1 – The Sun Shines (Too?) Brightly

1 is the singular and the exceptional, the leader, inventor and pioneer. It is the one who will not follow, nor be constrained. It does not belong as part of anything else and will often play merry hell when pigeon holed into conformity or subservience. This is because the number has a blessing and a curse. Its blessing – answering to no one – is matched perfectly by its curse, that it must lead and never follow.

When the number 1 is revealed through the compound number 19 then the matter is raised to a higher level where the karmic responsibilities and consequences of leadership and independence are magnified. The issue then becomes one of vision and focus. Does the subject have a realistic vision of how they might lead and a correct focus on what needs to be done to facilitate their independence? The suggestion, due to the 19, is that they do not and must work hard at attaining such, moving beyond all the excuses and justifications why they cannot do what they must.

Alongside this thirst for independence runs the quest for identity. If one is to stand alone, what does one stand for? Often this can only be worked out through trial, error, and mistake. Specifically, this may be learned through relations with others. Any form of unbalanced connection or incorrect partnership will be exposed for what it is and eventually come crashing down. Witness the absolute failure of Britain through the ages to co–operate internationally on an equal footing. In the modern world our reliance upon the Americans or our role within Europe will always be subject to the strong forces that pull us away on our own.

Through the constant presence of 1, and the frequency of 19/1, Britain in its various incarnations has held the enormous karmic responsibility of displaying global leadership through a strong sense of identity and an independent approach. Yet, like all individuals with 19/1 prominent, their efforts and words are prone to misunderstanding. This can grasped if we think about the Tarot, specifically The Magician (I) and The Sun (XIX). The interplay between these two images is what has made Britain and what influences all 19/1 people. The subject looks up to the Light, yet is blinded by it. The Light is external, in the sky, yet also internal in the solar plexus manifesting in a strong sense of sovereign individuality. The Light bestows power, yet power without wisdom is always misused. The subject is effectively trying to bring down the power and light of The Sun, yet this is such an enormous task that he fails to explain clearly himself to others or to execute his works effectively. Until he has learned all about himself and is no longer blinded by the Sun, he looks afar when he should be looking near. He misses the obvious while looking for the hidden and speaks of the grand when he should address the small. Yes, this is the ongoing story of the British and their Isles.

This is made all the more relevant when we think of the amount of significant players in British history marked with the 19/1, either in date of birth or in name. Such influential Prime Ministers as Asquith, Disraeli, Pitt the Younger, and Lord

Liverpool all bore this burden, as did numerous supporting influencers. Within the eras of the nation we see this number almost continuously – First Era Power Number 19/1, Second Era born on the 19th, Third Era First Road 1 in a Universal Year 1, Fourth Era born on the 19th, Sixth Era born on the 1st, and Power Number 19/1, and, as we shall shortly see, Seventh Era born on the first and Universal Year 1, and Eight Era Third Road 19/1. All these dates and people would imperfectly and messily play their part in the unfolding of this dynamic, which was described by Florence Campbell in the numerological classic 'Your Days Are Numbered',

"...debt is piled upon debt. This is the vibration of endurance. How much can we stand? All the life secrets are dragged into the Light, and we may find ourselves stripped at the finish of the race. We reap what we have sown and struggle with the burdens of the past. We are bound when we want to be free. We must pay with time, money and ourselves. Through all this we may see the Rising Sun of a New Dispensation."

These words have been true about Britain and the British ever since 1066, and will continue to be relevant until the nation incarnates once more.

The Seventh Era. Imperial Britain: 1801 –1922

UK of GB & I		E W S I	1 Jan 1801	Universal Year 1
First Road	*Second Road*	*Third Road*	*Fourth Road*	*Power Number*
3	1	11	5	2

The United Kingdom of Great Britain and Ireland (including the whole island of Ireland) came into formal being on 1st January 1801, and ceased to exist on 6th December 1922 with the establishment of the Irish Free State. This period encompassed the height of Empire, the Second Industrial Revolution, the colonisation of Africa Cape–to–Cairo, Queen Victoria, King Edward VII, and World War One.

Our first number here is 3, the number of communication, expression and self–confidence. A colourful force of language, art, and creativity, it profoundly wants attention and recognition, but can become surly, uncommunicative, and inexpressive if this energy is not channelled correctly. Here we see the British stiff–upper lip as much as we see the expressive genius of Oscar Wilde, Charles Dickens, the Bronte sisters and Arthur Conan Doyle. 3 is often very good at talking and dictating, but often not very comfortable with listening. Communication with a 3 can be very one sided, especially if pride and vanity are allowed to run free. The subject can then become vain, cynical and sarcastic. This can be dangerous and display an inability to accept that anyone else knows better. With ENGLAND also as 3 the confusion between Britishness and Englishness would be extended further. The continuation of 3 from the previous era allows for a great extension of the arts in public life, though its appearance sits in stark contrast to the necessary, but missing 8. It is like placing a Cavalier next to a Roundhead. Though they may need each other, they are unlikely to get on. The story of Britain is the national inability to reconcile these two natures.

The Second Road of the nation during this time (1) brings innovation, the buccaneering instinct, the pioneer, privateer, and entrepreneur, and puts leadership, impetus, and drive into play. Here there can be bullishness and aggression. Not so much a bulldog spirit, but intemperance, intolerance and a desire to lord it over others, though without thinking through how that might take place in practice. The 1 shouts 'Charge!' but it takes other numbers to make something worthwhile happen after the battle cry. This repeating 1 proves that the nation was always destined for leadership, but the consequences of a narrow–minded approach to dominating others without thought or compassion would prove severe.

The Third road of the Imperial Nation was 11. In its lowest form 11 is a fearful number, ungrounded, delusional and misguided – though of great inner power. The number can be very destructive to self and others and is always associated with extremes, be they of power, wealth, health or opportunity. Lack of self–confidence and suspicion of others can flow from this number and can lead its owner into over–compensation as they focus exclusively on power and protection. More positively this is the number of enlightenment and illumination – providing the lamp for others to follow – science, mathematics, discoveries of the mind, magic, mysticism and the occult. Looking back to the first appearance of 11 in the Statute of Rhuddlan we can see that these things are old within the nation.

The Fourth Road for Imperial Britain is 5, the number of travel, adventure, exploration and discovery. As the only number that can do anything and go anywhere, it seeks freedom and engages readily with diversity. It is the number that does not always practice what it preaches and can easily take on too much, moving out in all directions at once, over committed until the centre can no longer hold and the whole thing collapses in exhaustion.

The Power Number brings us to 2, connecting to the beckoning call of the peacemaker. But something must have gone very wrong, for the nation was pulling apart and World War One was round the corner. The self-destructive tendencies of the name of the nation – 22 – were increasingly showing themselves.

The Breach with Ireland

"To gain four is to gain everything, yet to lose one is to risk losing all."

The British Empire, drawing on all the incarnations of the nations before it, possessed numbers of great and expansive power – 1, 5, 11, 22 – but was destined to fail. The BRITISH EMPIRE (16, 7) saw lightning strike the The Tower (XVI) and The Chariot (VII) upturned. While the British were off around the world on various kinds of (sea) Chariot they assumed that the centre could hold and that all would remain well back at home. This was not to be, and the lightning, which caused the Tower's fall, struck in Ireland. As the British lost Ireland, they lost the Empire.

Ireland had been controlled, on and off, by the English since King John in 1199. Passing through periods of rebellion and inclusion (notably under Henry VIII and Cromwell) it was not until 1801 that Ireland was formalised into the Union. But even with this event it is hard to accept that Ireland was ever involved in the Union, as much coerced into it. Even if we try very hard not to fall into the common anti–British narrative the history of Ireland, certainly from Tudor times, does seem to be one of continual and repeated subjugation by the English. Given the name of the land, IRELAND (9, the number of humanity but victimhood, of love, openness and larger than life characters, naivety and innocence) this is hardly surprising. But the 9 character is strong and wild when roused, and will never remain lifeless, dim and subjugated forever. The English excuse has always been a religious one; to replace backward Catholicism with enlightened Protestantism, they said. Whether correct or not in intent, the methods were bloody and the results catastrophic. For Ireland might have been a great land as it had long recognised the Power of Four through its four provinces Connacht, Leinster, Munster and Ulster, as well as a fifth – the seat of power – Meath. Together with its long Druidic lineage it may have even been the original and true Nation of Fourness. But never under English rule.

Many attempts at a new, fairer settlement for Irish Catholics were made in the decades after the 1801 Acts of Union, but the more radical measures were overruled by the King or bogged down in debate without firm action. This is symptomatic of the 3 of Britain at that time.

Ireland, under British rule, was a country divided, where a small number of rich English Protestant absent landowners lorded it over a large population of poor and uneducated Irish Catholic workers. This class division was nothing new in Britain, but was made worse in Ireland by the lack of industry, the grip of the Catholic Church, and the reliance upon agriculture. Over time, Irish farm workers focused on raising cattle for export back to England, but themselves increasingly subsisted on potatoes. This monoculture crop had experienced multiple failures over the years, but the Potato Famine of 1845 – 1852 was the worst of all. Essentially simply a potato blight, it cost the lives of an estimated 1.5 million Irish, and reduced the population of the island to such an extent that it did not recover until the late twentieth century. The British government's response was slow and ineffective, and the Irish never forgave the British for it. Whether it was wilful neglect and arrogance, or mismanagement and incompetence, for one quarter of the homeland of the Empire to experience ruination on this scale, over such a protracted length of time, was a great Karmic error.

During the subsequent decades, while Britain involved itself in Crimea, India, Suez, Afghanistan, Sudan, South Africa, and then ultimately with Germany in Europe, the Irish independence movement gained ground. British politicians all knew the severity of the questions and even though Queen Victoria took direct interest in the matter, nothing was done. There was a collective failure to recognise the Power of Four – that Ireland was not just another conquered colony, but a necessary and integral part of the homeland. It was mistakenly treated with less urgency and vigour than matters half way around the globe. This would prove to be fatal for the Empire for, although the British were guilty of colonial mis–adventure, especially in India and South Africa, their cardinal sin was the treatment of what were now their own people, the Irish.

The Easter Rising, the Irish Civil War, the growth of the IRA, bombings on the mainland, and The Troubles in the North; the last third of the twentieth century were the direct consequences of all of this, and the British should have done better. Tony Blair eventually went some way to setting the Karmic record straight by a formal apology in 1997, but the damage had already been done. The forces unleashed by the Act of Union in 1801 were managed greatly on the world stage, but poorly at home. They allowed the British to create the greatest Empire the world had ever seen, yet that was doomed the moment they forgot the Power of Four.

To identify the Four Roads is to begin to walk them, but as the British fell over all their four roads turned negative. Their communicative 3 became a vain and pompous 3, and the Empress III, which should have led the British to value the home and the free expression of its entire people, was lost. They failed to harness correctly the 1, becoming selfish and narrow minded, failing to act to save the Irish people when they knew, because they had conquered the world, that they could if they but tried. But the greatest failings were in the third and fourth roads. What should have been positive expressions of justice, fairness, and equity (11) became rough justice and harsh treatment. The British had failed to control the very powers they had unleashed. The seeds, therefore, of World War One were planted decades before 1914, where the power the British had accrued over eight and half centuries had been mis–applied to such a great cost at home that they were bound to lose all that had been gained. It was therefore inevitable that the day would come when the homeland would fracture. This occurred through the renaming to the United Kingdom of Great Britain and Northern Ireland on 7th December 1922.

The Eras of Britain So Far

Everything runs in cycles of 9, and Britain is no exception. Each era conforms perfectly to the characteristics of its number. The First Era (1066–1284) saw the inception of the nation and the laying of its foundations. The Second (1284–1603) saw the nation play with balance and harmony and explore the invisible and spiritual. The Third (1603–1649) brought expansion and pomp, though much too much in the case of King Charles I. The physical chopping of his head at the neck in the Era of Expression (3) may be interpreted as leaving a wound in the character of the nation, turning what should be an expressive 3 into today's cynical and sarcastic one. When we had our First Road as 3 then we could overcome this, but not today.

The Fourth Era was the necessary correction (1649–1661) downwards, yet that proved too static and the dynamism of the nation could only be restored by a change into the Fifth Era (1661–1707) of gaiety, expansion and glory. This was

followed by the Sixth Era of Responsibility (1707–1801), where the productive forces of society were harnessed for progress, and successive governments became more responsible with the nation's finances. Then the Seventh (1801–1922), which as the number of the nation GREAT BRITAIN became the defining period of Empire. The Eighth Era of Reward followed, in 1922, where the nation reaped what had taken nearly 900 years to sow. So the 8 – the lesson of the nation – becomes important once more. This will be followed, soon enough, by the last period, the 9th where the nation will arrive at its Destiny, and nothing more, in its present form, can be achieved. But before we get to that we must explore a lot more about Britain post 1922, which itself was scarred almost at the moment of its birth.

The Curse of Tutankhamun

'As to anyone who violates my body which is in this tomb and who still removes any image from my tomb, he shall be hateful to the Gods and he shall not receive water on the altar of Osiris, neither shall he bequeath to his children, for ever and ever.'

This is the approximate translation of the words inscribed in the tomb of the Egyptian Pharaoh Tutankhamun, discovered on 4th November 1922. It is hard today to imagine an event with a comparable social or cultural importance. A Royal Wedding (or funeral) might possibly come close to the fever that was sparked by the discovery of the tomb and the removal of its contents. This phenomenon was fed, almost from the start, by the unnatural deaths of many of the exploring party, including the financier of the whole operation, Lord Carnarvon, who died from blood poisoning after a mosquito bite, four months after the tomb's discovery.

Much heat has been generated over the years by these curse stories, all of which focus on the existence of a mystical hex, or otherwise, upon individuals. But what if the curse actually fell upon Great Britain as a whole?

Consider how some of the key dates surrounding the tombs excavation chime in with the nation. Lord Carnarvon was born on 26th June 1866 (26 = 8. Also, 26+6+1866 = 1898 = 26 = 8). He was therefore motivated by money (of which he already had vast quantities), prestige and power. He employed as chief archeologist Howard Carter (H= 8. Also the letters of the full name sum to 8). This much 8 in just two men, involved in something so important, is too much. Their motives, together, were not altruistic.

The passageway down to the tomb was uncovered on 4th November 1922 (4+11+1922 = 1937 = 20 = 2), connecting into the Power Number of the United Kingdom at that time. A small opening into the tomb, through which Howard Carter peered and remarked upon 'wonderful things…' was made on 26th November 1922 (26 = 8). The first item was removed from the tomb on 27th December 1922 (27+12+1922 = 1961 = 17 = 8) where the intention of the explorers was proven. This was put beyond doubt when the seal to the burial chamber was broken on 16th February 1923 (16th = 7. 16+2+1923 = 1941 = 15 = 6).

To fully understand the effects unleashed by the breaking of the seal, consider the cataclysmic effects of pure and unpolluted intent upon the human psyche. The curse written at the time of burial was almost certainly introduced into oils and incenses of some kind, possibly sealed, waiting to be released. These things remained undiluted and untouched for over three thousand years, but they are not like milk or bread – they don't go off. If anything their strength increases over time, released only when their protective seal is broken. Thus the intentions and wishes of the Pharaoh were released through magical techniques we barely understand, in 1922. The direction of their expression moved beyond the individual explorers to touch the essence from which they originated – the British Empire.

Consider what happened next. From the moment of the tomb's discovery the nation was marked, ceasing to exist in its then current form within one month. Within 20 years Britain had been threatened with invasion and destruction but the curse of the tomb was not satisfied with this and struck again to deliver the final ruin of the Empire at Suez, in the Land of the Pharaohs, in 1957. Britain was touched again when the artefacts were exhibited at the British Museum in 1972, the same year that the country made the fatal decision to join the EEC. This exhibition opened on 30th March 1972 (30+3+1972 = 2005 = 7), plugging directly into the number of the nation. Then fast–forward to the artefacts' return to London, at the O2 on 15th November 2007 (15+11+2007 = 2033 = 8) where they spoke directly to the Karmic Number of the Nation, 8. The Financial Crisis and virtual bankruptcy of the nation followed very shortly after. These were the only two occasions that the artefacts visited Britain. We might hope not to witness another exhibition in our lifetime.

The Eighth Era of Britain: 1922 –

UK of GB & NI		E W S NI	**07 December 1922**	Universal Year 5
First Road	*Second Road*	*Third Road*	*Fourth Road*	*Power Number*
15/6	7	19/1	7	3

While Howard Carter was digging around in the Egyptian desert momentous changes were occurring back at home. 7th December 1922 was a step change in the history, with the introduction of an unfamiliar number to the fore that had only previously been in the background – 6. The tribe, the village, the community, the family, the class – these are all functions of 6, together with the modern inventions of society and socialism. It is no coincidence that the loss of Ireland connected directly to the loss of Empire and onwards to the rise of socialism in Britain in the form of the Labour Party and their prime instruments of influence – public service and the NHS.

Public Servants Old and New

Characterisations of the British establishment are usually confined to old–fashioned measures of education, class and wealth. But the British establishment is chameleon–like and manifests wherever there is the opportunity of a job for life. The teaching profession, the NHS, civil service, local councils, social services – all these are the modern establishment. Once upon a time the gatekeepers were exclusively public–school–tie Tory, but no longer. Management consultants, who converse in corporate speak, are now as much a part of the establishment as crusty old colonels ever were. The old nationalised industries – train operators, bus companies, anything with British in the title (Gas, Telecom) – also form part of the immovable blob that is anti–progress, anti–individual and anti–change. These organisations are often government funded, or shielded from commercial or common legal realities, such that they operate in protected bubbles, free to impose their version of 'customer service' and 'compliance' onto the many who have little choice about whether to use their provisions or not.

Today's establishment can be found wherever jobs are awarded primarily on the criteria of who you know, rather than what you know. We need look no further than TV, radio, and the media to see this in action.

The establishment, today, is The Devil (15) of the nation, and we should not pretend that just because an organisation prints the strapline 'transforming lives' underneath its logo that it possesses either the ability or interest to do anything other than regulate, confine and repress. Some advanced parts of the establishment seek to overwrite the individual conscience of their employees with a set of pre–programmed responses, such that many feel as though they are dealing with robots, rather than human beings. The noble idea of public service (6 – The Lovers, the root number of the current nation) has, in many places, been distorted by restrictive intolerances (15 – The Devil, the compound number of the current nation). Wherever we find these two numbers together we are dealing with the enemies of progress.

The great secret with The Devil though is that he relies upon the continued belief that his chains are solid. The moment we wake up to this fact and realise we have only enslaved ourselves, is the moment we are free from his influence.

The NHS: All That Is Best, Or The National Religion?

All religions are tools of The Devil (15). Their prime mission is to accumulate worshippers, those who will unquestioningly feed the beast and prostrate themselves at its feet. Many of the world's great religions deliver hope and comfort. But they do so on the foundations of belief and faith, not facts, evidence, experience, results or common sense. Given this characterisation of religion it is hard to look at the NHS today and conclude that it has become anything other than a faith–based organisation.

The National Insurance Act of 1911 was the first real attempt at universal health care in Britain. It came into force on 16th December 1911 (16th = 16 = 7), immediately connecting with the soul of the nation. Its birth into the organisation we now know took place on 5th July 1948 (5+7+1948 = 1960 = 16 = 7). Further good things can be discovered from the Destiny Number of the National Insurance Act, which is 22 (all things grand and transformative), and the words WELFARE STATE, which sum to 9 (pure humanitarianism).

However, repeated attempts by politicians to 'own' the NHS have contributed to its politicisation and movement away from its core values. A recent attempt at this took place with the release of the NHS Constitution on 21st January 2009 (21+1+2009 = 2031 = 6). This was perfectly in alignment with the number of its founder William Beveridge, born on 5th March 1879 (5+3+1879 = 1887 = 24 = 6), and with the Labour Party's own profusion of 6. Indeed the Welfare State's central principle, that all may pay so that all may benefit is a positive manifestation of 6.

But something else – beyond the love and compassion of 6 – is going on at the heart of the NHS. It is also an organisation dominated by 5. The name NATIONAL HEALTH SERVICE sums to 5, as does its abbreviation NHS. Both names begin with N (N =14th letter of the alphabet = 5). It was also born on the 5th, as was William Beveridge. 5 is the number of diversity, speed, adaptation and change. It is the number of variety and movement, the ability to do everything, but without purpose or direction the tendency to be overwhelmed and thus do nothing. This seems a perfect description of the recent state of the NHS, where everything is asked of it and change is imposed every five minutes. Given this presence of 5, deep within its DNA, the answers are not as simple as asking politicians and managers to back off, for the 5 will just find another way to show itself.

Instead solutions appear when all members and users of the organisation treat change as a friend, with multi–disciplinary approaches and a willingness to change and adapt along clear, defined parameters. This is what the 5 of the NHS needs – direction and guidance in what it should and should not do, and clear delineation of where it should and should not be. For to attempt to place it everywhere is to effectively place it nowhere. It is doubtful that this course will be taken without challenge. Gordon Brown's NHS constitution of 2009 seeds in to the future in the year 2031, and supposed fresh starts like the troubled Hinchingbrooke Private Finance Initiative (signed on 13th November 2011 = 1) seed in 2035. Resolution seems a long way off, but it should be noted that David Cameron does seem to have been touched by the NHS, energetically, when he himself was born on 9th October 1966 (9th = 9. And 9+10+1966 = 1985 = 23 = 5.) The numbers don't lie, whereas political hacks and propagandists always do. He has, innately within him, commonality with the NHS. Does this mean he is its saviour? We cannot say such a thing. But we can say that in terms of energy, numbers and karma – and nothing more – he is as necessary for the NHS as it was at one time for him and his family. Whether this cruel necessity is to break it up and sell it off, or to facilitate its full potential, only time will tell.

The Bank of England

The BANK OF ENGLAND sums to 7. Established in 1694 it is the lender of last resort to the country and its history is bound up tightly with that of the nation. Here are just a few snippets from its long history.

Black Wednesday, when the £ Sterling crashed out of the ERM causing terminal political damage to John Major's government and great financial cost to the Bank occurred on 16th September 1992 (16th = 16 = 7). The insolvency of the world's second oldest merchant bank, Barings, after disastrous speculation by Nick Leeson, took place on 26th February 1995 (26+2+1995 = 2023 = 7), while the Bank was formally granted independence over monetary policy by Gordon Brown on 1st June 1998 (1+6+1998 = 2005 = 7). Chancellor Brown announced the sale of much of the UK's Gold Reserve on 7th May 1999 (7th = 7) and – although only indirectly relevant – the American investment bank Lehman Brothers filed for bankruptcy protection in the US on 15th September 2008 (15+9+2008 = 2032 = 7).

Four of the last five Governors of the Bank of England have also possessed a prominent 16/7 in their date of birth. Gordon Richardson (Governor from 1973 – 83) was born on 25th November 1915 (25th = 7, also 25+11+1915 = 1951 = 16 = 7). Robin Leigh–Pemberton (1983 – 1993) was born on 5th January 1927 (5+1+1927 = 1933 = 16 = 7). He was followed by Eddie George (1993 – 2003), born 16th September 1938 (16th = 7) and after a notable interlude, since 2013 by Mark Carney, born 16th March 1965 (16th = 7).

The notable interlude takes us to the useful heart of Numerology – that while individuals shape and create organisations, once formed those organisations possess a life of their own, almost selecting for themselves the persons they require within them. Such individuals, as employees or leaders, are successful if they find themselves in resonance with the energies of the organisation. But sometimes an organisation experiences an interloper – an individual whose own personal energy and karmic requirements run counter to that of the organisation, though in harmony with a competing or overseeing organisation. Such individuals are disastrous in the life of the organisation they join. Enter the governor of the Bank who failed to foresee the 2008 financial crisis – Mervyn King.

Mervyn King was born on 30th March 1948. His First Road is therefore 19/1, which is in keeping with many previous Governors from the distant past, though not with the organisation itself, nor with any of its key dates. That is manageable; though it is also the number that can be blinded by the Sun unable see the wood for the trees. His Second Road is 3, the polar opposite of the Bank's 7, reflecting an individual better at talking than thinking, and out of step with the organisation he leads. His Third Road is 33 – the Master Number of Irresponsibility, perfectly in harmony with the number of the ruling party of government at the time, Labour. The presence of this man at the helm of the British financial system, under the rule of the Prime Minister of the Five of Pentacles during the Time of Earth created the perfect conditions for the financial crisis that engulfed the nation. With these forces in place how could it ever have been averted?

Lastly there is Gold. The seed year created by the announcement of the sale of the UK's Gold reverses on 7th May 1999 was 2011. Thus the issues thrown up by the events of that day were set forth to come home to roost in 2011. The decision to sell gold in 1999 was widely criticised for taking place at historically low prices of around $276/oz. The price of Gold would later rise to an all–time high of $1921.50/oz, on 6th September in the year previous seeded – 2011. The British might have robbed the gold from the Tomb of Tutankhamun, but they paid the financial price a thousand times over.

The Armed Forces

Other candidates for the establishment, old and new, are the Armed Forces, for the history of the nation is tightly stitched in with the history of the military. Battlefields, famous generals and key dates all form part of the fabric that decorates the nation. The Battles of Hastings, Agincourt, Bannockburn, the Armada, Waterloo, and the Battle of Britain retain resonance to this very day, as does the Falklands and the more recent but less successful encounters in Iraq and Afghanistan.

Modern Britain remains largely in the closet over its relationship with its armed forces. There are legitimate reasons why, since the Irish Troubles, UK military personnel have been discouraged from wearing uniform off duty. But is the nation also secretly ashamed of them, somehow not wishing to condone what is done in their name? Or is it because the British have lost all grasp of the reality of evil and the necessary steps that must sometimes be taken to tackle it?

The dispersal of the military from national life is a further sign of neglect of the Forgotten Lands. The British Army connects with Earth, the Royal Navy with Water and the Royal Air Force with Air. To ignore the military manifestations of a particular land is to ignore the land itself. And we do that at our peril.

Numerologically we see an enormous amount of 16 and 7 in the military. The forerunner of the modern Army was Cromwell's New Model Army, founded in 1645 (1645 = 16 = 7), whilst the name BRITISH ARMY sums to 7, as do the regiments of the GRENADIER GUARDS (16 = 7) and the IRISH GUARDS (16 = 7), while another famous regiment the COLDSTREAM GUARDS were founded on 23rd August 1650 (23+8+1650 = 1681 = 16 = 7). Conscription in World War Two began immediately upon the outbreak of war on 3rd September 1939 (3+9+1939 = 1951 = 16 = 7), and National Service, as it was later called, was abolished on 31st December 1960 (1960 = 16 = 7).

In each case no other number appears as frequently and the pattern continues with the other services. Both the ROYAL NAVY and RAF each sum to 16, then 7. As such the British Armed Forces touch – through those numbers – the soul of the nation, whether the inhabitants of the nation like it or not.

The matter develops further though. Our awareness of military campaigns tends to focus around decisive battles, and to some degree British self–image has been formed by its military victories and defeats. But could it be possible to tell, in advance, if a battlefield is favourable, and what aspects of the national character it would activate? On one level all war is war – the failure of negotiation and the beginning of death. But on another level all wars are not equal, with some carrying greater and different meaning into the future than others. The differences are worth knowing.

Battles of 8, such as the FALKLANDS, SUEZ and RORKE'S DRIFT seem to touch on National Karmic issues of power, to a degree that others do not, while Battles of 4 seem to go badly for Britain, or be places where the forces get bogged down, such as NORTHERN IRELAND, CRIMEA and MUSA QALA. In these three cases victory (of a sort) came, but not easily or without cost. Given this we might be wise to avoid modern military engagements in the Crimea, regardless of how many Russian sabres are rattled. Lastly, Battles of 7 seem to be the ones that connect beyond warfare, being the number closest to the national consciousness – HASTINGS and DUNKIRK being just two of these.

Music as Rebellion. Or as Conformity?

So far in this chapter we have looked at how the nation comes together, or fragments apart. Music plugs into this question. In terms of style, image, values and attitude bands such as Led Zeppelin and Coldplay, or The Beatles and Joy Division could not be further removed from each other. Yet, all these and more are Bands of 7, sharing an essential British–ness that is otherwise hard to define. Incredible though it may seem, these performers are all – numerologically – the same. Or at least they are operating with the same energy, trying to express essentially the same things. It gets much more messy when we start to think about dates of formation, dates of first gig and first number one hit, as well as names and dates of birth of the individual band members. These factors introduce differences that are not trivial, but those differences then come into play through the same prisms of 7.

JOY DIVISION (16, 7)	CLIFF RICHARD (16,7)
PET SHOP BOYS (16,7)	DIRE STRAITS
SIMPLE MINDS	THE WHO
10CC (16,7)	THE CORRS (16,7)
THE BEATLES	COLDPLAY
LED ZEPPELIN (16,7)	

By contrast, Bands of 4 are the awkward squad of Britain, those who would not lie down, go away or play nicely with others.

THE SMITHS (13,4)	MARILLION (13,4)
SIMPLY RED (13,4)	PINK FLOYD (13,4)
DAVID BOWIE (13,4)	MANIC STREET PREACHERS
THE CLASH (22,4)	HAPPY MONDAYS
FRANKIE GOES TO HOLLYWOOD (13,4)	

Take a moment to connect to these similarities and differences. Every single piece of music is of course different, every time you hear it. But, bands of like numbers are really very similar indeed. Listen, though not intently, and you will hear why.

The Numerology of the SNP

The SNP's approach to breaking up the nation is that it is somehow better, nobler, and fairer to be a Progressive Scot than a Tory Englander. This sense of exceptionalism is very common, but as much as it might be reflective of an inner knowing, it might just as easily be an illusion, the implementation of which would be doomed to failure. Any nation that professes something special but forgets this fact places itself in great peril. This has happened to many countries before (including, arguably to Great Britain itself) and it will happen again. Scotland is not great simply because some of its politicians assert it to be. For it to be truly great there most be something else taking place, in the letters and the numbers.

Not only does the word SCOTLAND sum to 7, but its vowels do too. The Treaty of Union, which pre–dated the formal Act of Union in 1707 (7's), was signed on 22nd July 1706, which sums to 7. This date provides Master Numbers 11 and 22, but all these numbers belong also to the Union, not merely to Scotland.

The Scottish National Party was formed on 7 April 1934 (7th = 7). The Kilbrandon Commission, which recommended Home Rule for Scotland reported on 31st October 1973 (7). The removal of the sacred Stone of Scone from Westminster took place on 25th December 1950 (25th = 7, and 25+12+1950 = 25 = 7) and its formal return to Edinburgh (7) took place in 1996 (7). The Queen formally opened the Scottish Parliament at Holyrood on 9th October 2004 (7) and the Independence Referendum took place on 18th September 2014 (7, and in the year 2014 = 7).

The SNP, at time of writing, has had 17 leaders, 7 of which had 7 prominent in their date of birth calculations. The current leader and First Minister Nicola Sturgeon was born on 19th July 1970, which sums to 7. It is often said that the SNP is not Scotland, but from this we can see that it certainly keys into it very effectively.

The frequency of 7 in all matters Scottish is remarkable, but 7 is also prominent in GREAT BRITAIN and the COMMONWEALTH, as well as being the number of two of the four roads in the date of birth of the current era of the nation. Numerologically Scotland *is* Great Britain. Yes, Scotland is at numerological odds with its neighbours (England 3, Wales 6, Northern Ireland 4) and maybe separation is another cruel necessity given the story of the nation. But the physical dispersal of the Four Lands will be ruinous for all four, not just for one. Exceptionalism will be proved at the point of separation, but it will be exceptional weakness, not exceptional strength.

In traditional elemental law the only two 'real' elements are the opposites of Fire and Water. Air is merely a separating medium, while Earth is a repository of the other three. Thus, elementally Scotland (Earth) holds the essence of everything else in the United Kingdom, the product of all hopes and fears, endeavours and failures. It is the summation of all that occurs in the land, yet also the basest vibration and the one least able to burn, flow, or move. In this sense there is no Scottish difference. Scottish success is British success, while British failure and Scottish failure walk hand in hand.

Four More Forgotten Lands

The Forgotten Lands of Earth, Water, Air and Fire also manifest within individual human beings, with each person living in one or more of those lands, though not geographically. Their life is then proscribed by the characteristics and qualities of those lands. Childhood developed personality as well as innate character go to define which land we start off in, but there is also a kind of 'sorting hat' which defines where we need to be, rather than where we think we want to be. Every individual can ultimately escape the land in which they were born and raised, but only through personal effort.

Those who live in the Land of Earth, regardless of their geography, status, wealth or health, are interested only in the material. Here life is sometimes heavy, but also simple. It is about 'stuff' and 'things' the accumulation and loss thereof. It is about having a new car, or wishing for one, clothes, jewellery, houses and gardens. Here life is a function of what is visible, and the influence of what is invisible – be it thoughts or feelings – is minimal. Life becomes all about the actions and experiences of the physical body in the material world. People who live in Earth might be long distance athletes or physically disabled. Either way it is all about the body. These people – whether mobile and successful or not – can be opposed to change and resistant to new ideas.

Many people live in the Land of the Earth, but an increasing number of people live in the Land of Water. For these people every moment of existence is subject to and a product of feelings and emotions. To simply be alive is not enough; their being must course through with sense and feeling. These people – wherever they geographically reside – live perpetually at sea, and very little is certain or concrete in their lives. Their condition in the morning will often be different to their condition in the afternoon and they have no idea what they will have to deal with from one moment to the next. This may produce a happy or a sad person but it will always produce a person who is looking for more than a mere existence. Reason, logic and thought are often not a major factor in these peoples lives, and although they may or may not be educated their decision–making is informed by changeable feelings and emotional reactions more than by facts or realities.

Others live in the Land of Air. These are the thinkers, the theorists and the dreamers. Everything that happens to them is passed through the medium of the mind and processed, analysed and measured against everything else that has ever happened to them. These people are ready to move on quickly, to adapt and adjust and find new ways whenever the unexpected strikes. They are able to stay cool, see the bigger picture and rise above whatever happens. They are everything that the people of Earth and Water are not.

A small number of people live in the Land of Fire. These people make things happen; they ignite others and generate change everywhere they go. They are active, fast moving, and busy. For them life is a process of activity, be it mental or physical and although these people can be destructive, they can, when channelled, be the ones to create the world that the other three experience.

Clearly most people move between the Lands as the requirements of life act upon them. But almost all live *mainly* in one Land or another, defaulting to one, returning to one time and time again, and/or see everything through the lens of a preferred Land. Each of these Four Lands are very real and they limit the experiences available to us. Most people, at first, cannot really do very much to move outside of their chosen Land. The person who has lived for years in the Land of Water has come to view everything – including themselves – through this prism. The entirety of life for them is about emotion, no matter how much they claim to apply reason. Everyone, unless action is taken to the contrary, is stuck in their own Land. But, three things can cause a person to move out of the Land of their dwelling – crisis, unexpected change, or self–exploration.

Crises present things that we do not want to deal with, probably emerging from unfamiliar and strange Lands. The degree of pain generated by the crisis is a direct function of the amount of resistance to change and the size of the brick wall we have constructed around our Land.

Unexpected changes are often mini–crises – chances to visit one of the other lands voluntarily, before we are forced to.

Self–induced personal transformation is of course the preferable route, but it should be carefully noted that the person residing in, for example, the Land of Water, cannot successfully experience the Land of Fire without in some way changing themselves. To merely *visit* the Land of Fire – to witness the possibilities that come from action, movement, speed and heat – is to view them through the prism of Water, and thus to water them down. The only real way to visit the Land of Fire is to become active, moving, fast and hot – even if to the resident of the Land of Water, this somehow 'feels' wrong.

All this is directly relevant to the Break Up of Britain because the separation between people is not just geographic, or even numerological. A larger problem exists where the People of Water develop contempt, dislike and resentment for the People of Fire. They somehow come to see them as evil, inhuman, greedy and selfish just because they aren't governed by emotion and compassionate like they are. Similarly the divorce is protracted further when the People of Fire grow impatient with the People of Earth and their resistance to change. The great rift comes when all four find that they can no longer find common ground, and isolate themselves to such an extent that they are unwilling to even try to see the world from the perspective of others. Whether the nation goes its four geographically separate ways or not, it is this invisible break up – which has already begun – that will cause the real damage. This is the story of the Fall of Rome, the ongoing, but not irreparable, Fall of Britain, and the eventual Fall of America, the inevitable outcome when people refuse to get on.

All these intangibles are made flesh during every type of flood, storm or drought, for all these things are cries from the Forgotten Lands, in the hope that they might be heard once more.

The Role of The Group Consciousness

Things happen when they are ready to happen. But they also happen when people make them happen, yet those people can only make them happen when they themselves are ready, and however much the initiators of change want things to happen, the masses only catch up much later on. If all this sounds like a backwards circle you would be right. Things happen when they are ready to happen, and they never happen sooner.

Names and dates of birth of nations are not formed solely on a whim, or only through planning and reason. They are downloaded from the group consciousness, which is itself formed from what we have previously uploaded. We are each and together guided on how to work with this group knowledge, but it is up to us whether and how we do so. Yet, paradoxically, in the end we all must do so.

The only way to break these circles is through the introduction of novelty – the appearance and presentation of things outside of existing patterns. This best happens through eccentricity (3, 7) and individuality (1, 5), two of the deepest traits of the British, yet the two that are under most threat today.

Since 1066, each national era has contained at least one number of non–conformance. For most of its history the nation has the numbers 1, 3, 5, 7 or 11 as the First Road or most powerful influence. This made the British spiky, disagreeable, creative, innovative and rebellious. But no longer, for these traits have been – and continue to be – watered down. The presence of the 6 in the date of the birth of the current nation promotes commonality, community and – when taken too far – sameness and homogeneity. All in the name of love thy neighbour. But this approach finds it hard to grow, to change or to bend. Yet these are the very things that are so desperately needed as the country approaches its ninth, and therefore last, era.

Britain & Europe

"If only we had thought of the idea we would be much more committed to it. The EU was devised by clever, Catholic, left-wing, European, bureaucrats. And the British have a problem with at least three out of those five." – Peter Hennessy, Professor, Queen Mary University of London.

Good things, freely adopted over time, endure. They can withstand virtually all attacks and demise only of natural causes. Good things, imposed, bend like straw at the first challenge. Due to their numbers anything imposed upon the British, even if it is good, breeds resentment and generates a backlash. Cooperation between nations (rather than conflict) is about the best idea ever. But it has been forcibly, and sometimes deceitfully, imposed upon the British. And as such there is much discontent.

The EU is only the latest episode in a long series of attempts to integrate the British Isles more closely with the continent, but only the open invasion of Julius Caesar, the raids of the Vikings, and the Norman Conquest of 1066 have ever actually succeeded. Three key occasions of resistance stand out, although there have been many more. Henry VIII's refusal to bow to the Church of Rome (albeit for selfish reasons), Elizabeth I's repulse of the Spanish Armada, and Churchill's last stand in the Second World War. All three drove the stake of British independence (19 and 1) deeper into the ground.

What is Europe anyway?

Britain's slow march into the European Union occurred under the name of the new nation, born in 1922. The Great Britain of the Empire, or Old England would never have countenanced it, but by 1922 the nation had changed, its First Road now 6 and the sacred bond of the Four Lands broken. After destruction within victory in the Second World War, and then its final embarrassment at Suez the leaders of the nation cast around for something, anything, to restore the nation. Only by looking at the matter of Europe through these lenses can we see what has driven the British into Europe, what keeps them semi–detached from it, and what might resolve the matter once and for all, one way or the other.

To the British many member countries of the European continent seem powerful, by function of their Numbers and Letters translated into English. But in many cases the numbers are very different in the English language to the language of the host nation. Are we sure that these countries are what the British think they are?

Just like Britain, Europe suffers from a confusion of names, causing it to present different faces to different people depending upon what it is called. This is exacerbated further within Europe by differences in language, and therefore of numbers.

Britain sees…		Host Nation projects…	
Belgium	33	Belgie	4
France	11	France	11
Germany	11	Deutschland	3
Italy	22	Italia	7

To those who refer to it as EUROPE (8), the EU (8) or the EUROPEAN ECONOMIC COMMUNITY (8) it is all a matter of money, trade and power. Whether they view this positively or negatively is a personal choice. Those who used to speak of the old EUROPEAN COAL AND STEEL COMMUNITY (6), or the COMMON MARKET (6), who now speak of the EUROPEAN UNION (6) or wistfully of a UNITED STATES OF EUROPE (6) see peace, togetherness and community. These are the two, key battlefields of argument and causes of confusion – what is it actually that the British are joining, or leaving? In a Europe ravaged by war and a country beset by economic difficulties Britain's entry into the Common Market (6) in 1972 was seen as the last bus that could not afford to be missed. But that 6–ness meant we were always joining something very different to our history.

The UK signed the Treaty of Accession to join the EEC on 22nd January 1972 (22+1+1972 = 1995 = 24 = 6), which after much debate was confirmed in a referendum on 5th June 1975 (5+6+1975 = 1986 = 24 = 6). Further 6–ness appears when the Single European Act setting up the single market came into force on 1st July 1987 (1+7+1987 = 1995 = 24 = 6) and again at the UK's ratification of the Maastricht Treaty on 22nd July 1993 (22+7+1993 = 2022 = 6). There is still more 6 energy in the introduction of the Euro on 1st January 2002 (1+1+2002 = 2004 = 6) and the implementation of the last big change, the Lisbon Treaty, on 1st December 2009 (1+12+2009 = 2022 = 6).

However, behind all this love and togetherness of 6 the EUROPEAN UNION actually compounds to 15, and then 6, thus represented in the Tarot by The Devil, not the Lovers. This number is shared with Edward Heath, the Prime Minister who took Britain in, born on 9th July 1916 (9+7+1916 = 1932 = 15 = 6) as well as with Britain's 1922 rebirth (7+12+1922 = 1941 = 15 = 6). There is that 666 again.

The evolution of the UK's relationship with Europe can be further traced by noting a few seed years. Formal accession to the EEC (1st January 1973) seeded forward to 1975, the year of the referendum, the date of which (5th June 1975) seeded forward to 1986, the year of the signing of the Single European Act. This in turn leapt through to 2005, when EU membership was enlarged to Romania and Bulgaria. Margaret Thatcher, once a euro–enthusiast had, very quickly after signing the Single European Act in 1986, begun to change tack. Her waking–up moment resulted in a kind of British Declaration of Independence in a speech she gave in Bruges on 20th September 1988 (20+9+1988 = 2017 = 1). Her words that day released much bad blood, which would in turn cause the Conservative Party to virtually self–destruct. But not before planting a seed year into the future. That seed is 2017 – the latest year promised by David Cameron for the in–out referendum.

Although there has been vocal British resistance to membership of the EU from Day One, it has rarely been the dominant voice. Mavericks like Enoch Powell and Tony Benn took the lead in the 70's, then in the late 80's and early 90's opposition was focused around the Eurosceptic wing of the Conservative Party, assisted by the likes of Sir James Goldsmith, who really put the matter on the map with his Referendum Party in 1997.

Goldsmith was born on 26th February 1933, and as such possesses a Double 8 (26th = 8, also 26+2+1933 = 1961 = 17 = 8). A double appearance of any number always sets up an imbalance, where the energy behind the number becomes so strong that its expression is distorted.

The energy of 8 is money and power, and this made Goldsmith a difficult, overbearing and arrogant man. Once he had accumulated enough money to last a lifetime he set about involving himself in politics, and courtesy of his dual nationality he was elected as a French member of the European Parliament. By the early 90's Goldsmith had become obsessed with the subject of power, both corporate and political – who held it, why, and in whose interests – and it was in that cause that he adopted a strong anti–EU stance in later life, raising the awareness about Britain's place in Europe to an alleged five million people to whom he mailed video tapes expressing his views.

Today we see the mantle of Euroscepticism carried on by, amongst others, UKIP's first MP Douglas Carswell, born 3rd May 1971 (3+5+1971 = 1979 = 26 = 8) and elected for the party in a by–election on 9th October 2014 (9+10+2014 = 2033 = 8), and the Conservative MEP Daniel Hannan, born 1st September 1971 (1+9+1971 = 1981 = 19 = 1). Hannan possesses a Double 1, the number of independence twice, as well as the 19, connecting him firmly back to the spirit of Margaret Thatcher's Bruges speech in 1988, and the energies of the old nation, pre–1922.

The tool remaining at the full disposal of these Eurosceptics is Fire. Should the other sacred lands be fully ceded to outside control, then the nation will be utterly lost. If foodstuffs are regulated and directed from Brussels then the British will have lost total control of Earth. If the bounty of the sea is lost then Water no longer falls under British jurisdiction. And if the airwaves, the commentary and discussion, all flow in support of the EU, then Air is lost too. How naïve and neglectful have the British been to relinquish control of their powers like this.

But the process of change has begun, with the passion (and sometimes anger) of Fire shown by sceptics across the continent. There are now also signs of a shift in the debate, where the airing of non–EU–compliant views is becoming more acceptable. The process will advance further when the emotional connection (Water) to Europe is polluted. Any other member country's exit from the Euro would do this by causing such misery as to destroy the illusion of togetherness forever. A further migrant crisis might also do the same. This will enable the emotional link of the British to Great Britain to be further restored. Earth – the actuality of reaffirmed membership or final departure – would follow after that. It took two hundred years from 1801 for the British to even partly resolve the Irish Question, which had been bubbling for centuries before that. It may take the same amount of time to fully resolve Britain's relationship with Europe. Exit might come as a result of financial prosperity or collapse, by seeming accident or by deliberate design, but so long as there is history there will always be the faint awareness that the British have before and can again prosper in their own way by themselves, and thus deliver unto the world that which only they – when unconstrained – can.

The Numerology of UKIP

The UK Independence Party was formed on 3rd September 1993 (3+9+1993 = 2005 = 7). It experienced a major electoral breakthrough at the European Parliament elections on 22nd May 2014 (2014 = 7) and a further breakthrough in terms of votes (but not seats) at the UK General Election on 7th May 2015 (7th = 7). 7, one of the numbers of the nation, does not conform, seeks solitude and often looks back to the past. Like it or not, UKIP taps into something very British.

The number 3 also features prominently. The party was founded on 3rd September, Nigel Farage was born on 3rd April, his Deputy Paul Nuttall on 30th November and the party's first MP Douglas Carswell on 3rd May. Additionally the letters UKIP sum to 3, as do the two vowels. 3 is the number of optimism, self–confidence and communication and is reminiscent of the SDP, which also had people, names and dates with repeated 3's. The media lauded the SDP in the same way that UKIP are reviled; yet media exposure is the result. But the air might well come out of the UKIP balloon as quickly as it did for the SDP.

It is hard to predict whether 2015 represented the high watermark of UKIP, or the start of something genuinely new in British politics. The possible parallel is with the Labour Party, which took 23 years to get its first Prime Minister, 29 years for its first majority government and 45 years before it really got anything done at all. Looking at the seed years for UKIP we can see 2033, 2041 and 2045 as potentially significant. There is no certainty in this though. Nigel Farage himself, born on 3rd April 1964 (3+4+1964 = 1971 = 18 = 9) is an archetypal 9, larger than life and immensely human (in other words, deeply flawed). In relation to his numbers he is an entirely authentic individual, but he has no marks of Destiny upon him. Indeed he runs the risk of subverting his own energy when · he is anything less than supremely positive and optimistic.

Religious Freedom

Britain has the vestiges of an established church, but the nation is not devout, and the land has always been teeming with agnostics and atheists, even before the modern scientific–rationalist age. This component of the national spirit will not easily be swept aside, for even under the aegis of state enforced religious tolerance there are many Britons, young and old, who are deeply resistant and suspicious of Evangelical Christianity, Catholicism and Islam. Care should taken to distinguish religious tolerance from religious freedom. The preservation of the right to say no to religion in any form is what matters here, not protecting the feelings of religious minorities.

Since the time of the Spanish Armada the British have forged a successful path by resisting the all–encompassing European religion of Catholicism. The struggle now takes on a different form as people wake up to the role that immersive religion plays in retarding human progress.

Belief in the invisible and unknown, of which this book contains a great deal, is not the cause of human misery. When it sits as simply a potential to be investigated then it stands or falls, over centuries, accepted or marginalised as people see fit. But the self–incantation processes of Catholicism and Islam provide genuine brakes on human progress. I cover the mechanisms of these in *Emergence Book Zero: Darkness*, but essentially when any form of worship involves a connection with the four lands, with the worshipper in close contact with others, eating, drinking and breathing the doctrine, then that worshipper is being brainwashed and radicalised. This programming says the same thing whether it is Islam or Catholicism. It says that ones loyalty must lie elsewhere (not to the nation, but to Rome or the Caliphate), that one must pray and act in accordance with the rules of the book (not the common laws of the land), and a reward for human efforts cannot be expected in this lifetime but must instead be reserved for the next. Thus under the dominance of these two religions the condition of the world today and tomorrow comes second to the condition of the worshipper in the afterlife. But this isn't even the worst of it.

All religions throughout history – including the Church of England – have been guilty of downplaying the uniqueness of the individual and disregarding the positive difference between individual people by emphasizing the negative differences between groups. The usual result of this has been war. But there is another way, and by accident or design Britain stumbled upon it.

Although the British of history seem a deeply religious people, in comparison to Central European Catholics, Eastern European Orthodox Christians and Arabian Muslims our British ancestors were positively heretical, and the Church of England a watered down version of the true word of God. Much criticism is reserved of the old religious for their Protestant work ethic, but at least it provided results and improvements in *this lifetime*. So much so that under the loose banner of the Church of England the rogue individual was able to flourish in a way that he was not on the continent. And I don't just mean the rogue individual at the top of his field, but the one who never received any attention or recognition, yet changed the way that life was lived in his village or town. The Church of England may not have outright facilitated this, but it allowed it, much more than Catholicism or Islam did.

Human difference is the stuff of evolution, essential if a nation is to prosper. Every single individual, whatever their education or social standing, can make a unique contribution to the life of the nation. Difference is often misunderstood as inevitably leading to conflict, but conflict is a product of the Dark Side, that innate destructive impulse within every man, woman and child. Difference is the stuff of life, it is evolutionary and creative, inventive and of the new. Commonality, not difference, is in the armoury of Darkness. Somehow Britain – more than any other country – got this, or at the very least quietly allowed it, and thus the modern world was born. The moral of the tale is that wherever a religion or orthodoxy dominates and the individual, discordant voice is silenced – as it was in the Holy Roman Empire and the Caliphate, and as it increasingly is on the European Union – then human progress is arrested, abandoned in the rush for safety and comfort. When a nation's mind is set to exploration, discovery and personal expansion (or at least when these things are tolerated) then many things become possible. Peace comes only from tolerance of divergent individuals, and never from attempts to suppress them.

Merlin's question must now be updated again – how is it that people are not all the same? Why do so many people think such profoundly different thoughts and have such wildly differing ideas? This should not be asked in the form of an exasperated complaint, but as a doorway to a truth – that the British eccentric is the cause of the prosperity of the nation.

Many people now believe that debate and disagreement are unwelcome and should be done away with. Evidence based policy, politically correct thought, appropriate speech and right education must sooner or later, in the view of some, bring everyone to the same correct points of view. But this is completely and utterly wrong. Difference is the stuff of life, disagreement is essential, and contrary – even polar opposite viewpoints – are beneficial, not regressive. The British House of Commons is derided for its knock–about debates, shouts and screams but what is the alternative? Government by decree and directive? Government by warm and fuzzy consensus, where by definition, bright ideas are extinguished? It is only among a free-thinking, pluralistic society that magic and its twin, human progress, can flourish.

But Does Europe Help Britain Resolve its Karma, or Fulfil its Destiny?

Margaret Thatcher, like many others, was slow on the uptake with regards to Europe, realising only too late what she had allowed to happen. After a lifetime with her eyes focused on one Devil – the Labour Party – she was slow to adapt when the Devil took on a continental European form.

Being so heavily embroiled with 6 the European Union must, by definition, be deeply involved in the business of redistribution, both of people and resources. But any organisation that does this without wisdom, oversight or accountability must inevitably wind up creating the very injustices they seek to eradicate.

Any redistribution of resources must, of course, be from the richest to the poorest. But the EU's approach to this does not cause the richest of the rich countries to have their resources redirected to the poorest of the poorest countries. No, it is the middle class of the richest countries who feed the middle class of the poorest countries, either directly through taxation or trade subsidies, or more indirectly through population flows. The effects of this are to slowly harmonise the living standards of hundreds of millions of people in the middle of society, below which persists a desperate underclass and above which prospers a fantastically wealthy elite. This is the EU's giant experiment in human stock equalisation, presented under the guise of togetherness. Yet if this is prosecuted to its conclusion we will find that no amount of good intentions will compensate for the bottomless pit that will open up as governments involve themselves en–masse in the minutiae of peoples' lives in order to ensure that everyone not only has an equal opportunity, but an equal outcome. Think what this means – no geniuses, no inventions and no new ideas, for all these things are the product of deviant minds, not conformist ones. Rulership by an unchecked EU is the end of progress in Britain, and, for that matter, Europe.

The EU is The Devil, literally the 15 hiding behind the 6, imprisonment lurking behind partnership. The Devil and The Lovers are intimately related, one constantly attempting to merge into and out of the other. It is not that they represent opposites – the unity of The Lovers is not simply counterbalanced by the separation of the Devil. It is that we mistake one for the other, or when connecting with one fail to see how close we are to being overwhelmed by the other. Acceptance of one always means the presence of the other. This is why the lessons of love are so hard, for love is intimately connected to hate, togetherness to isolation, and warmth to cold. In this paradigm responsibility and irresponsibility walk together, and attraction sits right next to repulsion.

Through the prism of The Lovers (6) Britain does not want to leave, it wants to stay, to move beyond itself and seek to contribute to and benefit from the group. Any group informed by 6 is governed by the quest for perfection (6 being mathematically a perfect number: $2 \times 3 = 6$. $3+3 = 6$), balance (the six–pointed Star of David consisting of two triangles merged together) and unity. But through the prism of The Devil (15) Britain wants to leave but feels it cannot, feels it is giving up more than it is gaining, and is increasingly hobbled with its freedoms curtailed. Yet all the time, in the land of The Devil the British are free to go. As in the card, their chains are not tight, and are self–imposed. They are free to leave the clutches of The Devil any time they like, but they do not see this, and they think they cannot. Fear is not then the presence of The Devil, but the thought of leaving him. The nation has enchanted itself under a mass of rationalisations and justifications about its involvement in Europe and can never be free until it gains the courage or maturity to escape. The question of

EUROPE (8) will bring forth a different answer than the question of the EUROPEAN UNION (15/6).

The Devil of the EU is not above resorting to flat out lies, but it much prefers subtle deceits and subterfuge. This is the history of all its treaties and agreements, where the small print is either concealed or glossed over, and its true intentions never openly revealed. This is not a conspiracy, simply a product of the conflation and development of Letters and Numbers over time.

A central tenet of numerology is that if you change your name you change your life. Once the land became the United Kingdom of Great Britain and Northern Ireland (7th December 1922 = 1941 = 15/6) the centuries long game of progress was up and initially The Devil was set loose. The Labour Party (33 –15 –6) grew in strength almost immediately afterwards and came to dominate the agenda of discussion in the country, even when for large chunks of the time it was out of office. The BBC (6) and the NHS (6) both developed during this time. A fight back was entered into during Thatcher's 80's but as she defeated one manifestation of the Devil so another one gained strength – the European Union.

While there is no doubt that some leading advocates of the EU are well intentioned and busy working positively toward reform, de–centralisation, and transparency, they cannot ever really get much done, because they are hobbled by the Letters and Numbers of The Devil. This Devil is persuasive and plays all the best tunes, offering great trivialities such as reduced mobile phone roaming charges and instant free treatment if you fall over drunk in Tenerife. Yet all the time he constrains our world in ways we no longer recognise, for we can no longer remember a time when it was otherwise. And what's to complain about anyway, we ask, as our attention is distracted by the latest crisis in the news.

The Devil also loves to play identity politics. He constantly reassures you that 'people like you' (open, liberal, tolerant) are under threat from 'people not like you' (nasty, racist UKIP types). He urges you to vote for and support people who look like you, sound like you, dress like you, and act like you, and to resist anyone who is different or divergent. Divide and rule, they used to call it. Now the division is perpetuated by The Devil, from his hidden position behind The Lovers. Mis–representing hate as love, promoting division as togetherness, encouraging discrimination behind the facade of inclusion and enforcing coercion under the mask of co–operation he raises commonality above uniqueness and over time stamps harder and harder upon the face of human innovation; unless, of course, that innovation can be harnessed to his own destructive ends. Technology does nothing to reduce this and, in fact, may itself become the ultimate tool of enslavement by the Devil.

All of the traits I have described exist currently in the 15/6 of the United Kingdom of Great Britain and Northern Ireland, but they are intermingled with others and have not quite overwhelmed the older and more positive traits of the historic nation of Britain. The EU is altogether more dangerous, as a new entity it is The Devil from Day One, unencumbered by dreams or memories that it might be anything else.

But the British are free, if they assert strongly enough that they are. The freak, the one alone, outside the norm is a necessity of life, for it is they who create change. Great Britain has succeeded when it has been individual and rebellious, non–conformist and against the flow. When Britain does this the whole world benefits. The direction and shade of government policy is secondary to the willingness of the British to go their own way, but none of this can happen until The Devil inside and outside the nation is quelled.

Every good idea originated by man has been sooner or later been corrupted by man. This is not because his ideas were wrong, it is because of the inherently destructive nature of human beings. Every constructive and positive idea – such as co–operation across borders – contains within it a hidden grain of darkness, waiting for a dark soul to activate it. It does not matter what team the dark soul plays for, what party he belongs to or what cause he espouses. The dark will find the dark and there is nothing that can be done about that, except to be aware of it and work, as individuals, to control those impulses. If those at the heart of the EUROPEAN UNION could recognise the Devil that is innately within the DNA of their organisation they might, just maybe, be able to invoke The Lovers more strongly. But a blind adherence to goodness and community, in tandem with a denial of the darkness within, can only mean that its course goes unchecked.

Powerless Britain?

Nothing that has been written thus far should be taken as constituting a wish to return to the past. Oliver Cromwell was right, when on 13th April 1657 he refused the Crown of England with the words, *"I would not build Jericho again!"* None of us can turn the clock back. And we should not want to. The future is much more interesting.

Yet the current episode in the long running story of the nation is proving to many very challenging. The nation, post–1922, has neglected the Four Lands and lives under the nexus of 15/6: The BBC, the European Union and the Labour Party. Even if we believe this nexus to be good, right, and correct then we must acknowledge our powerlessness in the face of it. Even the defeat of the Labour Party at the 2015 election does not break one leg of the stool, for the appeal of togetherness is strong, maybe even timeless.

All this, past and present, goes to show the dangers inherent in trying to construct Utopia. Whether it was Camelot, the Empire, or now the EU, every single decision, every date and every word uttered in the name of progress always comes back to bite the inhabitants of each New Jerusalem. While we utter an imperfect language, in an imperfect way, we will always seed imperfections into the future. One hopes to not repeat the mistakes of the past, but it is impossible to prevent new mistakes in the future. Utopia is less a function of beliefs and good intentions, and much more of the Letters and the Numbers.

Powerless Britain? The Numerology of Transnational Corporations

Transnational corporations are almost, now, the same thing as nations. They certainly possess, through letters and numbers, an expression, a soul, a direction and karma. A few examples, from the numerology of their names:

Corporations of 15/6: Embodiments of The Devil.
General Dynamics (US arms manufacturer), IBM, Walt Disney.
Disney is a perfect example of the operation of The Devil from behind The Lovers. The staple entertainment diet of families the world over it consistently interweaves its plots lines and characterisations with stereotypes and propaganda. It seems justified to refer to it, as some do, as Evil Disney.

Corporations of 8: Motivated, irredeemably, by money and power.
Pfizer, Coca–Cola, Tesco, Goldman Sachs.
To place Tesco in the same bracket as Goldman Sachs is to think anew about each.

Corporations of 4: Driven by order, measurement, tradition and restriction.
Carlyle (global private equity), Facebook, Roche (pharmaceuticals), JP Morgan Chase (investment bank), Blackrock (global investment), Chevron.

To see Facebook alongside such giants of conservatism and defenders of the status quo as JP Morgan Chase is to stare more deeply than ever before into the true heart of this leader in technology and social media. The picture that emerges is not pretty.

And lastly, the numerological score in the battle of technology between Apple and Samsung.
It is APPLE 5 – SAMSUNG 22.

Powerless Britain? USA! USA!

Britain has always stood out in the history of human development. It was the first truly global nation, the first to industrialise and then the first to de–industrialise. When something has been invented, it has historically come from, or been taken to another level, by the British.

But not so much recently. Since the American insistence that Britain dismantle her empire at the end of the Second World War the UK has grown even more comfortable as the junior partner. Yet in another sense it is America that has followed Britain, seeking at every turn to do that which Britain tried and failed. It experiences its own versions of the same problems faced by Britain, yet is hundreds of years behind in its development. The class divisions of Britain are the racial divisions of America, the projection of Imperial British military power overseas is the deployment of US troops across the globe. Due to common use of the Letters and Numbers it is America – and indeed the rest of the English–speaking world – that follows Britain.

America is the topic of another book, maybe requiring extensive study. It is a troubled land, though still exciting and vibrant where Britain, outside of London, is often tired and weary. Yet America too often acts like a spoilt child, with many of it inhabitants possessing acutely short attention spans and driven solely by emotion. And to stack up the achievements and follies of the American Empire against the British is to look upon a troubled picture. Yet, for all this it remains the world largest economy and has Silicon Valley, Wall Street, NASA and Hollywood leading the world. The rumours of America's degeneration and passing have, I think, been greatly exaggerated.

Powerful Britain? The Numerology of the Green Party

The UK Green Party is so young that we do not have a lot of data to go on. Three numbers repeat prominently though.

The word GREEN sums to 4. The Club of Thirteen, an early forerunner of the current UK Greens, was formed on 13th October 1972 (13th = 4, and the name itself = 13 = 4). The first public meeting of the Green Party in England took place on 13th June 1985 (13th = 4). Early prominent Green voices such as Jonathon Porritt, David Icke and Sara Parkin all have 13/4 prominent in their dates of birth. 4 is the number of rules, order and enforcement, appearing prominently in the numerology of the Conservative Party.

All the instances where 4 is prominent also have 6 prominent. The forerunner PEOPLE Party sums to 33, and then 6, the Club of Thirteen was founded on 13th October 1972 (13+10+1972 = 1995 = 24 = 6) and Jonathon Porritt was born on the 6, as well as having 3 x O's in his name (O = 15th letter of alphabet = 6). Additionally Caroline Lucas was elected as their first formal leader on 5th September 2008 (5+9+2008 = 2022 = 6) and then became their first MP on 6th May 2010 (6th = 6). Historic Green voice Mike Woodin was born on 6th November 1965 (6th, in the 60's) and one time Principal Speaker Sara Parkin was born on 9th April 1946 (9+4+1946 = 1959 = 24 = 6). Finally, the first public meeting of the UK Greens took place on 13th June 1985 (13+6+1985 = 2004 = 6). As we saw earlier, 6 is the number most associated with the Labour Party and the BBC and is the one most concerned with the concept of society.

9, the number of humanity – people, not stuff – is also worth highlighting. Sara Parkin, Keith Taylor (former Principal Speaker), Sian Berry (previous London Mayoral candidate), Caroline Lucas MP and Molly Scott Cato MEP have prominent 9's in their dates of birth. Molly Scott Cato also resonates with 6 (3 x O's in the name). The Greens also recorded their greatest electoral success ever at the European elections way back in 1989 (1989 = 9, and 9's).

Overall this reads that many Green politicians share Left–Labour–BBC–6 type values and are motivated by humanitarian concerns (9), rather than money. However the heaviness of 4 cannot be ignored. There is something in 'Green' that is repressive and authoritarian, and whatever the seemingly positive motivations of the movement it is in its heart all about imposition and regulation, not persuasion or encouragement. This is the 4 at work.

I have placed the analysis of the Greens toward the end of this book because so many people believe that the party represents a real break from the past. If so then it will combine the worst aspects of the two old parties. To be a genuine break from the old routine Greens might want to consider the following lessons from our excursions into numerology. Natalie Bennett, their most recent leader, might especially want to do this, given that she possessed not one scrap of 4, 6 or 9, the numbers of the party she purported to lead.

1. We create our institutions by what and when we name them. They then create us. *Within* any institution – and the Green party is an institution like any other – it is always hard to reinvent.
2. It takes people with Master Numbers – 11 or 22 – to effect lasting change in society. The Greens have only one – former Deputy Mayor of London and Member of the House of Lords, Jenny Jones, born 23rd December 1949 (23+12+1949 = 1984 = 22).
3. Institutions must have top–to–bottom connections. The PRIME MINISTER (6) must simply be a higher version of the MEMBER OF PARLIAMENT (6), the COMMISSIONER (8) must be as the

SERGEANT (8), the ADMIRAL OF THE FLEET (7) must be the MIDSHIPMAN (7) and the GENERAL (8) must be the CORPORAL (8)

4. Institutions attract like minds in order to self–perpetuate. Institutions develop minds of their own, which reject deviant ideas. In an organisation of 4 the resistance to new ideas is especially strong.

5. The need to belong is a very powerful force. A lot of people who join and support political parties do so in order to surround themselves with like minds and share common ideas. The correctness of those minds and the soundness of those ideas is secondary to the sense of belonging generated.

6. Bias, within any institution, is inherent. Greens are no exception to this, although they may believe themselves otherwise. When one interest group is elected – be it Conservatives, Labour, or Green – then contrary interest groups suffer. So what? Who cares about the privileged? Except they are human beings too.

Balanced Britain? The United Nations

There is a grand difference between a brotherhood of differently abled and differently inclined nations and a One World Government. One World Government can be nothing other than a hellish dictatorship, utterly incapable of taking into account the diversities of places and person. The argument that the challenges faced by the world are so great that they can only be solved at a global level is bogus – challenges are only ever really resolved when individuals change their behaviour, and any attempt to impose this from above simply leads to a flattening and dulling of the individual spark. The problems might be resolved, but the spark of the future is extinguished into the bargain. And then what is the point of solving the problems?

One World Government depends on a false belief, made stronger by constant assertion, that what humans have in common is not only greater, but more valuable than their differences. While it is true that differences can, and have, brought war, they have also brought invention and progress. Difference is evolution, growth and improvement. It is not difference that is the problem – it is the intolerance of difference and the hatred of the contrary that creates war and suffering.

Every nation serves its purpose, differently in different fields. This is what being human is all about. This was recognised even in the days of Empire, wherever the British went they built schools, implemented systems of government, improved the economy, and strengthened the law, generally enriching, but not changing the essential character of, places they colonised. This is evidenced by the post–colonial transition within 20 years of Southern Rhodesia from breadbasket and economic superpower of Africa into the hellhole that is modern day Zimbabwe. These matters are nothing to do with the colour of your skin, and everything to do with the content of your character, the application of the elements and use of the Letters and Numbers. The notable exceptions to this were, as we have seen, the mortal neglect and failure in Ireland, and the heinous spiritual arrogance in Egypt.

Some will say there were many more failings of Empire. This may well be true, but only those who worship at the altar of moral equivalence so hard that they fail to see evil when it presents itself can possibly believe that Great Britain has been the prime cause of human suffering in the world. Only virulent self–loathing could lead someone to believe that all the accomplishments of Britain – Magna Carta and common law, literature, music, government, exploration and discovery – are valueless. Only those twisted by propaganda and utterly lost in themselves can believe that Churchill was the evil one and that Hitler might not have been that bad really. It has on multiple occasions, for some of the reasons described and many more, fallen to Britain to advance the Light and to fight the Darkness. Though the British have not always succeeded in this, and occasionally failed catastrophically, they have frequently delivered benefit when it really counted. But no one nation, especially not Britain, can now do this alone, for we are in the Epoch of the Two.

In the 2000's we are governed by the influence of the High Priestess, Water and all things balanced and feminine. All 'follow me' revolutionary or redemption movements – political or religious – are the death rattle of the old ways. The mode of existence now is co–operation or death. Within this framework the balance must be found between being a strong and independent nation, within international structures of co–operation, and being a weak and dependent nation reliant upon international structures of coercion. The differences may be subtle and not at all apparent at first. Yet they are real and significant and set the tone for the kind of country we will live in.

The UNITED NATIONS (21/3) has two dates of birth. It was signed into being by treaty on 26th June 1945. This gives a First Road of 6, with a Second Road of 8. This treaty then came into effect on 24th October 1945. This produces a First Road of 8, with a Second Road of 6. The 6 of togetherness (without the Devilish 15), and the 8 of power each balance the other. Whilst this is still far from perfection it is an improvement on the numbers of Great Britain and the European Union, and as such it is this organisation into which we should invest our hopes for peace, togetherness and progress.

Britain's Gift to the World: Creative Language

Language is much more than a method by which we can express ourselves and connect with each other. It is our prime mode of manifestation, where our world is made flesh according to how we speak it into being. The more perfect the language we use to do this, the more perfected the world that is formed by us. Human languages are just like computer programming languages – C, Fortran, Java, and others. They actually make things happen.

Learned occult circles recognise the generative power of the Hebrew alphabet, but rarely are the principles of creative speech extended any further. Yet in amongst the lower planes of existence (the ones human beings think, feel and walk around in), we have at our fingertips a language that has exerted a far greater influence on the world than Hebrew. That language is English.

The English language – as distinct from the English people – has formed the modern world. Although the language itself is comprehensive and powerful its speakers are flawed and imperfect and thus are inclined to speak powerful everyday incantations into form, accidentally on purpose. These may either be destructive, or creative.

This is not to suggest that English is the one true language of the Gods, or that speakers of other languages are somehow inferior. It is simply to recognise the innate creative structure of the English language. Its alphabet contains 26 letters, composed of 21 consonants and 5 vowels. The five vowels AEIOU are the gates through which the elements Akasha, Fire, Air, Water and Earth show themselves, and almost every English word contains at least one of these elements. The 21 consonants are then reflected in the 21 numbered cards of the Major Arcana of the Tarot. The 22nd card – 0 The Fool – is the speaker of the creative words. Much more is said about this in *Emergence Book Three: Creation* but it is no coincidence that the greatest advances in human history have occurred through a language which can perfectly contain and project the 5 elemental principles and the 21 key storehouses of energy of the Major Arcana of the Tarot. The weak link in all English communication is the speaker himself, The Fool, who though potentially able to communicate his world into being more often than not babbles utter chaos into existence. Take some time to observe this in action, first with others, then with yourself. Then take another moment to observe the daily confusion of tongues that takes place where things are not only lost in translation between languages, but where Person A says 'now' and the Person B hears 'later' If the speaker does not understand what they are really saying – through failing to connect with the Forgotten Lands or to misunderstand the true nature of the world around them – then how can they hope to either communicate or create anything positive at all?

A Prescription for Renewed Government

National renewal must be based, as close as is possible, to the notion of 4.

All four of the constituent nations of Great Britain must be involved and harnessed. As one is weak, so are the others. Investment in Northern Ireland benefits not just Northern Ireland, but also London, Norfolk, Aberdeenshire and South Wales. As the Royal Family understand the importance of holding titles and maintaining residences and connections with every corner of the country, so government must do the same. A possible solution may involve a complete reorganisation of government so that the Prime Minister of Great Britain adopts a more Chairman like role with the bulk of decisions made by the First Ministers of England, Scotland, Northern Ireland and Wales, each attending cabinet and each possessing parity of authority in the nation. We could even go further with respective government departments for Earth, Water, Air, and Fire. Through doorways such as this we may find fractious unity.

It may also be that London is now too influential, but this imbalance is not corrected by pushing London down, but instead by pulling other parts of the country up. The answer is not to redistribute money and authority out of London, but to use London as a template for the generative forces that regional cities may adapt and personalise.

Institutions, places and organisations attract persons of like energy. When these things are disbanded, either through failure or natural degeneration then thought must be given to where those people go next. Otherwise dispossession is all that results, and when people cease to belong to something they will belong to anything. This is the lesson that Margaret Thatcher failed to understand, for there was never going to be a naturally occurring replacement for the industries, professions, and places that she necessarily decimated. Responsibility for progress is shared between individuals (who must themselves learn, develop, and move on) as well as governments (who must facilitate this in some way).

Britain must get back to an active involvement with the Land, the Sea and the Air, by recognising that all the people living in Britain are also the determining factors of Britain. If the country is rotten it is because the people are. Yet if the people are useless it is the fault of the country. Paradoxically both are true, yet the only solution, the only way to break the circle and arrest the decline is to start the change with the individual. Problems are therefore not societal, but primarily personal.

Britain must abandon the cult of sameness, and expect – even encourage – divergence of thought, word and action, and to appreciate when others do the same. Polite shouting might be a very British way to proceed. Everybody can share in this; indeed everyone must do something, for all must share in the failure as well as the success.

You are the Land and the Land is You

Every citizen is sovereign of his or her own lands. As they grow so the nation flourishes. As each individual manages their own personal four lands so the national four blossoms. If an individual can be sovereign then so can a nation, but if an individual is dependent then the nation is too. The external lands are healed when the internal ones are. A *sick* nation is a *sick nation*. If one is toxic then everyone is toxic.

Any vision of the future will always, if accurate, be a multi–dimensional one. It will be composed of bad as well as good. The clearer our vision the more likely we are to spot the necessary bad, especially if we are prepared to proceed in an unselfish manner. To see the good and the bad – as I have tried to lay out in this book – forces us to detach from particular outcomes and to work with all that we have. The purpose of seeing the bad is so that we become better equipped to carry on with the good. Constant assertion of rightness, virtue and goodness help no one.

Any successful individual, within a well-functioning society, is a product of the constructive application of the Forgotten Lands. It should be noted though that a great deal of technological and economic advance is doomed to failure when it involves an attempt to flee from the influence of these Elements. The longer the Forgotten Lands remain ignored, the more vigorous – and possibly destructive – they are when they finally manage to re-assert themselves.

Voting Matters

There is a great deal to complain about in the version of democracy operated within Britain, but rather than scream for changes in a system to suit the people, might we consider changes in the people to suit a system that has been copied the world over and has worked for centuries?

Voting in elections is an act of responsibility. By placing your mark next to a candidate every citizen grants power to someone to act on their behalf. Low voter turnout is a lack of appetite to do this, and a sign of irresponsibility. Many will say that low voter engagement is a commentary on the paucity of choice available, yet it also a function of a desire to not engage and not be held responsible when things go wrong. It is delusional to blame the politicians, for so long as there are human beings there will be imperfection and variance between deed and intention. What matters is that our representatives are more right than wrong on the things that are important. No society can do better than this.

On a BBC television repeat of the 1966 general election turnout was discussed at length and the common consensus formed that those who do not vote do not matter. Why should we form a more politically correct view today than we did fifty years ago? Because the truth is that we will either willingly hand over power of others to make decisions on our behalf in a parliamentary democracy, free to change our minds again later, or we will be governed by force and coercion. If enough people dodge their share of responsibility for who governs the country then who can blame the elites for doing what the hell they like?

One adjustment might be made however, small yet significant. In UK elections the mark voters are instructed to place upon the ballot paper is an X. This is negative mark, not a positive one, like a tick. So right from the start we are saying No, and then wondering why there is no enthusiasm for the process or those elected.

Notes on The Method

The sharp–eyed reader will have noticed that use of the Elements, Letters and Numbers enables us to project where, how, and when the factors set in motion will come up for resolution, but in no way does it enable us to say what that resolution will be. The factors described in this book enable us to comment, analyse and understand what happened in history, and even to shed some light on current affairs, but the method cannot provide certainty of outcome.

This is due to the omnipresence of human free will, the ability that men and women have, to a degree, to do as they please. This free will never lasts very long, and its bounds are already pre–drawn by what has gone before, but it has an effect, setting the margins of future possible outcomes. Free will therefore plays a crucial, though far smaller role in the workings of life than many would prefer to believe.

Another problem with the method is the potential bias of the interpreter and the weight of his or her pre–conceived notions, where the temptation is to make the numbers fit with what one wants to see. This problem is rife in all data–based functions, including far less esoteric ones that this. We should not misunderstand this as a wilful attempt by the operator to prove their prejudices. It is far more worrying than that, because it could happen automatically.

The Rumsfeld Paradox and Beyond

As it became clear, in the aftermath of the 2003 Invasion of Iraq, that WMDs were nowhere to be found, US Secretary of Defense Donald Rumsfeld gave a press conference answer, which caused much amusement and derision. Nonetheless, unwittingly or not, he had made a powerful insight,

"There are known knowns; there are things we know we know. We also know there are known unknowns; that is to say we know there are some things we do not know. But there are also unknown unknowns –the ones we don't know we don't know."

We can take his insight much further now. Any reading of a situation, event or person must, if it is to be complete and whole, take into account four distinct areas of knowledge:

Known Knowns: Straightforwardly, things that we know. The simple facts of life. When, where, and who? Here questions are all fully satisfied with answers. On what date did an event take place? How long was so and so Prime Minister for? When was X organisation founded?

Known Unknowns: These are the things that we are aware of not knowing, where we have questions without answers, and we are cognisant of the gaps in our knowledge. Why did X resign? When did they themselves decide to?

These two form the bulk of most attempts at analysis, understanding and commentary. But there are two more, which take us through illusion, fantasy and self–deceit and out the other side with unexpected insights and truths.

Unknown Unknowns: The things that we don't even know are possibilities. Here we don't have questions, let alone answers, because we have not considered that something could possibly be – we haven't even thought of the question. This is the area of discovery, where things that are ignored and disregarded live. Indeed it might not even be fair to call them 'ignored' as one cannot really ignore what one does not even know exists! Here live the things of mystery, but it is the job of all seekers to peer hard into this darkness, for here are found the answers and insights that we could not possibly imagine.

Finally, one not referred to by Rumsfeld at the time, *Unknown Knowns.* These are the things we know but do not wish to see, the things that are apparent but deliberately concealed or finessed out of view. Here live the conclusions that are inevitable but which are mostly explained away. This is the place where things that are *too true* reside. This may be the terrain of much of this book.

Any analysis that fails to tackle all four, must, by its very nature, be incomplete and, whilst possibly correct in what it says will inevitably be, in totality, incorrect and unhelpful, due to what it misses out. My analysis of the life of the nation has attempted to incorporate all four of these aspects, leading me to conclusions that I had not expected, and many insights that I found troubling. Nonetheless I excluded nothing, however uncomfortable I found it.

No Method is 100%

Throughout this book I have effectively treated the nation as an organism, and used the microscopes of Letters, Numbers and Elements to delve into its very soul. Many patterns have been seen and insights gained, but never perfectly, for there is always novelty – the event, person or thing that 'should' fit to the pattern, but does not.

In these small, but significant, cases we must first check our expectations. Why should the pattern be replicated in the way that we expect? It might be our expectations that are adrift, rather than the pattern. But there is also another explanation, that no method is ever 100% accurate 100% of the time. Not economics, not weather forecasts, not medical science. Nothing, devised by humans, can ever hope to explain everything, everywhere, at all times. If this were so then there would never be any surprises, never any strangeness, never any newness, and although many people like to claim that 'there is nothing new under the Sun' the fact is that every single day brings a sprinkling of the unexpected, seeming to derive from the creative impulse at the heart of everything and everyone. Given this, the patterns of the past suggest, intone, and fuse together to form the future, but that future never turns out quite as expected. As there are rules so there are exceptions that prove those rules, as well as those which break them.

As such, the patterns identified are not meant to be all encompassing or in any way comprehensive. They do not tell us everything. I accept this possibility, for however hard we look we can never see it all. But, the process is what matters. The process of looking with different eyes at old problems, of refusing to accept group–think and being open – not eager, just open – to see whatever presents itself. These are the prizes on offer in all fields of study and walks of life, the gold that is available to simply pick up off the floor when using the prisms and the patterns of the Letters, Numbers and Elements.

The Secret Conclusion

This will be made available upon the death of the author.

APPENDIX A
Places of Britain

Countries & Names

GREAT BRITAIN	7
UNITED KINGDOM	2
BRITAIN	1
ENGLAND	3
SCOTLAND	7
WALES	6
NORTHERN IRELAND	4
IRELAND	9
EUROPE	8
EUROPEAN UNION	6
UNITED STATES OF EUROPE	6

SHIRE	5
VALLEY	5
ISLAND	5
ISLE	9
PEAK	6
BRIDGE	9
ISLANDS	6

Counties of the UK

AVON	7	LONDON	11
BEDFORDSHIRE	5	CITY OF LONDON	8
BERKSHIRE	5	MERSEYSIDE	5
BRISTOL	5	MIDDLESEX	5
BUCKINGHAMSHIRE	4	NORFOLK	1
CAMBRIDGESHIRE	4	NORTHAMPTONSHIRE	6
CHESHIRE	3	NORTHUMBERLAND	3
CLEVELAND	33	NORTH HUMBERSIDE	8
CORNWALL	8	NORTH YORKSHIRE	5
CUMBRIA	4	NOTTINGHAMSHIRE	9
DERBYSHIRE	5	OXFORDSHIRE	6
DEVON	6	RUTLAND	9
DORSET	9	SHROPSHIRE	9
DURHAM	11	SALOP	9
EAST SUSSEX	8	SOMERSET	33
ESSEX	9	SOUTH HUMBERSIDE	7
GLOUCESTERSHIRE	4	SOUTH YORKSHIRE	4
GREATER LONDON	22	STAFFORDSHIRE	4
GREATER MANCHESTER	9	SUFFOLK	9
HAMPSHIRE	7	SURREY	7
HEREFORDSHIRE	3	SUSSEX	8
HERTFORDSHIRE	9	TYNE AND WEAR	4
HUMBERSIDE	5	WARWICKSHIRE	3
HUNTINGDONSHIRE	5	WEST MIDLANDS	8
ISLE OF ELY	9	WESTMORLAND	9
ISLE OF WIGHT	7	WEST SUSSEX	3
KENT	5	WEST YORKSHIRE	6
LANCASHIRE	9	WILTSHIRE	6
LEICESTERSHIRE	11	WORCESTERSHIRE	5
LINCOLNSHIRE	3	YORKSHIRE	11

Counties of the UK (contd)

ANTRIM	3
ARMAGH	3
BELFAST	2
DOWN	2
FERMANAGH	1
LONDONDERRY	9
DERRY	7
TYRONE	7

ABERDEEN	9
ABERDEENSHIRE	5
ANGUS	8
ARGYLL	3
AYRSHIRE	4
BANFFSHIRE	7
BERWICKSHIRE	4
BUTE	3
CAITHNESS	8
CLACKMANNANSHIRE	11
DUMFRIESSHIRE	1
DUNBARTONSHIRE	6
DUNDEE	8
EAST LOTHIAN	7
EDINBURGH	7
FIFE	8
GLASGOW	3
INVERNESSSHIRE	4
KINCARDINESHIRE	3
KINROSSSHIRE	11
KIRKCUDBRIGHTSHIRE	2
LANARKSHIRE	8
MIDLOTHIAN	6
MORAY	9
NAIRNSHIRE	7

ANGLESEY	7
CARDIFF	11
CARDIGANSHIRE	8
CEREDIGION	8
CARMARTHENSHIRE	7
CLWYD	22
DENBIGHSHIRE	9
DYFED	8
FLINTSHIRE	3
GLAMORGAN	7
GWENT	6
GWYNEDD	1
MID GLAMORGAN	6
MONMOUTHSHIRE	7
MONTGOMERYSHIRE	6
PEMBROKESHIRE	9
POWYS	8
SOUTH GLAMORGAN	9
WEST GLAMORGAN	11

ORKNEY	7
PEEBLESSHIRE	6
PERTHSHIRE	9
RENFREWSHIRE	4
ROSS AND CROMARTY	5
ROSSSHIRE	4
ROXBURGHSHIRE	1
SELKIRKSHIRE	9
SHETLAND	11
STIRLINGSHIRE	5
SUTHERLAND	5
WEST LOTHIAN	11
WIGTOWNSHIRE	8

Former Colonies

ADEN	6
AUSTRALIA	3
CANADA	6
CEYLON	11
HONDURAS	1
JAMAICA	2
NEW ZEALAND	6
RHODESIA	7
UGANDA	3
INDIA	1
BERMUDA	1
CAYMAN ISLANDS	9
GIBRALTAR	7
FALKLAND ISLANDS	4
SOUTH GEORGIA	1
TURKS AND CAICOS	5
JERSEY	1
GUERNSEY	6
SARK	4
ISLE OF MAN	4
HONG KONG	1

Place Names of Britain – England

London Boroughs	
LONDON	11
GREATER LONDON	22
BARKING & DAGENHAM	8
BARNET	6
BEXLEY	1
BRENT	5
BROMLEY	9
CAMDEN	22
CROYDON	4
EALING	3
ENFIELD	1
GREENWICH	11
HACKNEY	4
HAMMERSMITH & FULHAM	9
HARINGEY	6
HARROW	11
HAVERING	3
HILLINGDON	5
HOUNSLOW	1
ISLINGTON	11
KENSINGTON & CHELSEA	11
KINGSTON UPON THAMES	7
LAMBETH	7
LEWISHAM	9
MERTON	4
NEWHAM	1
REDBRIDGE	9
RICHMOND UPON THAMES	9
SOUTHWARK	1
SUTTON	1
TOWER HAMLETS	6
WALTHAM FOREST	8

WANDSWORTH	1
WESTMINSTER	3
CITY OF LONDON	8

Greater London & Commuter	
HEMEL HEMPSTEAD	8
WATFORD	33
WOKING	7
HARLOW	5
ST ALBANS	7
BRACKNELL	33
CHELMSFORD	4
SLOUGH	1
HIGH WYCOMBE	1
READING	4
SOUTHEND ON SEA	7
LUTON	1
CRAWLEY	33
AYLESBURY	11
BASILDON	4
BASINGSTOKE	5
BRENTWOOD	8
CHESHUNT	8
GUILDFORD	6
GRAVESEND	5
HARLOW	5
HORSHAM	1
MAIDENHEAD	1
MAIDSTONE	1
ROYAL TUNBRIDGE WELLS	8
TUNBRIDGE WELLS	9
SITTINGBOURNE	11
STEVENAGE	8

Place Names of Britain – England (contd)

Merseyside & surrounding	
LIVERPOOL	7
BIRKENHEAD	5
BOOTLE	6
CROSBY	1
ELLESMERE PORT	1
KNOWSLEY	7
RUNCORN	4
SOUTHPORT	8
ST HELENS	3
WALLASEY	8
WARRINGTON	4
WIDNES	11

Manchester & NW	
MANCHESTER	7
GREATER MANCHESTER	9
STOCKPORT	11
TAMESIDE	4
OLDHAM	8
ROCHDALE	3
BURY	3
BOLTON	6
WIGAN	9
SALFORD	3
TRAFFORD	7
GOLBORNE	7
GLOSSOP	4
NEWTON LE WILLOWS	5
BURNLEY	7
BLACKBURN	3
BLACKPOOL	33
CARLISLE	7
CHESTER	33

Potteries	
STOKE ON TRENT	5
STOKE	7
NEWCASTLE UNDER LYME	3

Birmingham, WM and beyond	
COVENTRY	5
BIRMINGHAM	4
EDGBASTON	33
ERDINGTON	7
HALL GREEN	1
HODGE HILL	8
LADYWOOD	9
NORTHFIELD	3
PERRY BARR	4
SELLY OAK	1
SUTTON COLDFIELD	8
YARDLEY	9
DUDLEY	8
SOLIHULL	9
WALSALL	8
WEST BROMWICH	5
WOLVERHAMPTON	11
WORCESTER	9
TELFORD	8
HEREFORD	7
LICHFIELD	5

Leeds	
LEEDS	9
BRADFORD	5
DEWSBURY	9
HALIFAX	7
HUDDERSFIELD	7
KEIGHLEY	1
WAKEFIELD	4

Teeside	
MIDDLESBROUGH	11
STOCKTON ON TEES	6

Brighton	
BRIGHTON	3
HOVE	5
WORTHING	6

Places Names of Britain – England (contd)

Sheffield	
SHEFFIELD	11
ROTHERHAM	7
DONCASTER	9
BARNSLEY	33
DERBYSHIRE	5
CHESTERFIELD	6

Tyneside & NE	
NEWCASTLE UPON TYNE	7
GATESHEAD	7
SOUTH SHIELDS	6
WASHINGTON	4
SUNDERLAND	4
HULL	8
HARROGATE	3
GRIMSBY	3
YORK	6
DURHAM	11

Nottingham & East Mids	
NOTTINGHAM	4
BEESTON	8
DERBY	9
MANSFIELD	11
LEICESTER	6
NORTHAMPTON	1

South	
SWINDON	8
SALISBURY	9
WINCHESTER	7

Bournemouth	
BOURNEMOUTH	8
POOLE	9
CHRISTCHURCH	3

East of England	
NORWICH	9
IPSWICH	6
GREAT YARMOUTH	1
CLACTON	5
HARWICH	7

South West	
PLYMOUTH	4
BRISTOL	5
TAUNTON	6
GLOUCESTER	8
CHELTENHAM	8
EXETER	5
BATH	4
CIRENCESTER	11

South East	
GILLINGHAM	11
CHATHAM	9
COLCHESTER	9
FOLKESTONE	5
CANTERBURY	1

Central	
MILTON KEYNES	9
OXFORD	1
PETERBOROUGH	6
CAMBRIDGE	8
LINCOLN	7
BEDFORD	9

Southampton	
PORTSMOUTH	3
GOSPORT	11
FAREHAM	7
WATERLOOVILLE	7
SOUTHAMPTON	9
EASTLEIGH	5

Place Names of Britain – Scotland

GLASGOW	3
EDINBURGH	7
ABERDEEN	9
DUNDEE	8
PAISLEY	33
EAST KILBRIDE	7
INVERNESS	8
LIVINGSTON	6
HAMILTON	11
CUMBERNAULD	6
DUNFERMLINE	4
KIRKCALDY	4
PERTH	4
KILMARNOCK	8
COATBRIDGE	3
GREENOCK	6
GLENROTHES	6
AIRDRIE	1
STIRLING	9
FALKIRK	5
IRVINE	5
DUMFRIES	5
MOTHERWELL	5
RUTHERGLEN	11

Place Names of Britain – Wales

CARDIFF	11
SWANSEA	1
NEWPORT	3
WREXHAM	11
BARRY	1
NEATH	3
CWMBRAN	11
BRIDGEND	9
LLANELLI	5
MERTHYR TYDFIL	3
CAERPHILLY	1
PORT TALBOT	4
PONTYPRIDD	6
ABERDARE	9
COLWYN BAY	3
PONTYPOOL	4
PENARTH	1
RHYL	9

Place Names of Britain – Northern Ireland

BELFAST	2
DERRY	7
LONDONDERRY	9
LISBURN	5
NEWTOWNABBEY	5
BANGOR	3
CRAIGAVON	9
BALLYMENA	4
NEWTOWNARDS	3
NEWRY	4
COLERAINE	1
ANTRIM	3
OMAGH	8

Place Names of Ireland

IRELAND	9
EIRE	1
IRISH FREE STATE	9
DUBLIN	8
CONNACHT	33
LEINSTER	3
MUNSTER	11
ULSTER	5
MEATH	2

Fictional Places in the UK

CAMELOT	6
WEATHERFIELD	8
WALFORD	7
ALBERT SQUARE	4
CORONATION STREET	4
HOLLYOAKS	1
BROOKSIDE	8
CAMBERWICK GREEN	11
TRUMPTON	11
EMMERDALE	4
FULCHESTER	9
HOLBY	8
MIDDLEMARCH	9
ROYSTON VASEY	9
WALMINGTON ON SEA	11
AMBRIDGE	5

Spiritual Mystical Places in the UK

GLASTONBURY	1
AVEBURY	4
STONEHENGE	4
LINDISFARNE	3
ROSSLYN	5

APPENDIX B
Foreign Relations

Title	X
Country	8
Nation	1
Colony	3
Dominion	3
Territory	4
Dependency	5

Country (English)	X	F
Former Colonies		
Australia	3	1
Canada	6	3
Jamaica	2	1
India	1	9
Singapore	5	1
Hong Kong	1	8
British Hong Kong	5	2
South Africa	4	1
New Zealand	6	5
Africa	11	1
Rhodesia	7	9
Southern Rhodesia	1	1
Zimbabwe	9	8
Overseas Territories & Dependencies		
Jersey	1	1
Sark	4	1
Guernsey	6	7
Isle of Man	4	9
Bermuda	1	2
British Virgin Islands	8	2
Cayman Islands	9	3
Falkland Islands	4	6
Gibraltar	7	7
Turks and Caicos Islands	11	2

X = Expression
F = First Letter

Country (English)	X	F	Country (Own Language)	X
			Europe	
Austria	8	1	Österreich (German)	6
Belgium	33	2	België (Dutch)	8
			Belgique (French)	6
Croatia	4	3	Hrvatska (Croatian, Latin script)	1
Cyprus	3	3	Cipros (Greek transliteration)	8
Czech	9	3	Česká (Slavic, Latin)	8
(Czechoslovakia)	6	3		
Denmark	3	4	Danmark	8
Estonia	11	5	Vabariik (Finnic, latin)	1
Finland	33	6	Suomi (Finnish, Latin)	5
France	11	6	France	11
			République française	4
Germany	11	7	Deutschland	3
			Bundesrepublik Deutschland	9
			Deutsches Reich	3
			Großdeutsches Reich	9
Greece	7	7	Elláda (translit)	9
Hungary	4	8	Magyarország (Uralic, Latin)	6
Ireland	9	9	Éire	1
Italy	22	9	Italia	7
Latvia	2	3	Latvijas (Baltic, Latin)	3
Lithuania	5	3	Lietuvos (Baltic, Latin)	33
Luxembourg	3	3	Lëtzebuerg (Lux)	8
			Luxembourg (French)	3
			Luxemburg (German)	6
Malta	11	4	Malta (Maltese, Latin)	11
Netherlands	3	5	Nederland	5
The Netherlands	9	2	Koninkrijk der Nederlanden	2
Poland	8	7	Polska (Polish, Latin)	2
			Rzeczpospolita Polska	5
Portugal	11	7	Portuguesa (Port, Latin)	8
Romania	8	9	România (Romanian, Latin)	7
Slovakia	9	1	Slovenská (Slovak, Latin)	9
Slovenia	7	1	Slovenija (Slovene, Latin)	8
Spain	5	1	España	6
Sweden	7	1	Sverige	4
Europe	8	5	Europa	4

Country (English)	X	F	Country (Own Language)	X
Significant Others				
United States of America	3	3		
USA	5	3		
America	5	1		
China	8	3	Zhōngguó (Chinese, translit)	5
Peoples Republic of China	5	7		
Brazil	5	2	Brasil (Port, Latin)	7
Japan	6	1	Nippon (transliteration)	3
			Nihon (transliteration)	7
Russia	6	9	Rossiya (transliteration)	7
Afghanistan	1	1	Afġānistān (Pashto translit)	
			Afġānestān (Persian translit)	
Sudan	5	1	Sūdān (Arabic translit)	
Egypt	11	5	Miṣr (Arabic translit)	
Norway	33	5	Norge	5
Switzerland	7	1	Schweiz (German)	3
			Suisse (French)	2
Argentina	8	1	Argentina (Spanish)	8
Iraq	9	9	ʿIrāq (Arabic translit)	
			ʿÊraq (Kurdish translit)	
Saudi Arabia	5	1	Arabiyah as-Saʿūdiyah (Arabic, translit)	
Israel	1	9	Yisrāʾel (Hebrew translit)	
Iceland	3	9	Ísland (Icelandic Latin)	

The Numerology of the names containing foreign language characters or accents is speculative only, though it serves to highlight the potential differences between perception by the UK and projection by the host country.

APPENDIX C
British General Elections

Pre-1918 (and again in 1945) elections took place over multiple days.
Dates, since postal voting was legalised in 2001, are symbolic rather than actual.

No.	Polling Day	Day Compound	Day Root	Connecting with...	Destiny Compound	Destiny Root	
1	14 Dec 1918	14	5			9	
2	15 Nov 1922	15	6	W	22	4	
3	6 Dec 1923		6	W	15	6	
4	29 Oct 1924	11	2	UK	19	1	
5	30 May 1929		3	E		2	
6	27 Oct 1931		9			6	
7	14 Nov 1935	14	5		16	7	
8	5 July 1945*		5		22	4	
9	23 Feb 1950		5		22	4	
10	25 Oct 1951		7	S, GB		6	
11	26 May 1955		8	K		6	
12	8 Oct 1959		8	K		6	
13	15 Oct 1964	15	6	W		9	
14	31 Mar 1966		4	NI		2	
15	18 Jun 1970		9			5	
16	28 Feb 1974		1			6	
17	10 Oct 1974		1			5	
18	3 May 1979		3	E		7	
19	9 Jun 1983		9			9	
20	11 Jun 1987	11	2	UK		6	
21	9 Apr 1992		9			7	
22	1 May 1997		1			5	
23	7 Jun 2001		7	S, GB		7	
24	5 May 2005		5			8	
25	6 May 2010		6	W		5	
26	7 May 2015		7	S, GB	11	2	
27	*7 May 2020*		7	*S, GB*		7	

* election took place over multiple days.

Key: *Scotland (S) 7. England (E) 3. Wales (W) 6. Northern Ireland (NI) 4. United Kingdom (UK) 2, 11, 20. Great Britain (GB) 7. Karma (K) 8.*

Connecting with...	Universal Year Compound	Universal Year Root	Connecting with...	Seeded Year	Seed to Root Timespan
	19	1		1944	26
NI	14	5		1948	26
W	15	6	W	1941	18
	16	7	S, GB	1963	39
UK		3	E	1964	35
W	14	5		1968	37
S, GB		9		1960	25
NI	19	1		1957	12
NI	15	6	W	1975	25
W	16	7	S, GB	1986	35
W		2	UK	1986	31
W		6	W	1977	18
		2	UK	1989	25
UK	22	4	NI	2000	34
	17	8	K	1994	24
W		3	E	2004	30
		3	E	1994	20
S, GB		8	K	1987	8
		3	E	1998	15
W		7	S, GB	2004	17
S, GB		3	E	2005	13
		8	UK	2003	6
S, GB		3	E	2014	13
K		7	S, GB	2015	10
	21	3	E	2021	11
UK		8	UK	2027	12
S, GB	*22*	*4*	*NI*	*2032*	*12*

APPENDIX D
The Full Names and Numbers of the Nation

	Expression		Soul Urge		
	Compound	*Root*	*Compound*	*Root*	
GREAT BRITAIN	16	7	7	7	
UNITED KINGDOM	11	2	5	5	
ENGLAND	3	3	6	6	
SCOTLAND	7	7	7	7	
WALES	15	6	6	6	
NORTHERN IRELAND	22	4	8	8	
ULSTER	5	5	8	8	
IRELAND	9	9	15	6	
BRITISH EMPIRE	16	7	10	1	
BRITANNIA	7	7	20	2	
COOL BRITANNIA	7	7	5	5	
LITTLE BRITAIN	16	7	33	6	
ALBION	8	8	16	7	
BRITISH ISLES	5	5	5	5	
UNION	10	1	18	9	
COMMONWEALTH	7	7	18	9	
PROTECTORATE	12	3	5	5	
UNITED KINGDOM OF GREAT BRITAIN AND IRELAND	22	4	7	7	
UNITED KINGDOM OF GREAT BRITAIN AND ULSTER	18	9	9	9	
UNITED KINGDOM OF GREAT BRITAIN AND NORTHERN IRELAND	8	8	9	9	

All individual words and dates are summed to between 1-22, or 33
They are then added and reduced to a compound (10-22) and root (1-9).

This provides two levels of understanding:
Compounds 10-22 only show lessons inherent in the words, what is trying to show itself through them. (The numbers 23-78 are less important)
Roots 1-9 are the most important factor, with additional consideration given to compounds 11, 22, 33.

	Secret Desire			
Compound	*Root*	*1st Letter*	*Rpt Numbers*	*Missing Numbers*
18	9	G (7)	9	3, 4, 6, 8
33	6	U (3)	4, 5	1, 8
6	6	E (5)	5	2, 6, 8, 9
18	9	S (1)	1, 3	7, 8, 9
9	9	W (5)	1, 5	2, 4, 6, 7, 8, 9
5	5	N (5)	5	7
15	6	U (3)	3	4, 6, 7, 8
21	3	I (9)	5, 9	2, 6, 7, 8
6	6	B (2)	9	3, 6
5	5	B (2)	9	3, 4, 6, 7, 8
11	2	C (3)	9	4, 7, 8
19	1	L (3)	2, 9	4, 6, 7, 8
10	1	A (1)	none	4, 7, 8
9	9	B (2)	9	4, 6, 7
10	1	U (3)	5	1, 2, 4, 7, 8
7	7	C (3)	5	7, 9
7	7	P (7)	2	4, 8
15	6	U (3)	5, 9	8
9	9	U (3)	5, 9	8
8	8	U (3)	5, 9	none

For example, Great Britain:

Expression: Great = 6. Britain = 10. Thus Great Britain = 16/7
Soul Urge: Great = 6. Britain = 19. Thus Great Britain = 25/7
Secret Desire: Great = 9. Britain = 9. Great Britain = 18/9

APPENDIX E
The Tarot of the Union Jack

Just like the Letters and the Numbers, the Tarot exists as an alphabet, the arrangement of which enables a new language to be spoken. Once the cards are positioned in a meaningful arrangement a variety of techniques can be used to read them. One can read outwards from a central card, or observe the cards at the farthest position from the centre. We can read in lines, shapes or circles, allowing us to see different things as the pattern takes us. The benefit of turning numbers into cards is that the energy becomes more dynamic and a whole new world of meaning presents itself, where cards with matching colours may form groups, and images from cards may begin to talk to one another.

A Suggested Arrangement

Arrange the cards along the vertical, horizontal and diagonal lines of the image of the Union Jack.

The Chariot VII, the most frequent number of the nation, may take the central position, the intersection of the crosses. Either side of this, above and below, sits The Devil XV and The Lovers VI. The vertical sequence is completed at the foot by The Fool 0 (representing every man and woman of the nation) and at the head by Judgement XX, the marker for the century we are now in.

Across the middle we have The Hierophant V (for the BRITISH ISLES), The Hermit IX (for IRELAND), the Empress III (ENGLAND) and The Emperor IV (NORTHERN IRELAND).

The top left cross is filled with Justice XI (so frequent in Britain's previous roads) and Strength VIII (Karma). You might wish to reverse either of these cards depending on how you see the nation expressing them. The top right is then filled with The Magician I and The Tower XVI, both key numbers in the Nations. Lastly the whole of the bottom area contains the cards of the most recent and soon to be Prime Ministers, the Five, Six, Seven and Eight of Pentacles. Again one or more of these could be reversed to add depth to the reading.

Once you have the arrangement in the shape of the Union Jack start to remove and transpose cards. How is the reading affected by removing the central VII representing Scotland, or by moving to one side the XV of the EU? Try substituting numbered Major cards for their numbered equivalents in the Minors, for example swap the Hermit with the Nine of Swords. You could even re–arrange the cards entirely from the pattern of the Union Jack into the flag of the EU. How will you deal with having too many cards? Which ones would be left out, or how could they be included, given the twelve stars of the flag?

In another method you might look to the people of Britain – the animal lovers and the eccentrics (7 – Chariot), the innovators and entrepreneurs (1 – Magician), the buccaneer adventurers (5 – Hierophant), the writers and musicians (3 – Empress) and the peacemakers (2 – High Priestess). Endless visual permutations now become possible, and when you alight upon something that makes you go "mmmm" then note it and try to recall it when you next watch or read the news. You will be surprised at what you might discover, and you may even come to understand my thought process in writing this book.

Finally, when we reach the next election try to find the dates of birth of the candidates. Calculate their Four Roads and match them up to the Four Roads of past and current incarnations of Britain. To which do they speak? Which values do they therefore reflect? Then match these numbers up to the numbers of the nation. Include the date of the election and the numbers that reveals. Transfer all this to a Tarot layout and glance into the future of the nation. Best to perform a protection ritual first though.

Cards of Destiny

Every Tarot card, through the sequence of the 75/78 Prime Ministers, connects the reader back to the issues of Britain's past. When we draw the Seven of Wands we are immediately transported back to the time of Charles Dickens' Bleak House of 1852, with all the issues of that time revived in the present. When we draw the Nine of Cups the self-satisfaction of Peak Empire under Lord Salisbury is again invoked. Thus the appearance of a card delivers the opportunity to heal our wounds and strengthen our understanding of Britain's past, present and future.

BIBLIOGRAPHY

History (Actual & Mythical)
A History of Britain – E H Carter and R A F Mears
The Quest for Arthurs Britain – Geoffrey Ashe
The Lore of the Land – Jennifer Westwood & Jacqueline Simpson
On the Ruin of Britain – Gildas The Wise
Arthur and the Sovereignty of Britain – Caitlin Matthews
The History of the Kings of Britain – Geoffrey of Monmouth
Empire – Niall Ferguson
The Decline and Fall of the British Empire – Elliott Evans Mills
The Lion & The Unicorn – George Orwell
A History of the English Speaking Peoples – Winston Churchill
John Dee – Charlotte Fell Smith
The Limits of the British Empire – John Dee
The Perfect Arte of Navigation – John Dee
The Illustrated Book of Flags – Alfred Znamierowski

Politics
The Conservatives: A History – Robin Harris
Liberals – Roy Douglas
Sir Robert Peel: The Life After 1830 – Norman Gash
A History of the British Labour Party – Andrew Thorpe

Occultism
The Aquarian Guide to Legendary London – John Matthews and Chesca Potter
London's Curse – Mark Beynon
Merlin: The Prophetic Vision and The Mystic Life – R J Stewart
The Old Straight Track – Alfred Watkins
Numerology & Your Future – Dusty Bunker
Practical Elemental Magic – David Rankine & Sorita d'Este
The Destiny of The Nations – Alice A Bailey
The Magical Battle of Britain – Dion Fortune, with Gareth Knight
The Dark Star – Lord Hugh Dowding
Seven – Rod Chapman
Nostradamus and the Third Antichrist – Mario Reading
The Pictorial Key to the Tarot – A E Waite
Magic – David Conway
Occult Reich – J H Brennan
The Book of English Magic – Philip Carr–Gomm & Richard Heygate
Dragons – Joyce Hargreaves
London's Mystical Legacy – Toyne Newton & Jonathan Tapsell
London's Ley Lines – Christopher E Street